Postcard History Series

Homes of
Hollywood Stars

FRONT COVER: JIMMY DURANTE'S HOME. Pictured is comedian Jimmy Durante's Beverly Hills residence in the 1950s. He bought the house in 1944. In 1963, he had it completely remodeled into a more contemporary residence. The grounds also included a guesthouse, swimming pool, and a dry sauna. By Hollywood standards, it was quite modest. (Author's collection.)

BACK COVER: PICKFAIR. Shown is a classic 1920s postcard of the legendary mansion known as Pickfair, the home of silent film stars Douglas Fairbanks and Mary Pickford. The 25-room mansion was flanked by formal gardens and a swimming pool. Inside were splendidly designed English windows, rich wood paneling, parquet floors, and high frescoed ceilings. Its location afforded stunning views. (Author's collection.)

POSTCARD HISTORY SERIES

Homes of Hollywood Stars

Barry Moreno

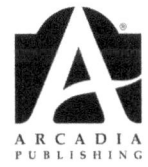

ARCADIA
PUBLISHING

Published by Arcadia Publishing
Charleston, South Carolina

Library of Congress Control Number: 2017937439

For all general information contact Arcadia Publishing at:
Telephone 843-853-2070
Fax 843-853-0044
E-mail sales@arcadiapublishing.com
For customer service and orders:
Toll-Free 1-888-313-2665

Visit us on the Internet at www.arcadiapublishing.com

In memory of my grandmother

CONTENTS

ACKNOWLEDGMENTS

I have been fortunate in finding many helpful sources in the course of researching this book. Among them are period newspapers, magazines, and special architectural publications, many of which highlight the houses or homelife of well-known actors. Also helpful were original interviews and commentary by theatrical columnists, such as Adela Rogers St. John, Hedda Hopper, and Sheilah Graham. Not surprisingly, archival sources were of immense value. Among them are the following: the US Censuses of 1900 through 1940; the New York State Censuses of 1905, 1915, and 1925; US Army draft registrations of World Wars I and II; city directories; US immigration records; American and British ships' passenger lists; New York and California federal naturalization records; death certificates; and British probate records. Among the books I have consulted are the following: *An Architectural Guidebook to Los Angeles* by David Gebhard and Robert Winter; *California in the 1930s: The WPA Guide to the Golden State*; *Hollywood at Home: A Family Album, 1950–1965* by Richard J. Schickle; *Hollywood Death and Scandal Sites* by E.J. Fleming; *Souvenir Map Guide to the Fabulous Homes of the Stars* by Vance Kabourek; *Movie Star Homes: The Famous to the Forgotten* by Judy Artunian and Mike Oldham; *The Ultimate Hollywood Tour Book* by William A. Gordon; and *Picture Postcards of the Golden Age* by Tonie and Valmai Holt. A number of biographies and memoirs were also invaluable, especially those of the lives of Jean Arthur, Joan Blondell, Fannie Brice, Eddie Cantor, Maurice Chevalier, Claudette Colbert, Bing Crosby, Marlene Dietrich, Jimmy Durante, Alice Faye, Pauline Frederick, Clark Gable, John Gilbert, Corrine Griffith, Bob Hope, Van Johnson, Adolphe Menjou, Ray Milland, George Murphy, Ramón Novarro, Mary Pickford, William Powell, Ronald Reagan, Gloria Swanson, Robert Taylor, Rudolph Valentino, and Mae West. I have been fortunate in receiving assistance from knowledgeable friends, such as North Peterson regarding Priscilla Dean's retired life in Leonia, New Jersey, and from Doug Treem on the lives of certain Hollywood actors.

All the images in the book are from my own private collections.

INTRODUCTION

Life in old-time Hollywood was a mixture of many things: the movies, the studios, and the lives of stars. And the latter included the private residences in which actors made their homes during the palmy days of their success. As a visible object of material accomplishment, this gave rise to a whole sideline industry of a certain kind of Hollywood memorabilia—the production, printing, and selling of picture postcards. *Homes of Hollywood Stars* showcases the postcard folders, single postcards, and related imagery of some of the leading players of motion pictures during the Golden Age of Hollywood. Different publishing firms created them, and different techniques were used in their creation and printing. Some of the cards in this book, all originals, date back to the very early 1920s. In all, the postcards span six decades of Hollywood history.

It comes as no surprise that Pickfair, the luxurious mansion of Hollywood's uncrowned king and queen, Douglas Fairbanks and Mary Pickford, was regarded as the supreme social center of the movie community. The 14 acres of land in Benedict Canyon where it was built was purchased by Douglas Fairbanks prior to his marriage to Pickford for $35,000 in March 1919; the grounds included a hunting lodge. From 1920 on, a mansion was built for the newlyweds. It fitted the couple's marked preference for English architecture over Mediterranean and consisted of four stories and 25 rooms. Further, the estate included servants' quarters, stables, a swimming pool, and tennis courts. The address was 1143 Summit Drive. Screen beauty Corinne Griffith's ivy-covered Tudor Revival mansion at 1033 Summit Drive was built just down the road from Pickfair. Comedian Harold Lloyd also built his vast estate, Greenacres, in the same Benedict Canyon neighborhood. His 44-room mansion was designed by architect Sumner Spaulding in the Italian Renaissance style. Completed in 1927, the Lloyd estate was exquisitely landscaped by Archibald Hanson and included a golf course; a fishing stream, stocked with bass and trout; and the largest swimming pool in Southern California.

The origins of Hollywood go back to its discovery by pioneering filmmaker David Wark Griffith. In 1910, he realized its possibilities as a movie-making paradise while filming the first movie ever made there, *In Old California*. Soon, studio after studio opened for business in Hollywood and other districts of Los Angeles. To moviemakers, the place was fitting in just about every way. With its sunny climate and diverse terrain, it was a veritable oasis for photoplay production. In the early years, from 1911 to 1917, most actors only stayed for the shooting season, after which they bustled back to the East Coast to fulfill pressing stage engagements, perhaps on Broadway or in one of the many flourishing vaudeville circuits. During their stay in Hollywood, actors found temporary lodgings in boardinghouses, small hotels, and in bungalows. But with the proliferation of film studios and the profitability of both short films and full-length features, actors began to have a good reason to find permanent residences there. By 1919, there were 37 motion picture studios operating in Hollywood and its environs.

During this period, nearby Beverly Hills, a pristine terrain of flat and hilly land, began attracting settlers, and following the opening of the Beverly Hills Hotel on May 12, 1912, more new residents began moving nearby. Two years later, Beverly Hills became an independent city. Situated in the foothills midway between the movie capital and the sea, it was regarded as the most beautiful residential area near Los Angeles. As well, it was not far distant from the Santa Monica Mountains from whence it afforded superb views of the lowlands and the placid waters of the boundless Pacific. Middle-class professionals—lawyers, doctors, businessmen, and the like—built the first private residences near the hotel. This class of neighbor gave tone to the rising community, and actors, deeply impressed, followed. Its flatlands and rolling hills would soon become the principal domestic setting for the movie community, and with the design and construction of many charming and luxurious homes, it became the nesting place to which actors retired to after the grueling hours of shooting a picture. Although not every star chose to live there, a great many did, and so, by the 1920s, to fans in America and abroad, Beverly Hills was the quintessential home of the stars. The first well-known film personalities to have homes there were French comedian Max Linder in 1917; American actors Douglas Fairbanks, Charles Ray, and Pauline Frederick in 1918; and then Australian actress Enid Bennett in 1919.

With all of these developments, it did not take long for the canny entrepreneurs of the postcard trade to note how tourists were drawn to Hollywood. In the 1920s, $2 motor coach sightseeing tours of Hollywood were already well organized. The buses would halt in front of the private residences of actors, and the tour operator would make droll comments while speaking through a megaphone. Souvenirs were in demand, and the cheapest to buy were picture postcards of Hollywood and the homes of the stars. Prominent postcard entrepreneurs in Los Angeles involved in this development included Theodore Sohmer (1880–1938) and Morris Kashower (1883–1920), both of whom had emigrated from Eastern Europe, the former hailed from Romania and the latter from Russia. In 1912, the two men, along with Sohmer's brother Philip, founded the Western Publishing and Novelty Company. In 1914, they dissolved their partnership, and the Sohmer brothers kept the company's name. Kashower left to form his own postcard business, known as the M. Kashower Company.

And then, the world of silent film was struck by an innovation that changed everything—the revolution in sound! The first warning was the release on October 6, 1927, in New York City of Sam Warner's dream, *The Jazz Singer*. Audiences heard music, singing, and the speaking voice, however briefly, of its star, Al Jolson. Jolson's voice and the music heralded a new age in motion pictures.

In 1928 and 1929, Hollywood made the dramatic transition from silent films to making films with recorded sound. This "talking picture revolution" changed lives and livelihoods. Many established actors, unable to live up to vocal expectations, found their careers on the downswing or even in ruins. Many lost heart and threw out their film careers entirely, but in some cases, an actor's career took on a surprising twist, and he or she rose to even greater acclaim, such as William Powell and Adolphe Menjou. In his 1948 autobiography *It Took Nine Tailors*, Menjou devoted an entire chapter to the subject. He underscored how he and other panic-stricken silent film favorites in 1929 reacted at the prospect of the "microphone voice test," which they had to undergo in order for movie moguls to decide whether their voices were suitable for talking pictures.

Homes of Hollywood Stars highlights actors that rose and fell through the years with the changes in industry and the affection of fans. Since this book is arranged in semi-alphabetical order, it makes it easy for readers to look up screen actors and to compare their homes. Even though these cards were designed to celebrate fame and popularity, they are now also a reminder of how fickle and fading fame is.

One

ABBOTT AND COSTELLO TO BURNS AND ALLEN

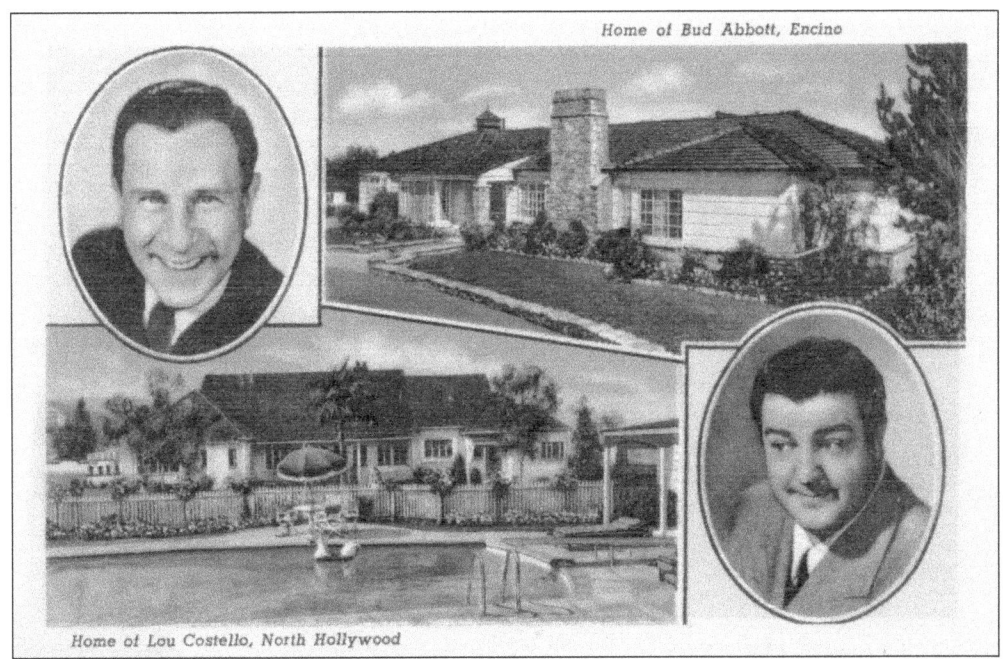

ABBOTT AND COSTELLO. At the height of their fame in the 1940s, the beloved comedy duo of Bud Abbott (1895–1974) and Lou Costello (1906–1959) lived at 4505 Woodley Avenue in Encino and 6935 Longridge Avenue in North Hollywood, respectively. Their films made at Universal Studios include *Buck Privates, In the Navy, Hold That Ghost, Keep 'Em Flying, Who Done It?, The Naughty Nineties,* and *Mexican Hayride.*

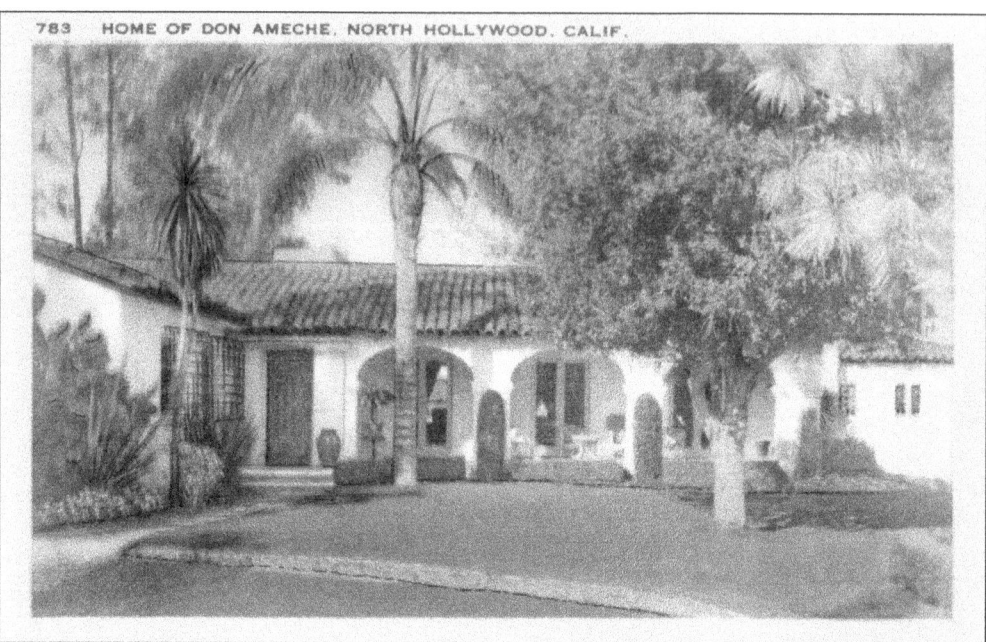

DON AMECHE. Before buying Al Jolson's estate in Encino (1939), Ameche and his family lived in this North Hollywood house. The enumerator for the US Census 1940 listed its value as $150,000. The half-Italian and half-Scottish Don Ameche (1908–1993), born Dominic Amici, starred in many films, including *Gateway*, *The Story of Alexander Graham Bell*, *Down Argentina Way*, *Something to Shout About*, *Happy Land*, *Picture Mommy Dead*, and *Cocoon* (Oscar, 1985).

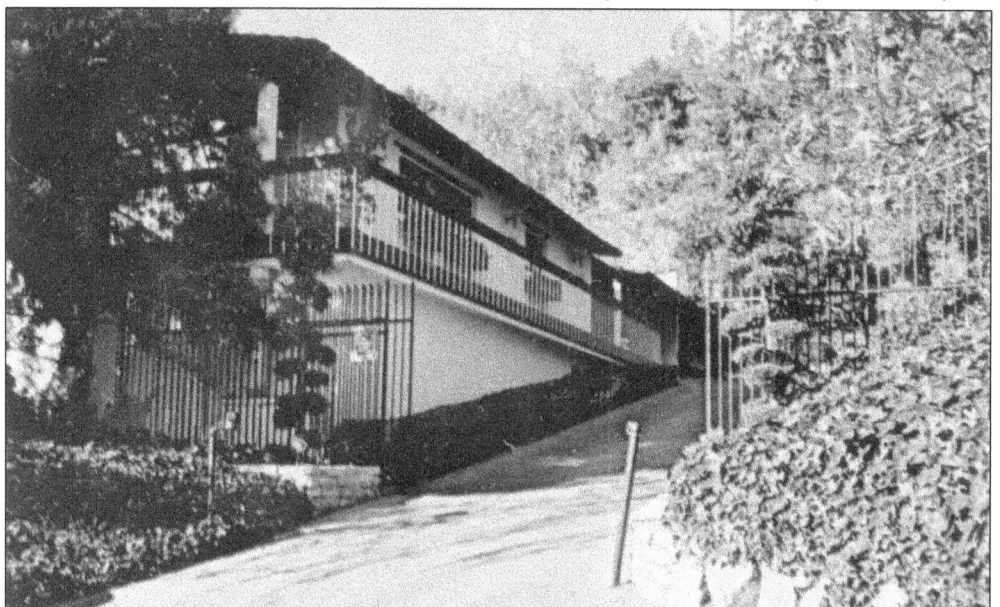

JULIE ANDREWS. The British actress Dame Julie Andrews (born 1935) became a sensational star on Broadway with *My Fair Lady* (1956) and *Camelot* (1960) and on screen with *Mary Poppins*, for which she won an Oscar (1964). The delightful English stage actress had proved to be so perfect in films that she achieved further acclaim with *The Americanization of Emily*, *The Sound of Music*, and *Thoroughly Modern Milly*. This is her Beverly Hills home.

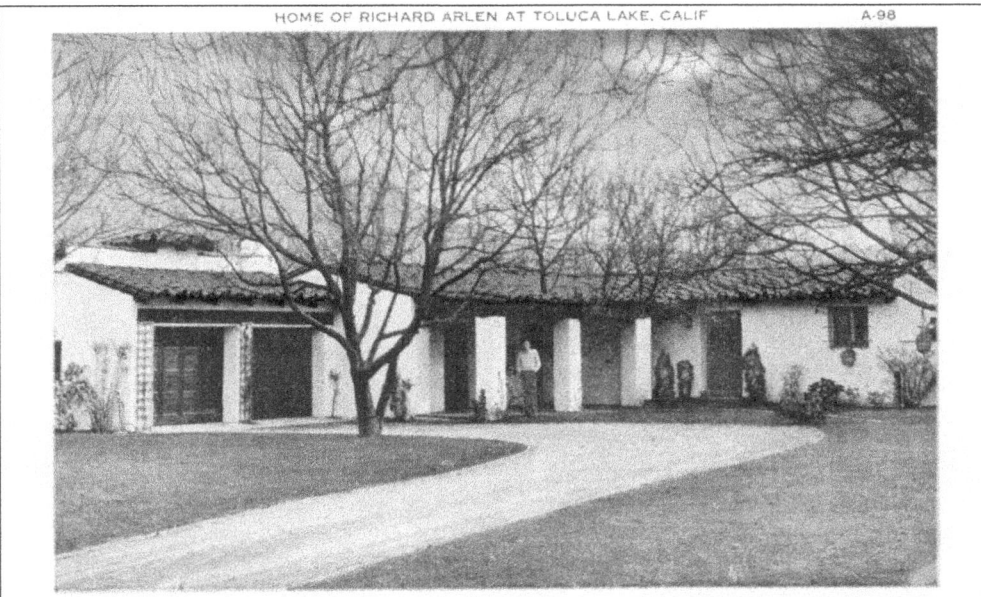

RICHARD ARLEN. Born in Minnesota as Sylvanus Mattimore, Richard Arlen (1899–1976) was one of Hollywood's most popular stars of the late 1920s and early 1930s. Among his films are the silent aviation classic *Wings* and talkies such as *The Four Feathers*, *Island of Lost Souls*, *Three-Cornered Moon*, and *The All-American*. In 1930, Arlen and his wife, actress Jobyna Ralston, lived in this house at 10025 Toluca Lake Avenue.

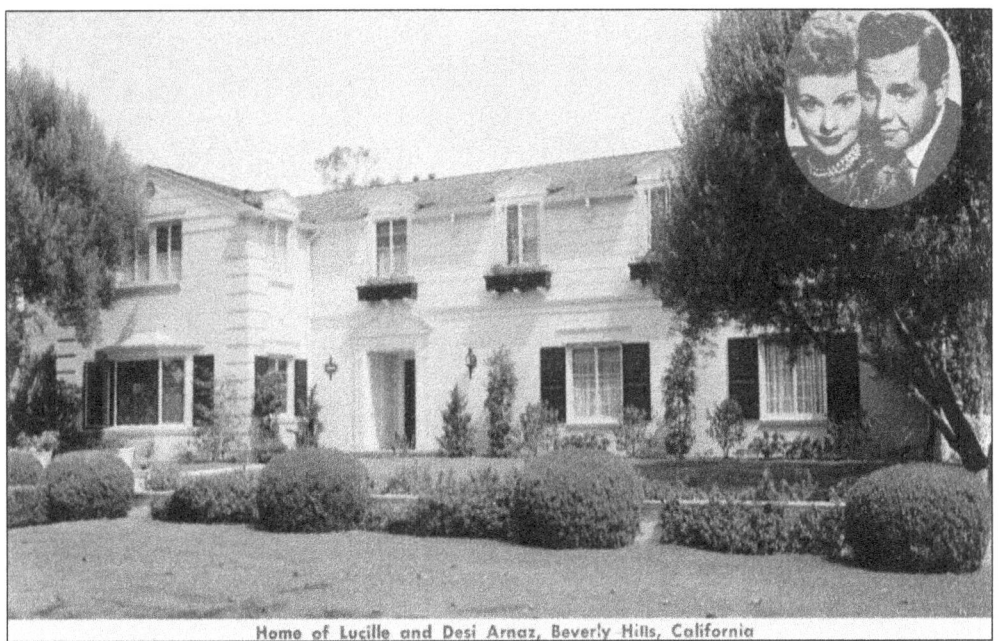

Home of Lucille and Desi Arnaz, Beverly Hills, California

DESI ARNAZ AND LUCILLE BALL. In 1955, Desi Arnaz and Lucille Ball moved into this mansion at 1000 North Roxbury Drive, Beverly Hills. Aside from their popular television show *I Love Lucy*, Lucille Ball (1911–1989) starred in movies, such as *Beauty for the Asking*, *Best Foot Forward*, *The Dark Corner*, and, opposite Franchot Tone, *Her Husband's Affairs*. Aside from films with his wife, Desi Arnaz (1917–1986) starred in *Cuban Pete* and *The Escape Artist*.

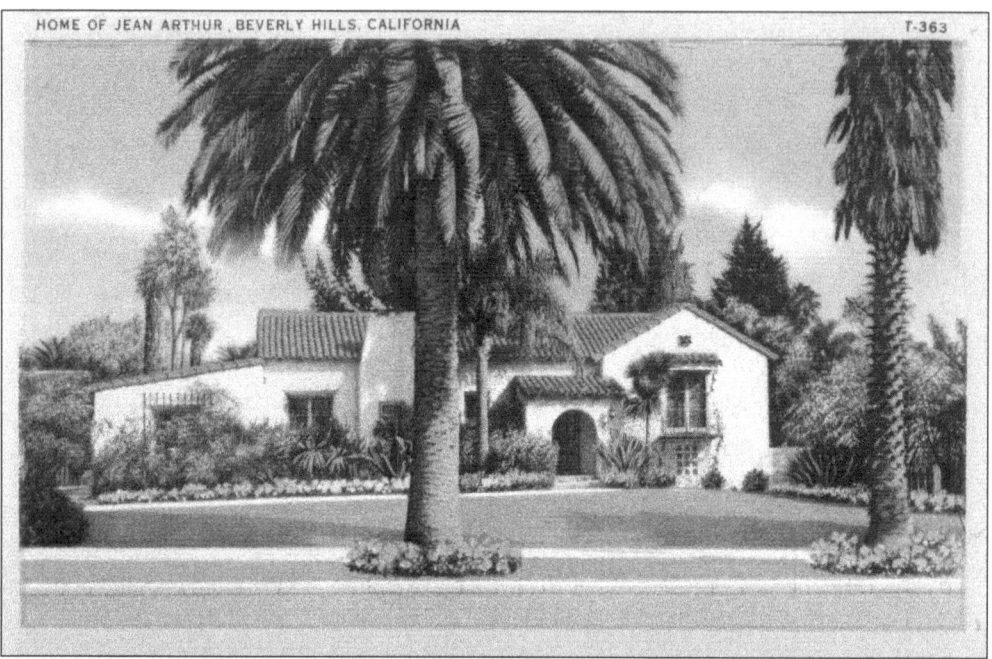

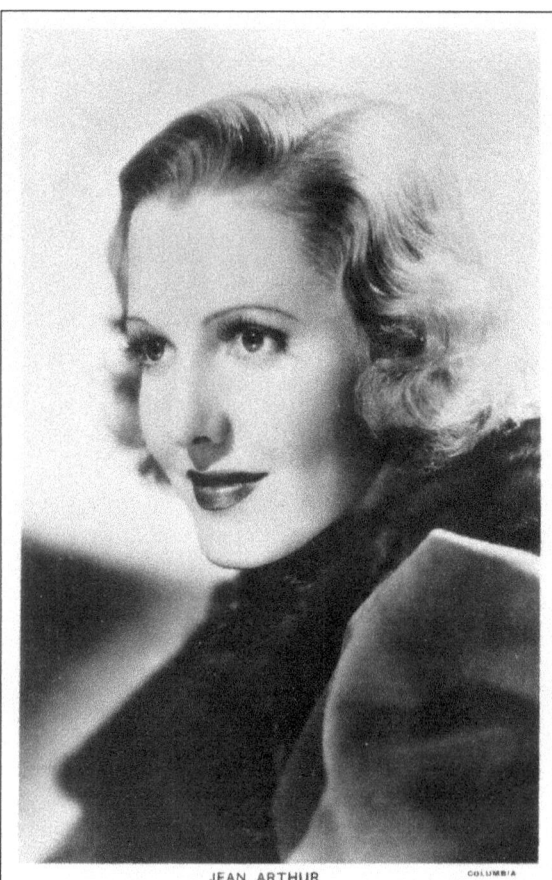

JEAN ARTHUR

COLUMBIA

JEAN ARTHUR. Jean Arthur (1900–1991), the effervescent star of classic screwball comedies, rented this Beverly Hills house at 512 Beverly Drive in the 1930s. In 1938, she and her husband, Frank Ross, moved to Brentwood. Among her best films are *The Whole Town's Talking, Mr. Deeds Goes to Town, The Ex-Mrs. Bradford, The Plainsman, Easy Living, Only Angels Have Wings, You Can't Take It with You, The More the Merrier,* and *Shane.*

JEAN ARTHUR PICTURE POSTCARD. Jean Arthur had a career stretching back to silent films. However, her career faltered after talkies came in, so she left for New York to learn how to master dialogue as a stage actress. Two years later, she return to Hollywood with confidence and would eventually became one of its most successful stars. This real-photo postcard was published in the "Picture-Goer Series" by Kinematograph Publications of London.

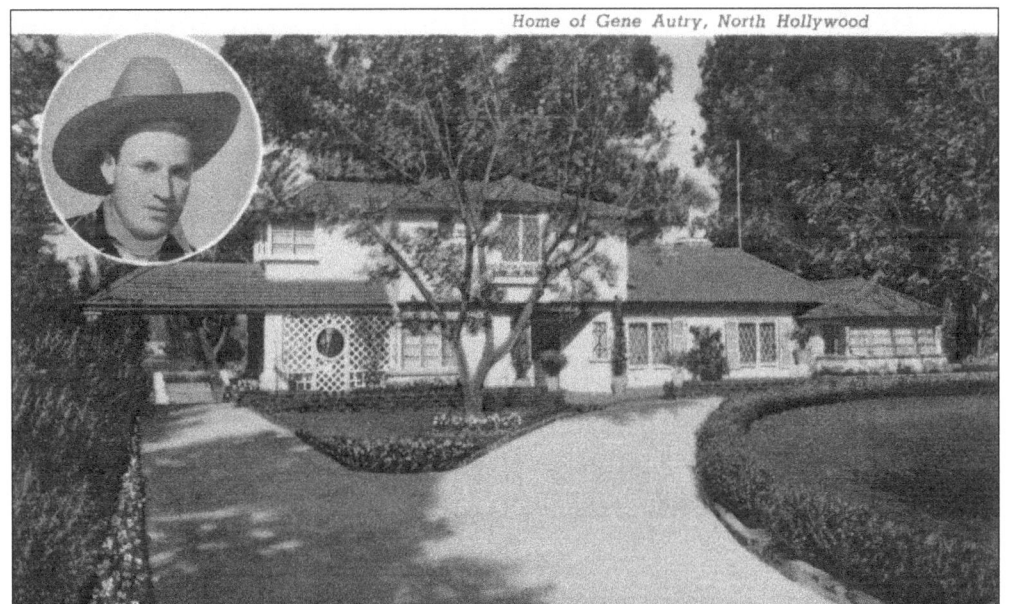

GENE AUTRY. This was the Singing Cowboy's home, presumably in Whitley Terrace, North Hollywood, in the 1930s. A unique talent who remained popular for decades, Gene Autry (1907–1998) was the star of 93 films, including *The Phantom Empire*, *Tumbling Tumbleweeds*, and *Springtime in the Rockies*, and had a successful CBS television series, *The Gene Autry Show* (1950–1956). Autry's hit songs include "Rudolph the Red-Nosed Reindeer" and "Here Comes Santa Claus."

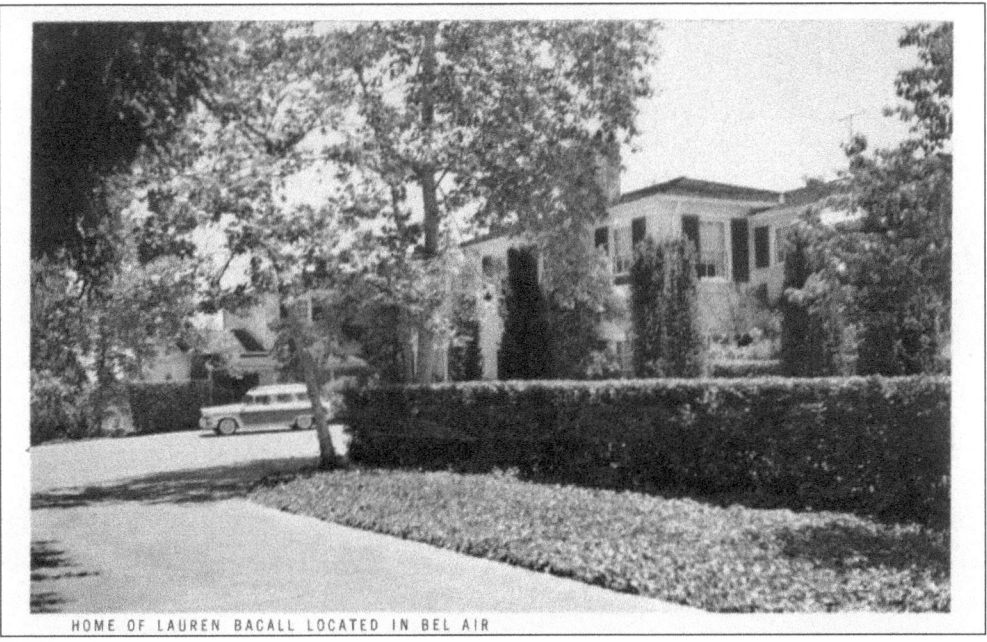

HOME OF LAUREN BACALL LOCATED IN BEL AIR

LAUREN BACALL. Lauren Bacall (1924–2014) lived at 232 North Mapleton Drive with her husband, Humphrey Bogart, and continued to live there for several years following his death in 1957. Bacall began as a model and, following her marriage to Bogart, launched a long career on screen and stage. Her films include *To Have and Have Not*, *Confidential Agent*, *The Big Sleep*, *Dark Passage*, and *Written on the Wind*.

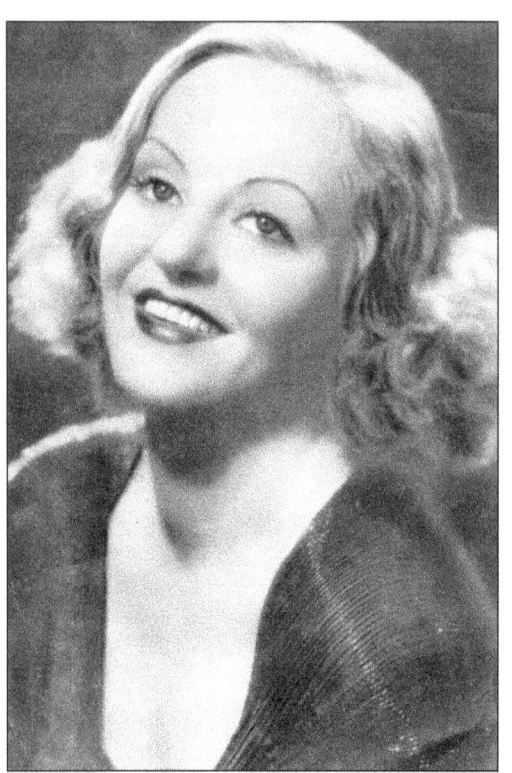

TALLULAH BANKHEAD. In 1931, Paramount Pictures brought Broadway star Tallulah Bankhead (1902–1968) to Hollywood. For them, she starred in *Tarnished Lady* (with Clive Brook), *My Sin* (with Fredric March), *The Cheat* (with Harvey Stephens), *Thunder Below* (with Charles Bickford), *Devil and the Deep* (with Cary Grant and Charles Laughton), and *Faithless* (with Robert Montgomery). At the time, Bankhead was renting 1712 North Stanley Avenue, Hollywood Hills, from actor-designer William Haines.

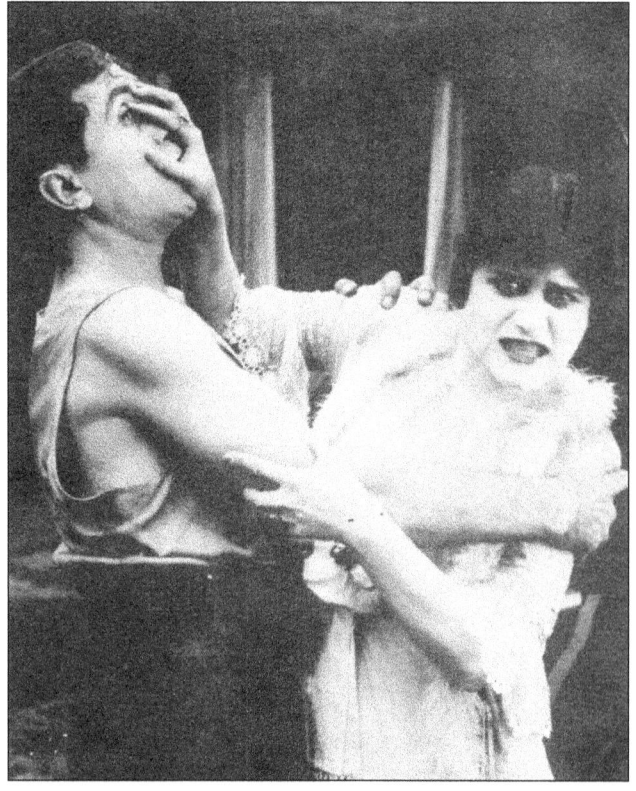

THEDA BARA. Silent screen vamp Theda Bara (1890–1955) lived at 649 West Adams Boulevard, Los Angeles, from 1917 to 1919; she later moved to 632 North Alpine Drive, Beverly Hills. The greatest silent screen temptress, Bara shocked but secretly thrilled audiences with such wicked offerings as *A Fool There Was*, *Lady Audley's Secret*, *Cleopatra*, *The Eternal Sappho*, *The She-Devil*, and *The Siren's Song*. This scene from *Destruction* (1915) shows Bara with costar Johnnie Walker (1894–1949).

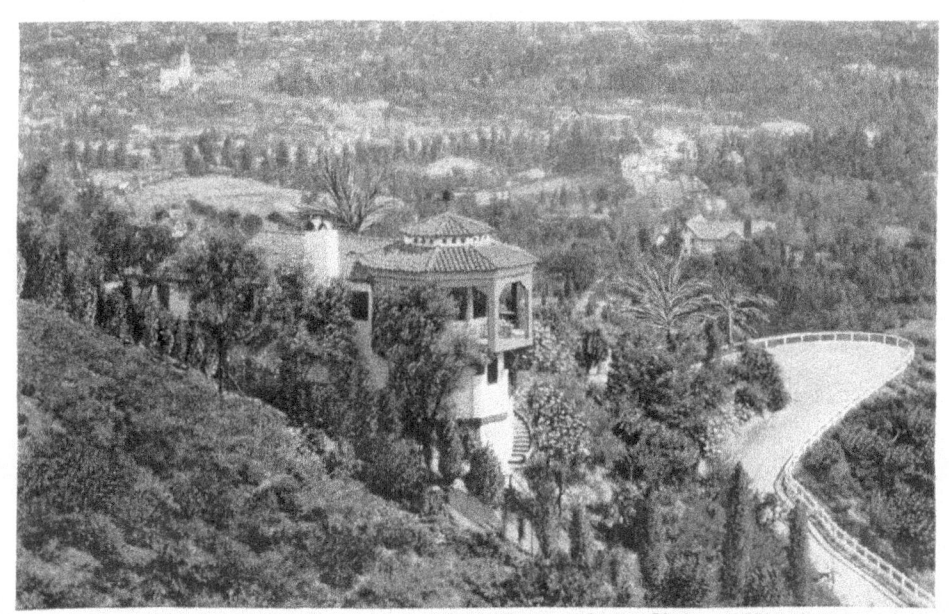

RESIDENCE OF MR. AND MRS. JOHN BARRYMORE (DOLORES COSTELLO), BEVERLY HILLS

JOHN BARRYMORE AND DOLORES COSTELLO. This Barrymore estate overlooked Beverly Hills. On November 24, 1928, John Barrymore married Dolores Costello (1903–1979), his leading lady in *The Sea Beast.* They lived here and had two children; unfortunately, they divorced in 1934. In her later years, Dolores Costello owned an avocado grove near San Diego, California. Among Barrymore's films are *Svengali, Grand Hotel, Topaze, A Bill of Divorcement*, and *Twentieth Century.*

JOHN AND LIONEL BARRYMORE. Celebrated as the "Royal Family of Broadway," John and Lionel Barrymore, as well as their sister Ethel, were also acclaimed in Hollywood. Pictured here are John (1882–1942) and Lionel (1878–1952), who lived at 6 Beverly Grove and 802 Roxbury Drive, Beverly Hills, respectively. In the 1940s, their sister Ethel (1879–1959), who had long reigned on Broadway, finally settled in Hollywood as well. In 1932, Metro-Goldwyn-Mayer (MGM) made a coup when all three of them starred in *Rasputin and the Empress.*

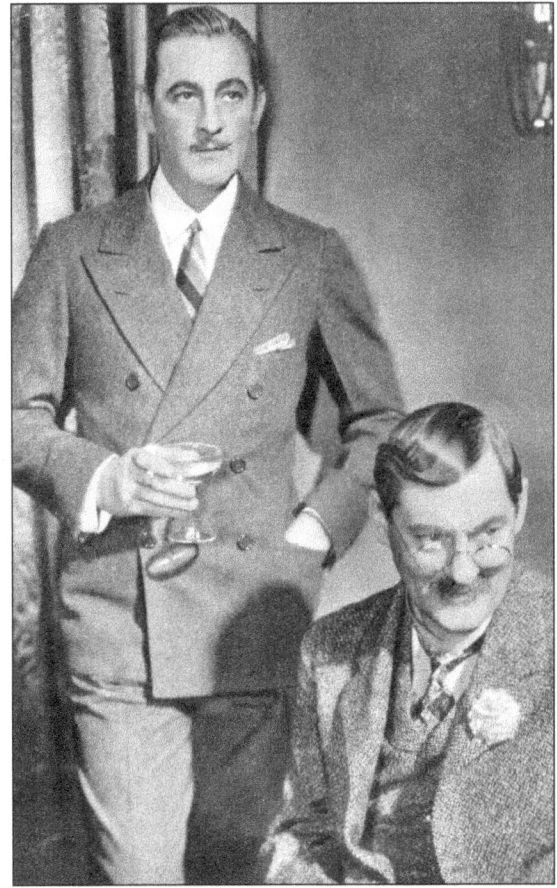

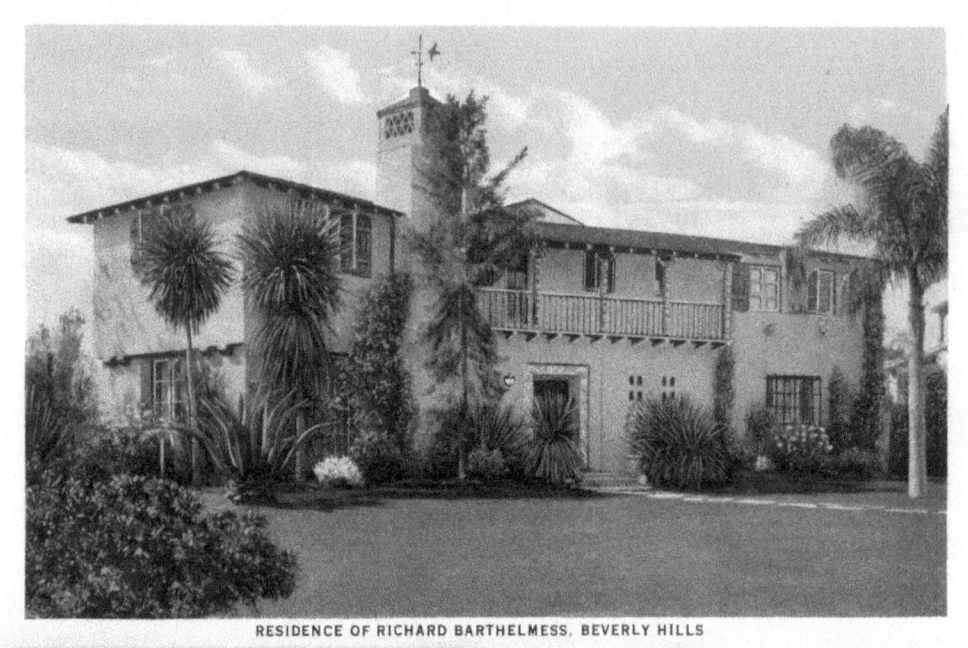

RESIDENCE OF RICHARD BARTHELMESS, BEVERLY HILLS

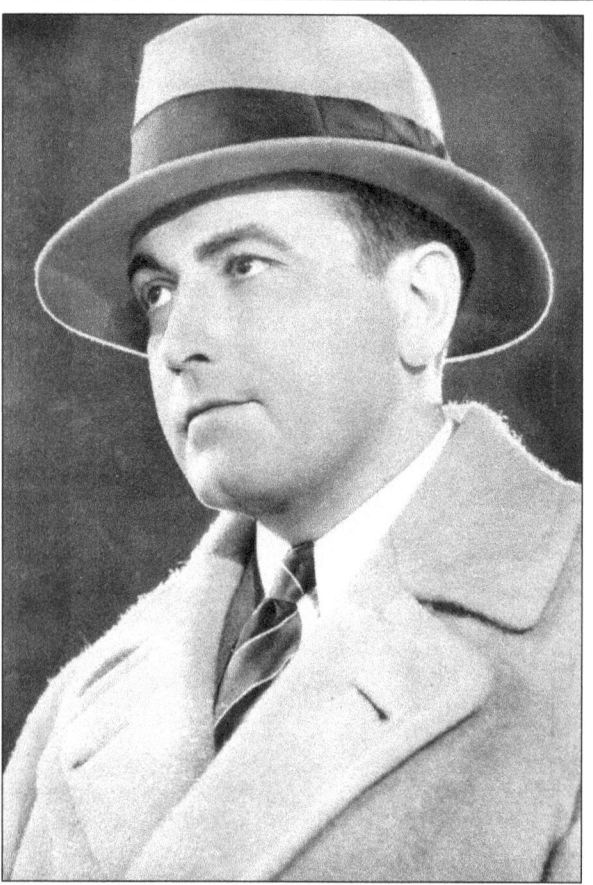

RICHARD BARTHELMESS. Located at 905 North Roxbury Drive, Beverly Hills, this Spanish-style estate was the home of silent screen star Richard Barthelmess (1895–1963). He was famous for his leading roles in such classic films as *Broken Blossoms*, *Way Down East*, *Tol'able David*, *The Noose*, *The Patent Leather Kid*, and *The Drop Kick*. Although he made the transition to sound films, his popularity waned following his initial success with *The Dawn Patrol* (1931).

RICHARD BARTHELMESS PORTRAIT. As a screen star, Richard Barthelmess was the very embodiment of the clean-cut American hero. He produced 12 movies of his own as well as starred in films for First National Pictures. In his last years, he retired to his lavish estate in Southampton, Long Island, New York.

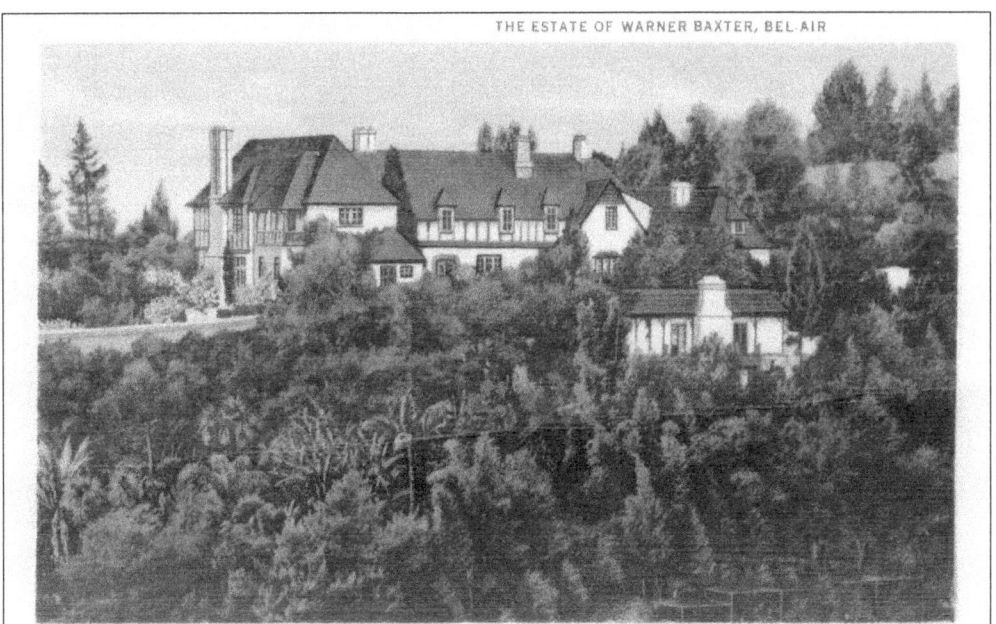

WARNER BAXTER. Warner Baxter lived in this mansion at 688 Nimes Road, Bel Air. Baxter had this Tudor-style estate built for him in 1933 at the height of his fame. In 1929, Warner Baxter (1889–1951) won an Oscar for playing the Cisco Kid in *In Old Arizona*. He also starred in *The Great Gatsby*, *42nd Street*, *Broadway Bill*, *The Prisoner of Shark Island*, *Kidnapped*, and, in the 1940s, 10 Crime Doctor mysteries for Columbia Pictures.

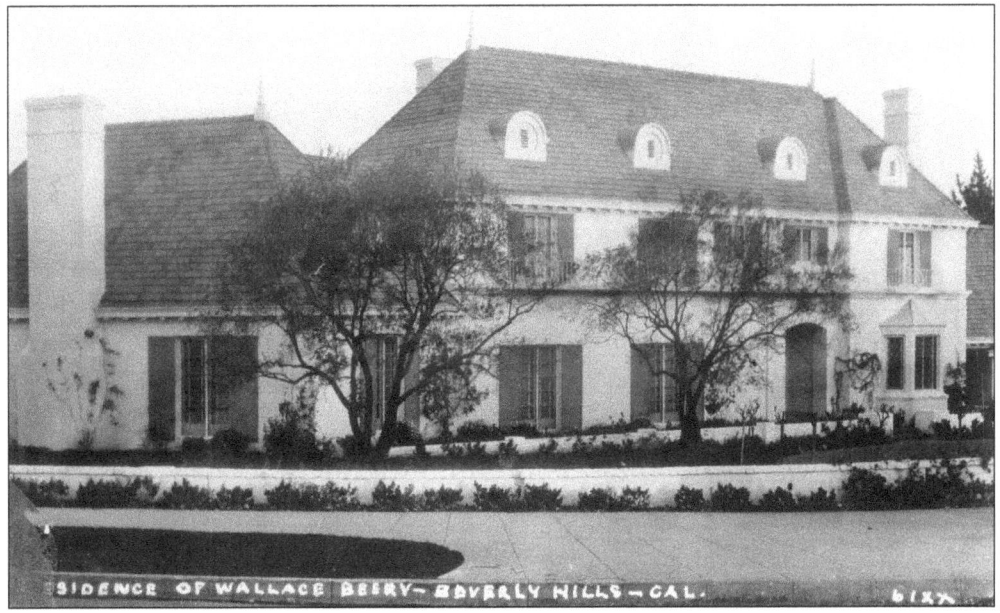

WALLACE BEERY. In 1935, Wallace Beery (1885–1949) had this French-style mansion at 816 North Alpine Drive, Beverly Hills, built for him. After years playing villains in silent pictures, he went on to stardom when Metro-Goldwyn-Mayer found that his gruff voice and rough charm delighted audiences; thus, he became the screen's "lovable old rascal." Beery's films include *Min and Bill*, *The Champ* (Oscar, 1931), *The Bowery*, *Treasure Island*, and *Viva Villa!*

17

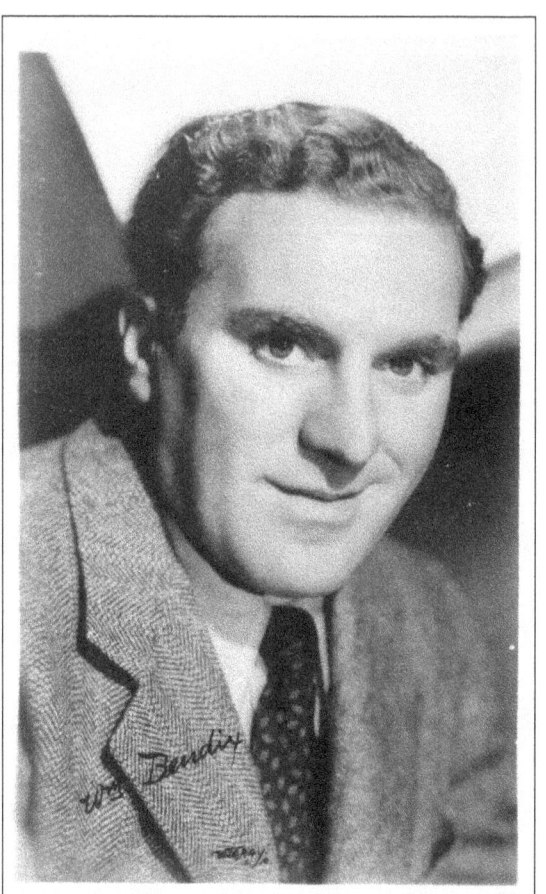

WILLIAM BENDIX PICTURE POSTCARD. Actor William Bendix (1906–1964) was noted for his dramatic performances in dozens of films as well as his work on the television series *The Life of Riley* (1953–1958). His movies include *Lifeboat*, *The Hairy Ape*, *Wake Island*, *The Babe Ruth Story*, *Cover Up*, and *Idol on Parade*. In the latter film, he convincingly played a British army sergeant major. Bendix lived at 5031 Encino Avenue, Encino.

ENID BENNETT. Australia's Enid Bennett came to America in 1915. In 1918, she married movie director Fred Niblo (1874–1948). In the 1920s, they lived in this mansion at 805 North Crescent Drive, Beverly Hills. Enid Bennett (1893–1969) had starring roles in *Fuss and Feathers*, *What Every Woman Learns*, *Robin Hood*, *The Sea Hawk*, and *The Red Lily*. In 1931, she had supporting roles in two talkies, *Waterloo Road* and *Skippy*.

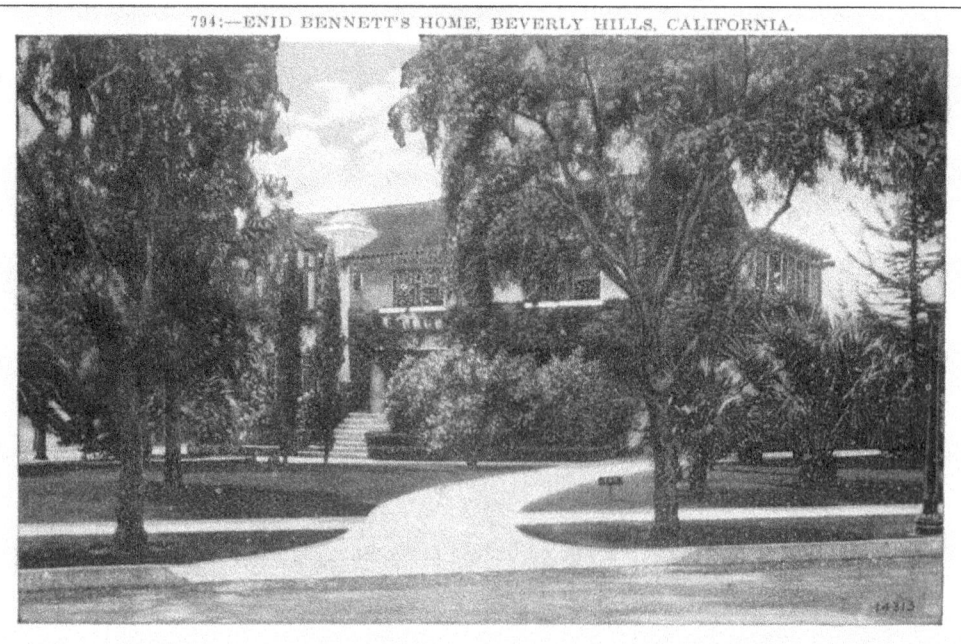

794:—ENID BENNETT'S HOME, BEVERLY HILLS, CALIFORNIA.

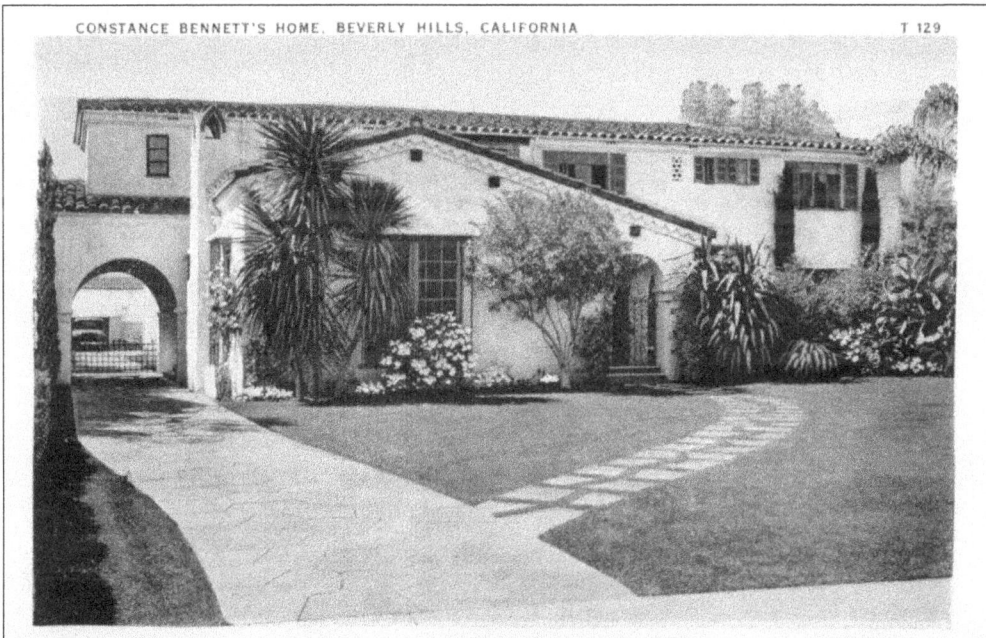

CONSTANCE BENNETT. In 1931, Constance Bennett (1904–1965), a member of the famous theatrical Bennett family, lived in this Spanish-style residence at 903 North Roxbury Drive, Beverly Hills. She later moved to Carolwood Drive. Constance Bennett's starring vehicles include *Three Faces East*, *Common Clay*, *The Easiest Way*, *Bed of Roses*, *Lady with a Past*, *Our Betters*, *Topper*, *Merrily We Live*, and *Madame Spy*. Her final performance was in *Madame X*, which premiered in 1966.

CONSTANCE BENNETT PORTRAIT. Willowy blonde Constance Bennett was the daughter of famed stage actor Richard Bennett and the sister of Joan Bennett (1910–1990). As the highest paid star in Hollywood (1931), Constance Bennett was at the top of the lists for box office popularity and appeal. Her best-known films are *What Price Hollywood* (1932) and ethereal comedies *Topper* (1937), with Cary Grant and Roland Young, and *Topper Takes a Trip* (1938).

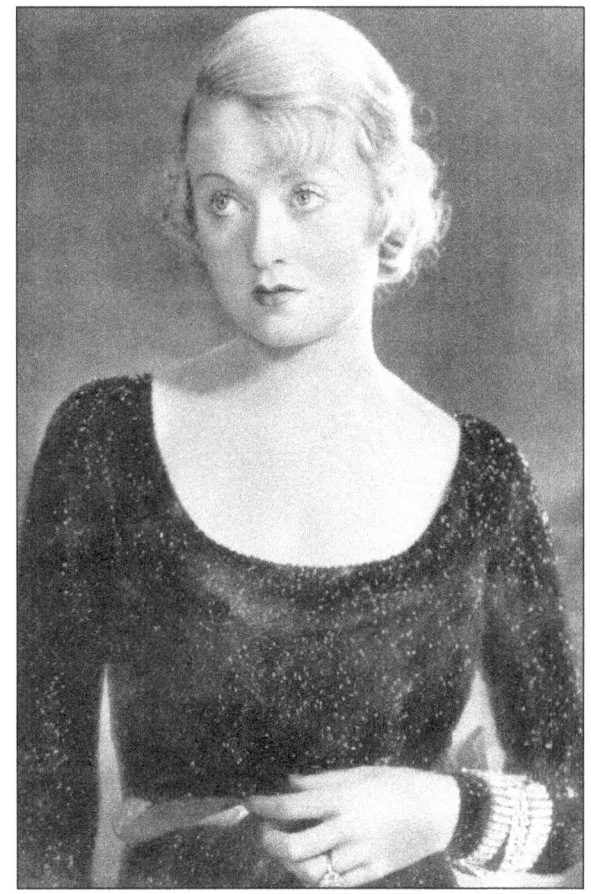

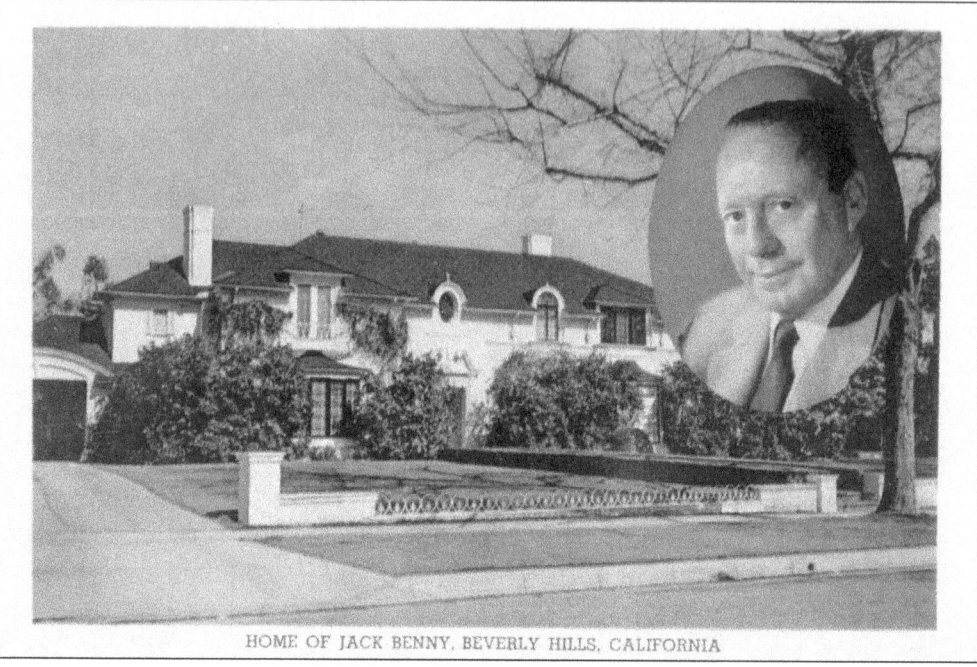

HOME OF JACK BENNY, BEVERLY HILLS, CALIFORNIA

JACK BENNY. The master of comedic timing, Jack Benny (1894–1974) lived with his wife, Mary Livingstone (1905–1983), born Sadya Marcowitz, at 1002 North Roxbury Drive, Beverly Hills, for 25 years. Jack Benny was a vaudeville headliner long before going to Hollywood, where his radio and television shows were especially popular. His films include *Broadway Melody of 1936*, *Charley's Aunt*, *To Be or Not to Be*, and *The Horn Blows at Midnight*.

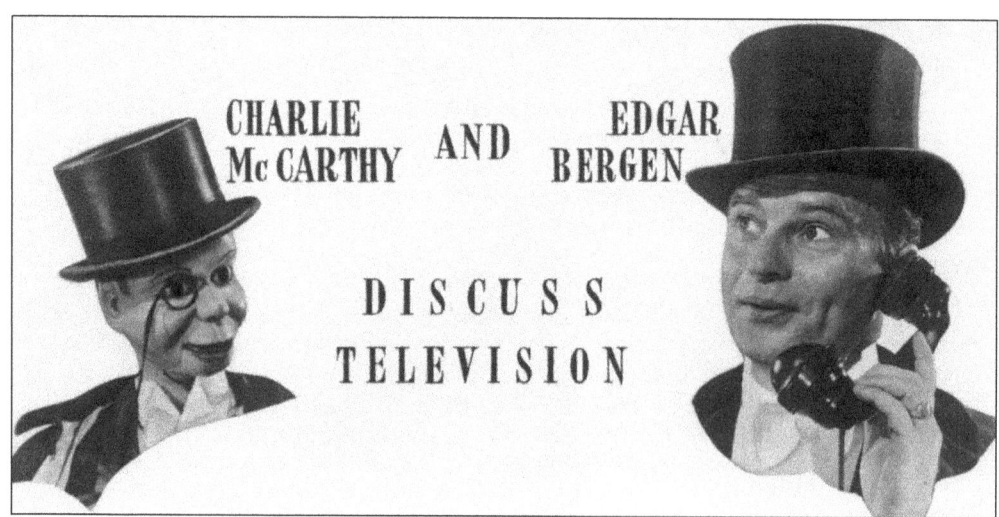

CHARLIE McCARTHY AND EDGAR BERGEN

DISCUSS TELEVISION

EDGAR BERGEN AND CHARLIE McCARTHY. Ventriloquist Edgar Bergen (1903–1978) delighted millions with the cunning wit of his dummy, Charlie McCarthy. This photograph of the pair appeared in 1949 when they were stars of the CBS-Radio program *The Charlie McCarthy Show*. The weekly show lasted until 1956. Bergen and his daughter Candice lived in his hacienda-style house, Bella Vista, at 9876 Beverly Grove Drive, Beverly Hills.

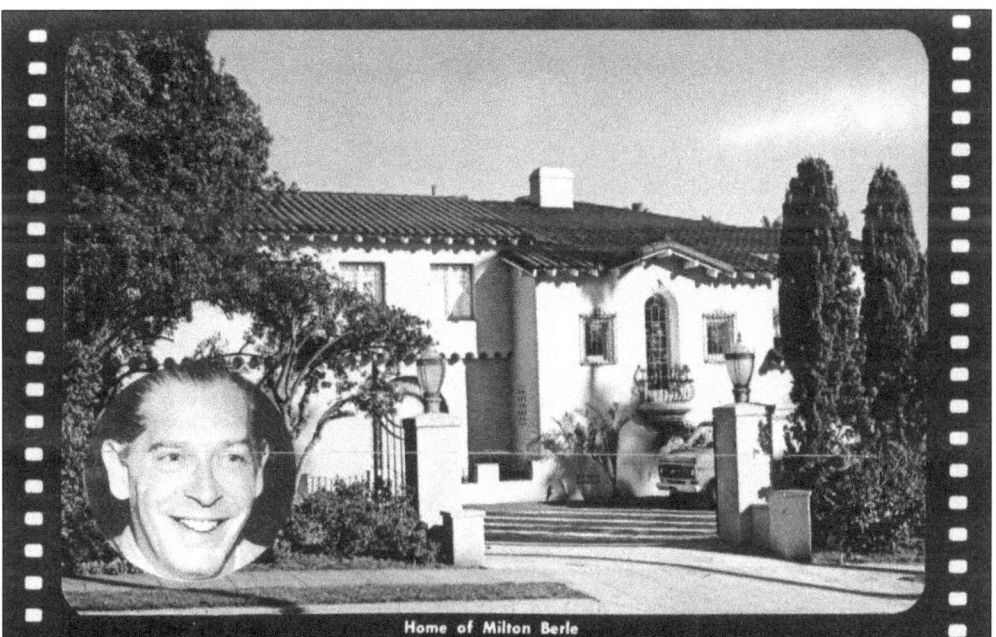

Home of Milton Berle

MILTON BERLE. Television's first superstar, Milton Berle, known to his adoring fans as "Uncle Miltie," reigned with *The Texaco Star Theatre* (*The Milton Berle Show*) (1948–1956). Because he was a phenomenally successful host, countless Americans rushed out to buy a television set just to see his show. Berle, who lived at 908 North Crescent Drive, Beverly Hills, was also in films, such as *Whispering Ghosts*, *Over My Dead Body*, *Always Leave Them Laughing*, and *The Oscar.*

JOAN BLONDELL. From 1936 to 1939, during the first three years of her marriage to actor-crooner Dick Powell, Joan Blondell (1906–1979) lived at 711 North Maple Drive, Beverly Hills. Built in 1926, the English-style six-bedroom house also had a swimming pool. In 1939, they moved to Fay Wray's former house on Selma Avenue in Hollywood. Blondell's films include *Footlight Parade*, *Stage Struck*, *East of Heaven*, and *A Tree Grows in Brooklyn.*

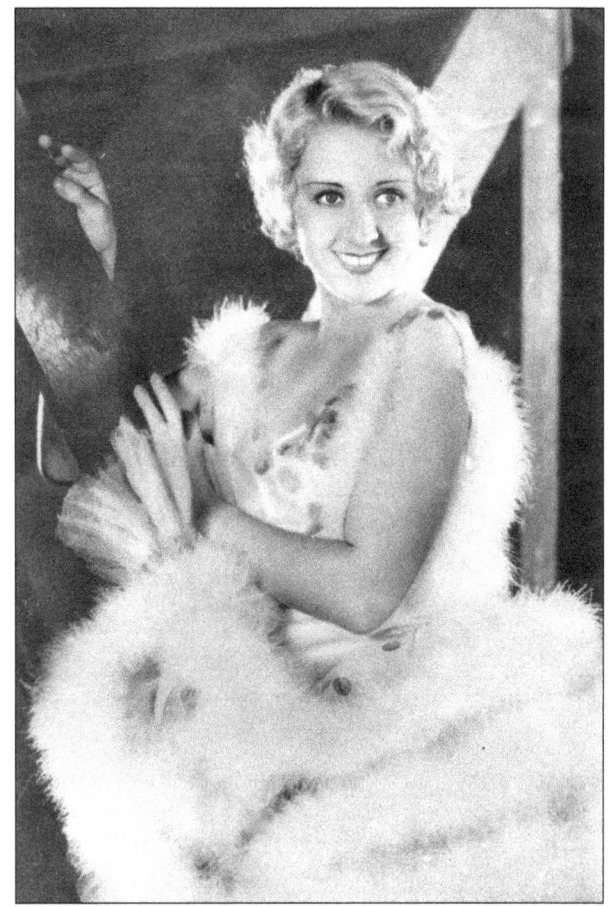

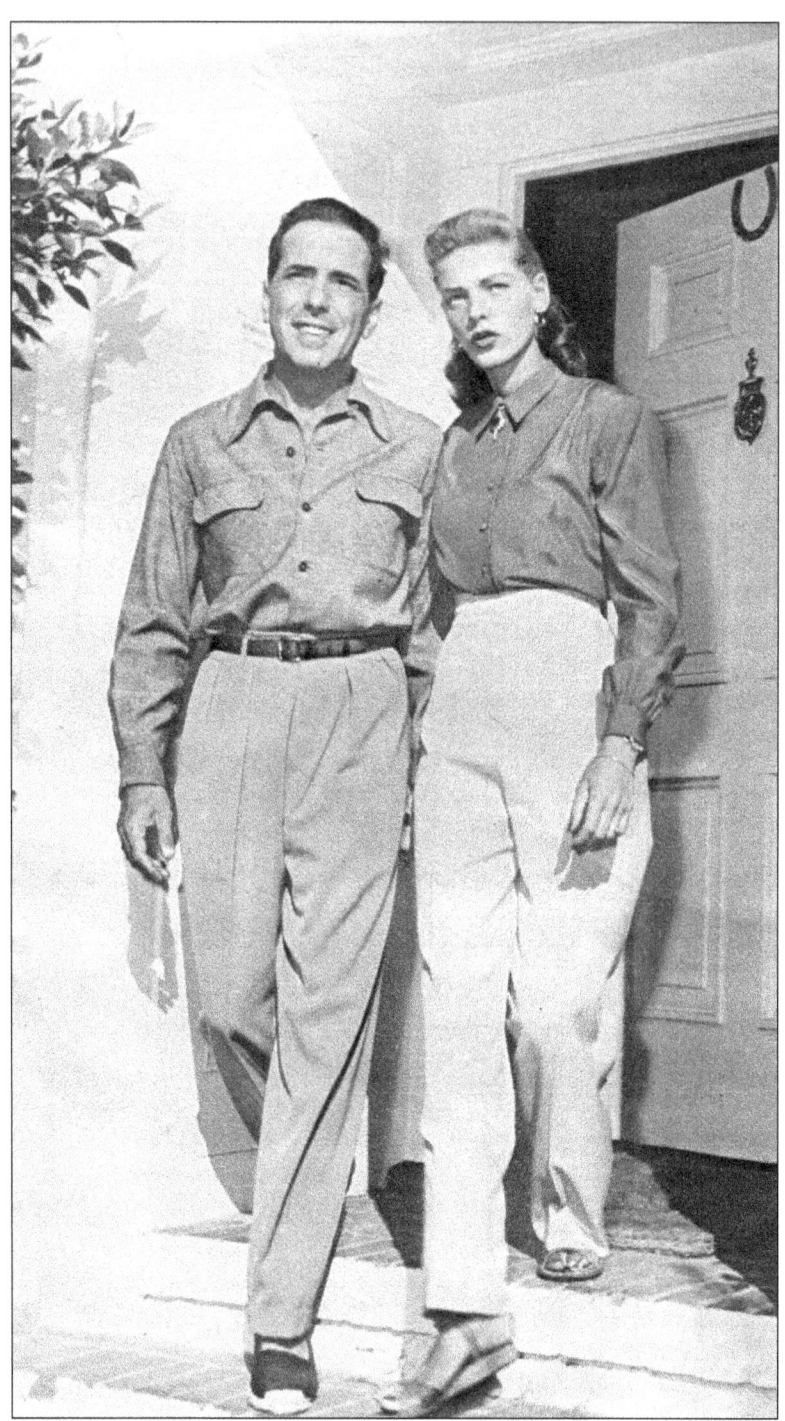

HUMPHREY BOGART AND LAUREN BACALL. Here, Humphrey Bogart and his wife, Lauren Bacall, are seen stepping out of their Beverly Hills home in 1949 to greet a guest. Bogart (1899–1957) said that he liked cozy homes. The couple, though 25 years apart in age, married on a farm in Ohio on May 21, 1945. They costarred together in *To Have and Have Not*, *The Big Sleep*, *Dark Passage*, and *Key Largo*.

JOHN BOLES PORTRAIT. Texan John Boles was educated at the University of Texas at Austin, where he studied French and German as well as premed, and then served in the Army during World War I. His education and abilities, including fluency in French, resulted in his reassignment to intelligence under Gen. John J. Pershing. Boles lived at 259 South Roxbury Drive, Beverly Hills.

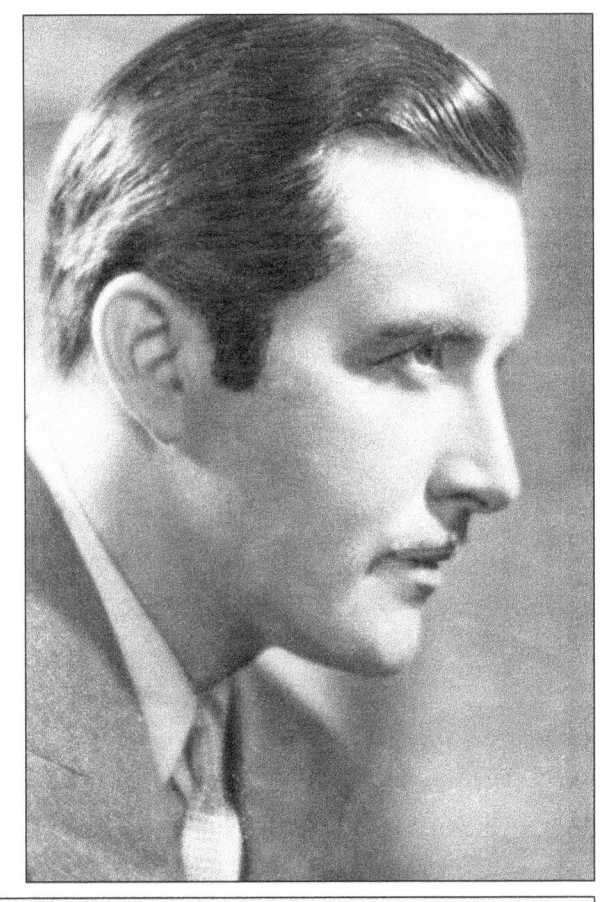

JOHN BOLES. Actor and singer John Boles (1895–1969) first won acclaim in Gloria Swanson's hit silent drama *The Loves of Sunya* (1927). With the advent of sound, Boles's star rose in musicals, like *The Desert Song, Rio Rita, Captain of the Guard,* and *One Heavenly Night.* Later, he successfully transitioned to such well-known dramas as *Frankenstein, Only Yesterday, Back Street, A Message to Garcia, Craig's Wife,* and *Stella Dallas.*

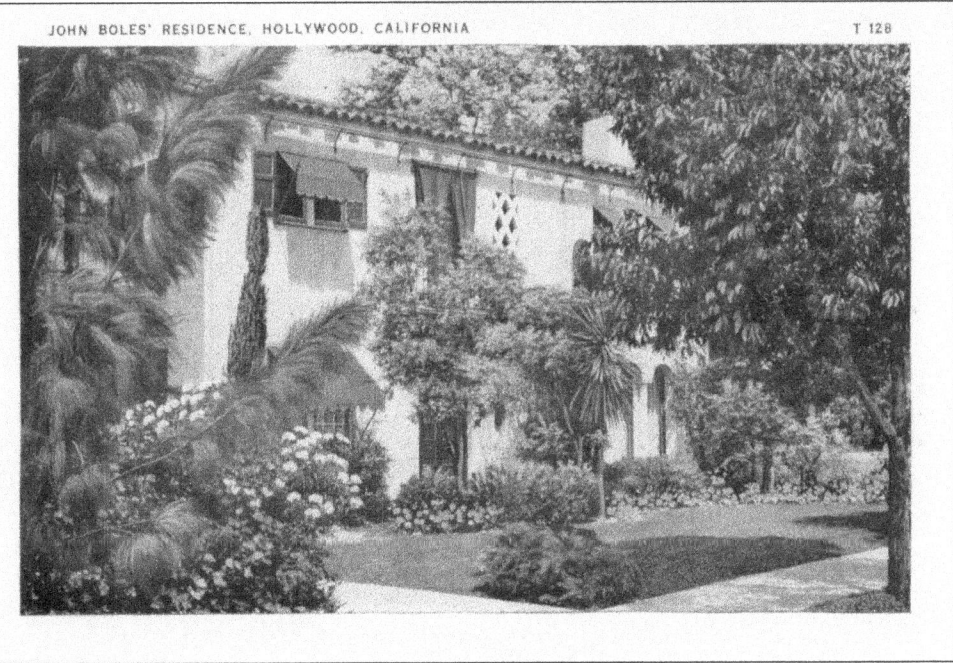

JOHN BOLES' RESIDENCE, HOLLYWOOD, CALIFORNIA   T 128

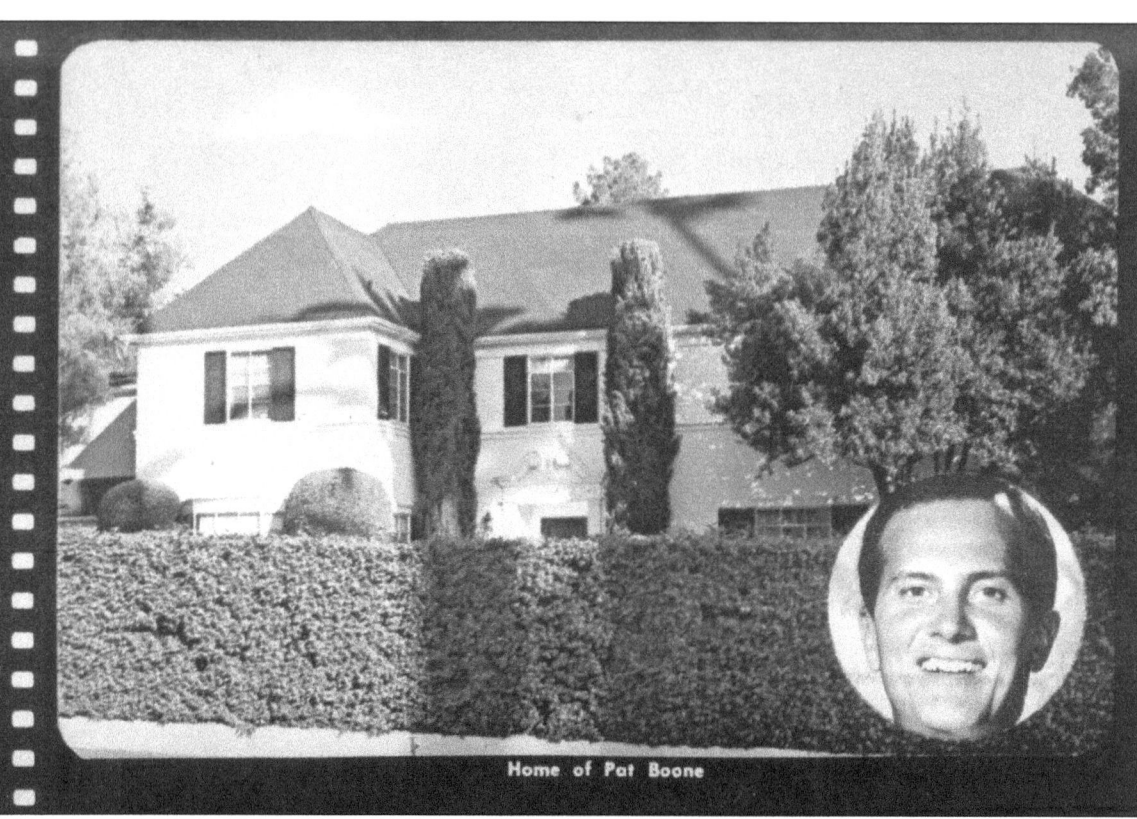

Home of Pat Boone

PAT BOONE. Pictured here is crooner Pat Boone's mansion at 904 North Beverly Drive, Beverly Hills. Boone (born 1934) rose from singer and composer to film star in the 1950s. His musical talent and wholesome image were helpful to his career. Boone's films include *Bernardine*, *April Love*, *Journey to the Center of the Earth*, and *State Fair*. On television, he starred in *The Pat Boone Chevy Showroom*.

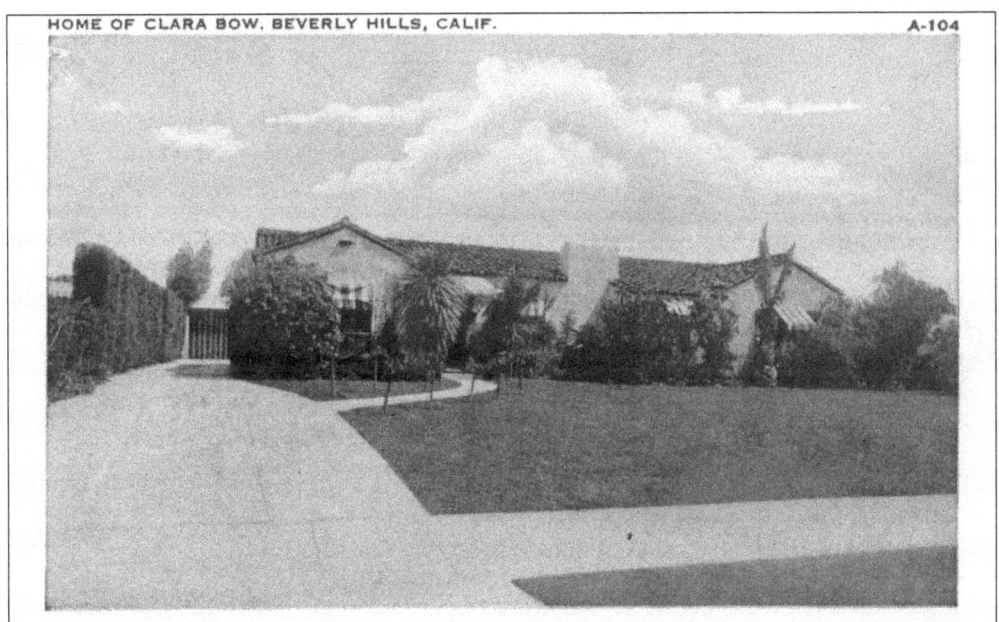

CLARA BOW. Although there were many Hollywood flappers, Clara Bow (1905–1965) is certainly the most iconic. Shown here is her home at 512 North Bedford Drive, Beverly Hills. "The It Girl," as she was called, was one of the brightest stars of the Roaring Twenties. Her films include *Parisian Love*, *The Plastic Age*, *Fascinating Youth*, *Mantrap*, *It*, *Rough House Rosie*, *Wings*, *Her Wedding Night*, *No Limit*, and *Call Her Savage*.

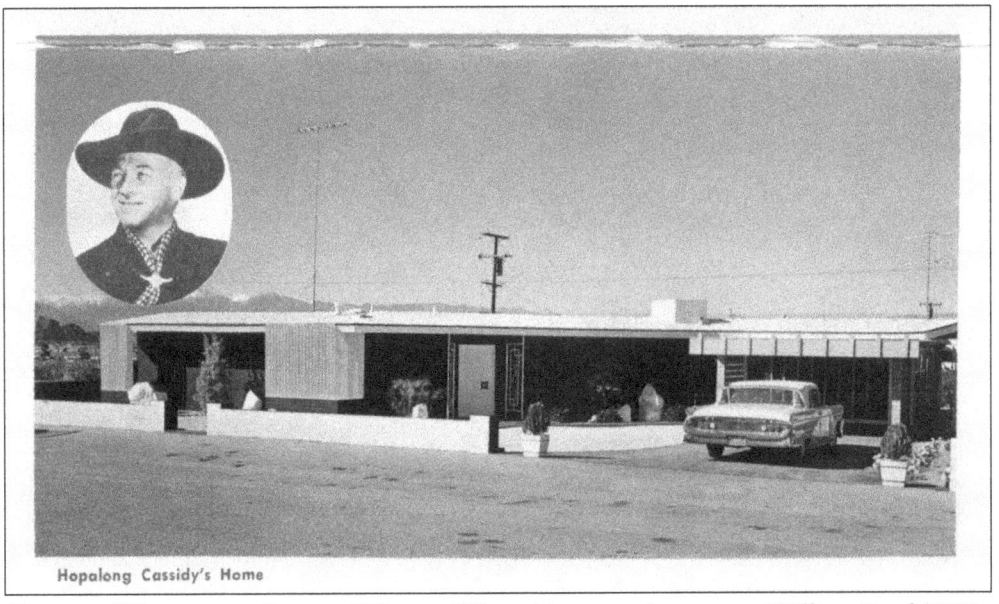

Hopalong Cassidy's Home

WILLIAM "HOPALONG CASSIDY" BOYD. When this postcard came out, William Boyd (1895–1972) had already retired from a successful career playing cowboy hero Hopalong Cassidy in a series of 66 movies, beginning with *Hop-Along Cassidy* (1935). In 1949, executives released these old films to television viewers. At the same time, a new television series for the actor was in production, called *Hopalong Cassidy* (NBC, 1949–1954). After retiring, he lived in this house on Verba Santa Drive, Palm Desert.

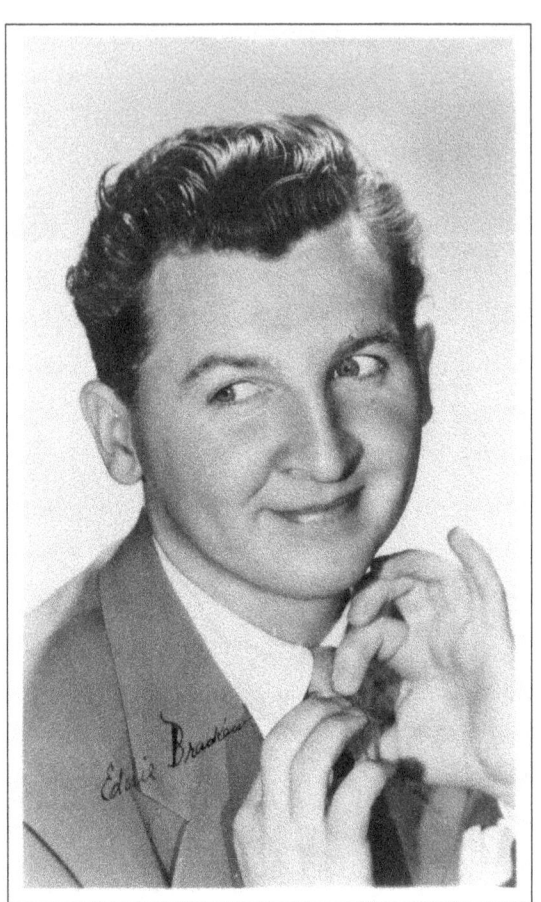

EDDIE BRACKEN PICTURE POSTCARD. Originally a New York stage and radio comedian, Eddie Bracken made an even greater mark on Hollywood with his memorable performances in *Hail the Conquering Hero* and *The Miracle of Morgan's Creek*, both released in 1944. His other films include *Bring on the Girls*, *Out of This World*, and *Hold That Blonde*. In the 1950s, Bracken (1915–2002), his wife, and children lived at 207 North Saltair Avenue, Brentwood Heights.

GEORGE BRENT. Irish immigrant George Brent (1904–1979) was a Hollywood leading man for years. He came to North America as a stage actor before settling down in Hollywood. His first film was *Under Suspicion* (1930). His later films include *42nd Street*, *The Painted Veil*, *The Rains Came*, *The Spiral Staircase*, and *Man Bait*, with Diana Dors. He lived at 727 North Bedford Drive, Beverly Hills.

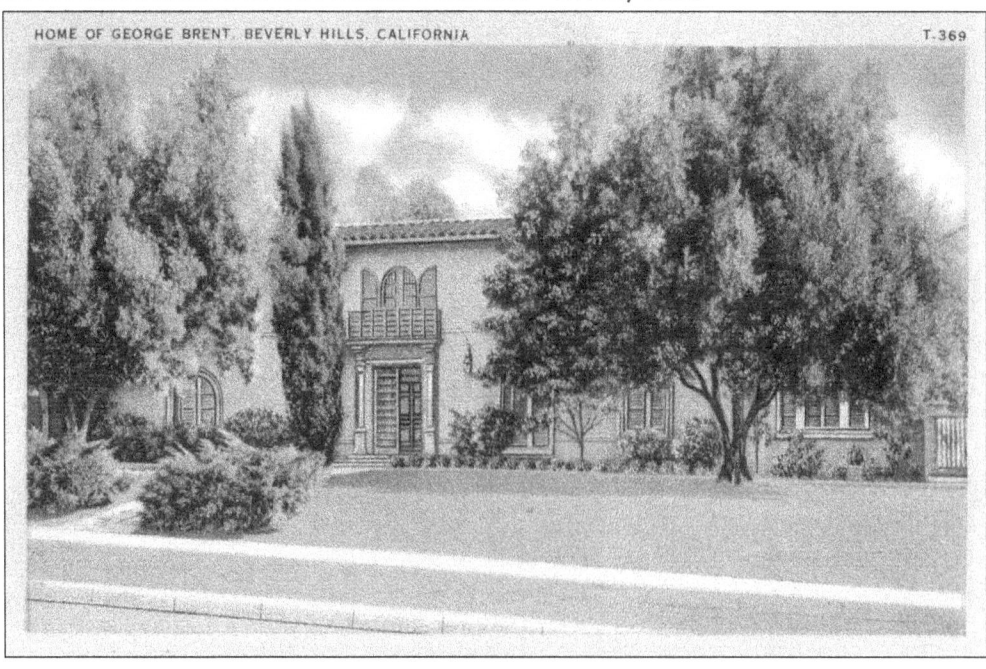

HOME OF GEORGE BRENT, BEVERLY HILLS, CALIFORNIA   T-369

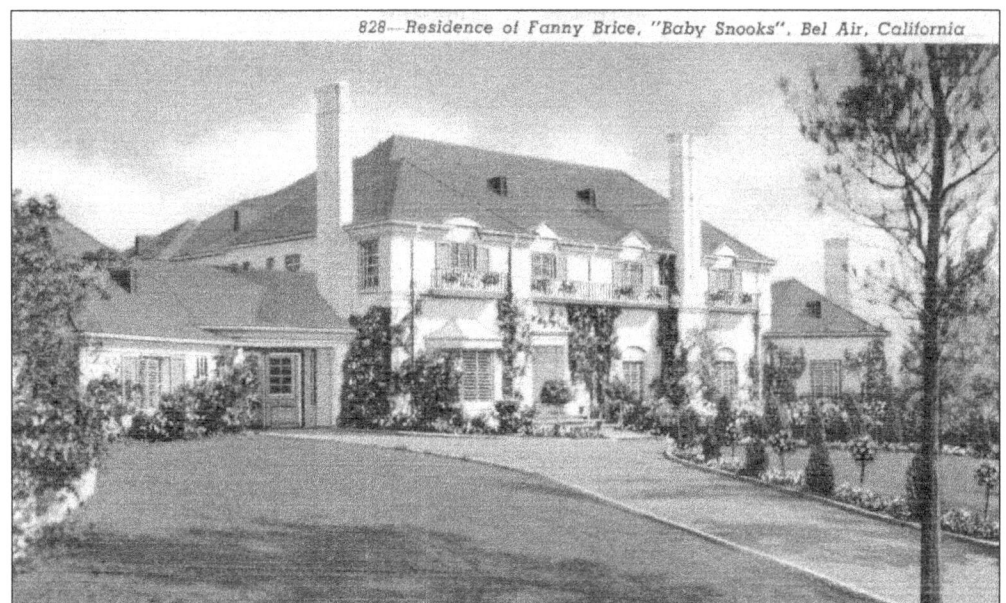

FANNY BRICE. After years in vaudeville and in *Ziegfeld Follies* on Broadway, legendary comedienne Fanny Brice (1891–1951) brought her old act "Baby Snooks" to various radio programs, which culminated in *The Baby Snooks Show* (1944–1951), a tremendous hit. From 1938 until 1951, Fanny Brice lived in this mansion at 312 North Faring Road, Bel Air. Her films include *My Man*, *The Great Ziegfeld*, *Everybody Sing*, and *Ziegfeld Follies*.

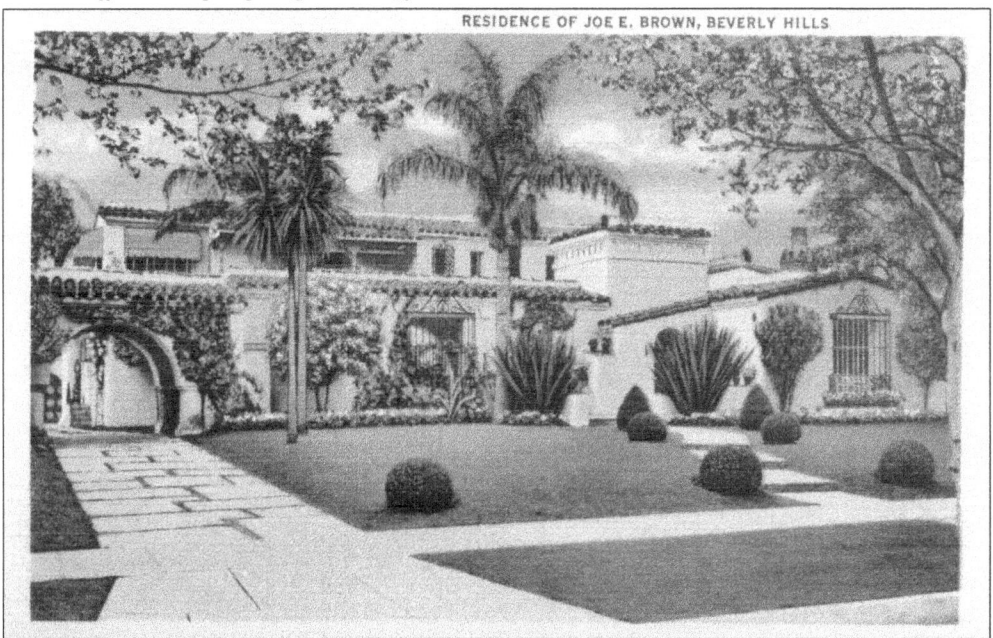

JOE E. BROWN. This is Joe E. Brown's mansion at 707 North Walden Drive, Beverly Hills. He commissioned Rene Rivierre (1899–1953) to design the Spanish Revival house, and Brown lived there from 1931 to 1938. Noted for his amiability and comedic timing, Joe E. Brown (1891–1973) was one of the top comedians of stage, screen, and radio. Among his films are *Alibi Ike*, *Elmer the Great*, and *Some Like It Hot*.

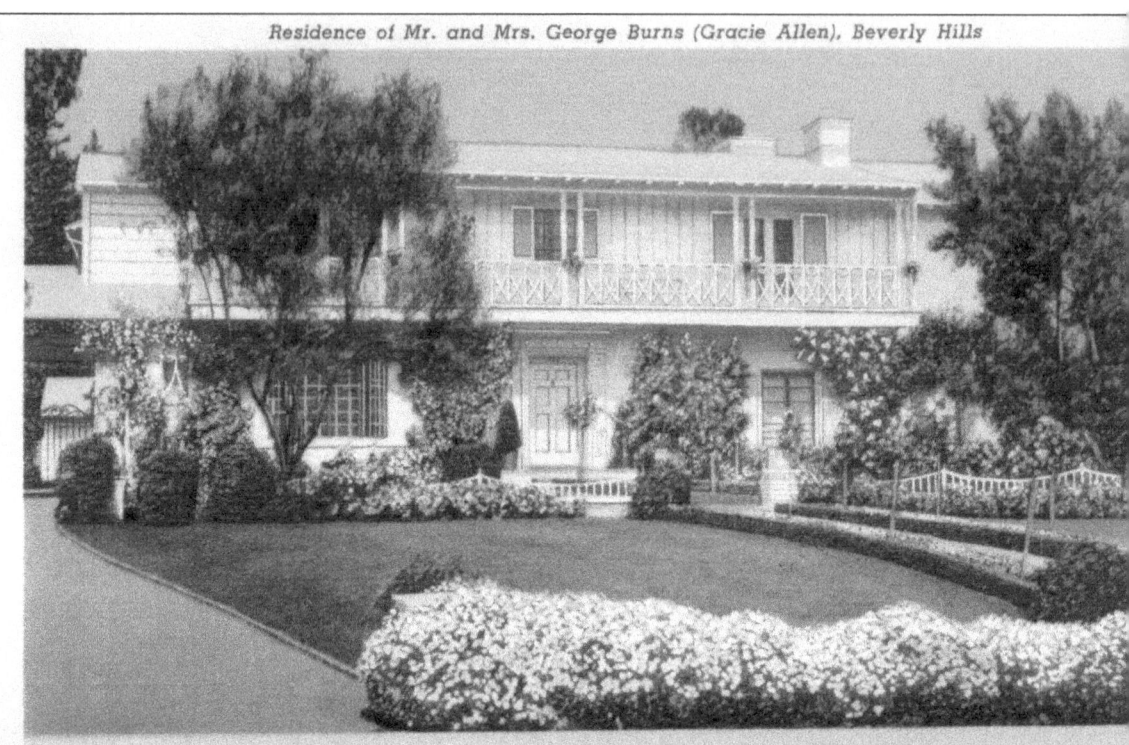
Residence of Mr. and Mrs. George Burns (Gracie Allen), Beverly Hills

GEORGE BURNS AND GRACIE ALLEN. In 1936, comedians George Burns (1896–1996) and Gracie Allen (1895–1964) moved into their newly built Old California–style mansion at 720 North Maple Drive, Beverly Hills. Old-time stars from the days of vaudeville, they struck gold in radio, motion pictures, and television. Their films include *Six of a Kind*, *We're Not Dressing*, *Many Happy Returns*, *College Holiday*, *A Damsel in Distress*, and *College Swing*.

Two

James Cagney to
Pauline Frederick

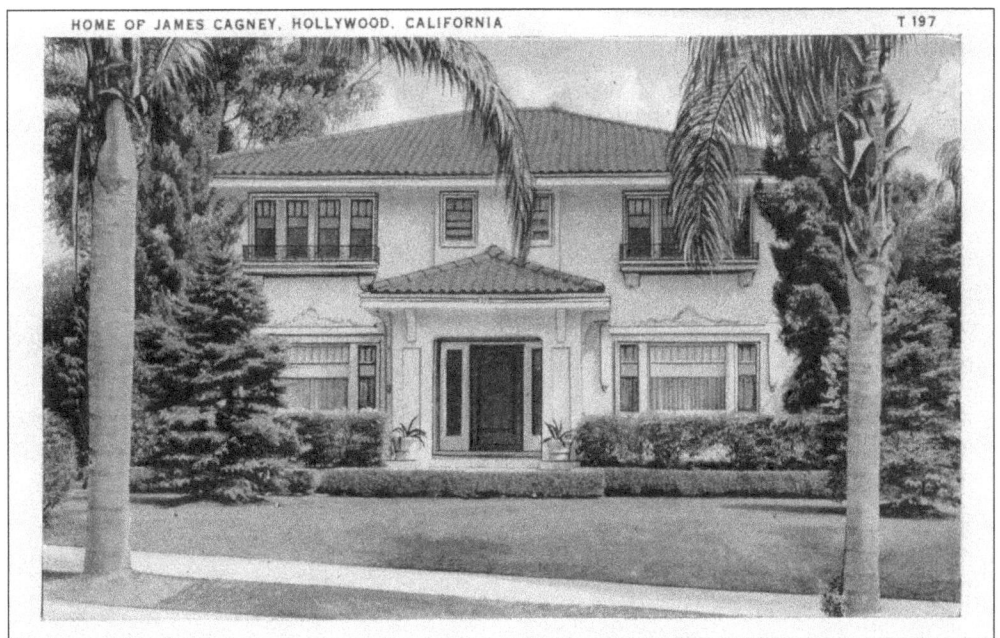

HOME OF JAMES CAGNEY, HOLLYWOOD, CALIFORNIA   T 197

James Cagney. Tough guy James Cagney (1899–1986) shot to fame in *The Public Enemy* (1931), a crime drama. Cagney was one of many New York stage actors imported by studio chiefs to replace silent film actors who could not handle dialogue convincingly. Cagney's triumphs include *G Men*, *The Fighting 69th*, *Yankee Doodle Dandy* (Oscar, 1942), *White Heat*, *Mister Roberts*, *Ragtime*, and *One, Two, Three*. He lived at 2069 Coldwater Canyon Drive, Beverly Hills.

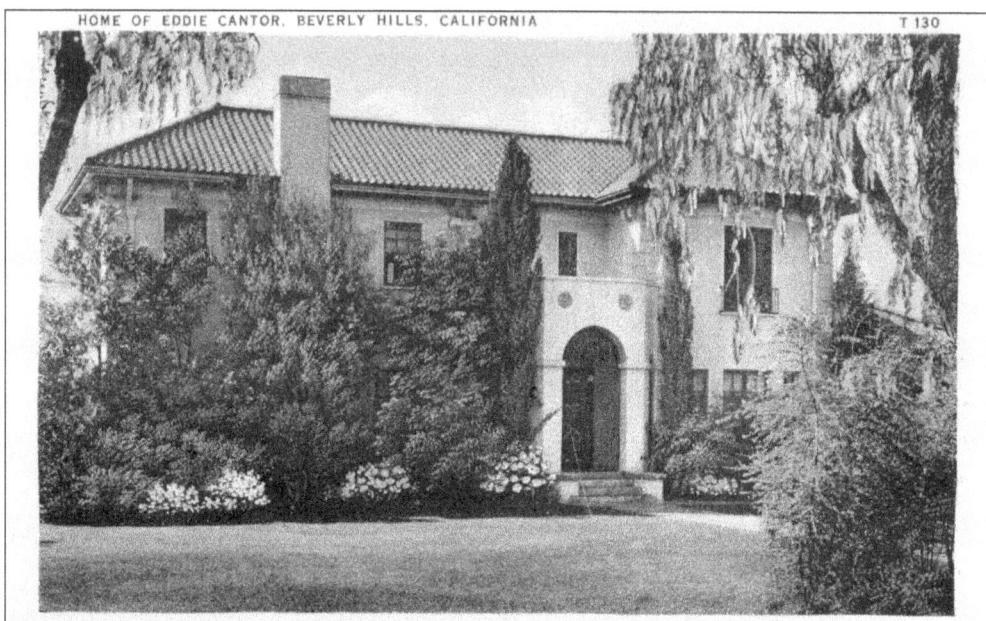

EDDIE CANTOR. Beginning as a vaudeville comedian, Eddie Cantor (1892–1964) rose to stardom in Broadway's celebrated *Ziegfeld Follies*, which led to further success in motion pictures, radio, and television. This postcard shows the house he lived in after moving from 807 Crescent Drive, Beverly Hills, but before moving to 1012 Roxbury Drive, in 1936. Cantor's films include *Kid Boots*, *Whoopie!*, *Palmy Days*, *Roman Scandals*, and *Strike Me Pink*.

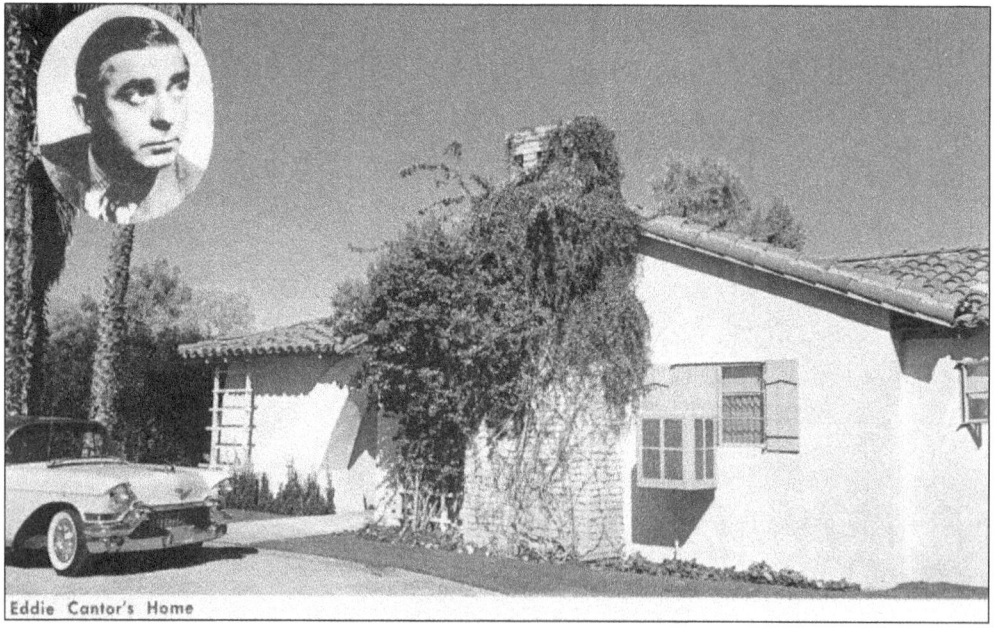

Eddie Cantor's Home

CANTOR'S PALM SPRINGS HOME. As early as 1944, Eddie and Ida Cantor had lived in this house at 720 Paseo El Mirador, Palm Springs. Late in 1952, after collapsing on stage in New York from exhaustion, the overworked comedian with the "Banjo Eyes" recuperated at his Palm Springs home. That same year, he recorded his old songs for Warner Bros.'s new movie, *The Eddie Cantor Story*.

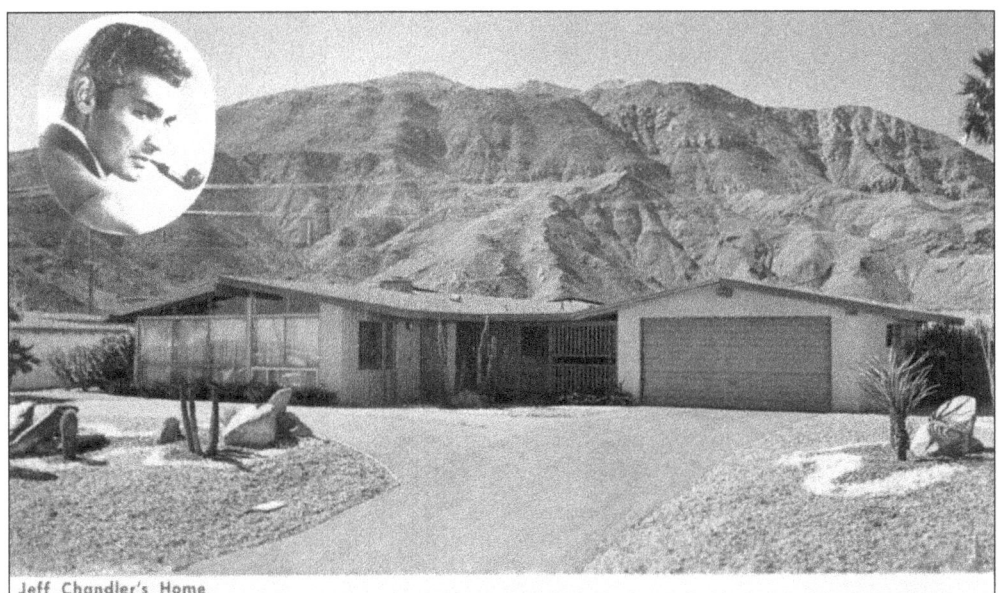

Jeff Chandler's Home

JEFF CHANDLER. Although Jeff Chandler (1918–1961) owned a home in West Los Angeles, he also had this house on Tangier Road, Palm Springs. The prematurely grey-haired actor was popular and talented. A stint on radio led to screen roles, most notably in *Sword in the Desert* and *Broken Arrow*, which helped him emerge as a major star. Other films include *Deported*, *Sign of the Pagan*, *Drango*, *Jeanne Eagles*, and *Away All Boats*.

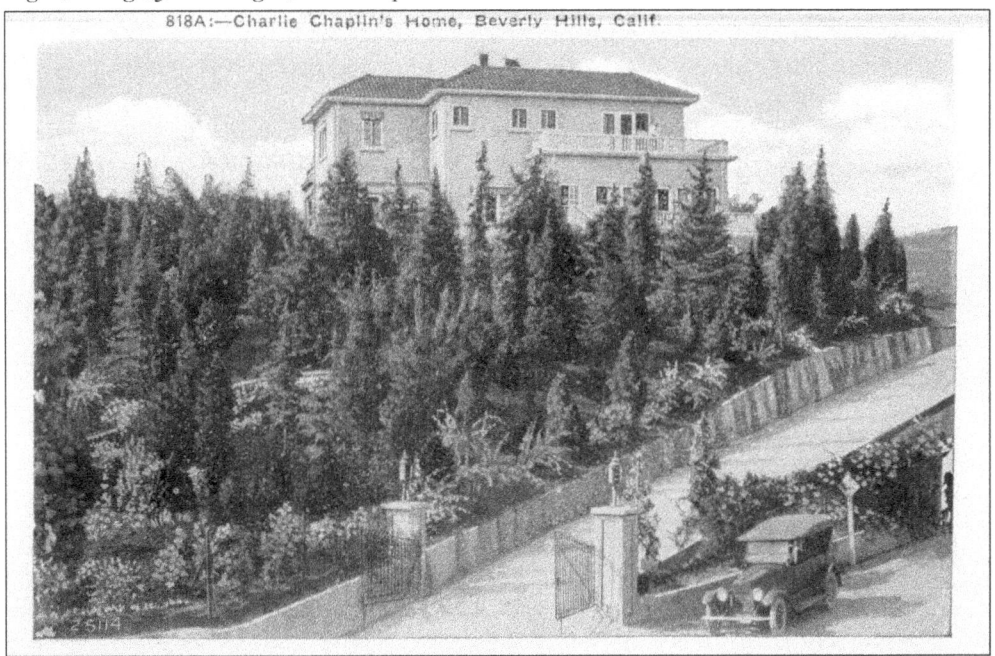

818A:—Charlie Chaplin's Home, Beverly Hills, Calif.

CHARLIE CHAPLIN. Sir Charles Chaplin (1889–1977) lived in a number of mansions during his Hollywood days, including the Beverly Hills residence on this postcard. The celebrated English actor made a fortune in Hollywood playing the Little Tramp in dozens of sparkling silent comedies, including *Easy Street*, *The Vagabond*, *The Idle Class*, *The Gold Rush*, *The Circus*, *City Lights*, and *Modern Times*. His first talkie was *The Great Dictator* (1940).

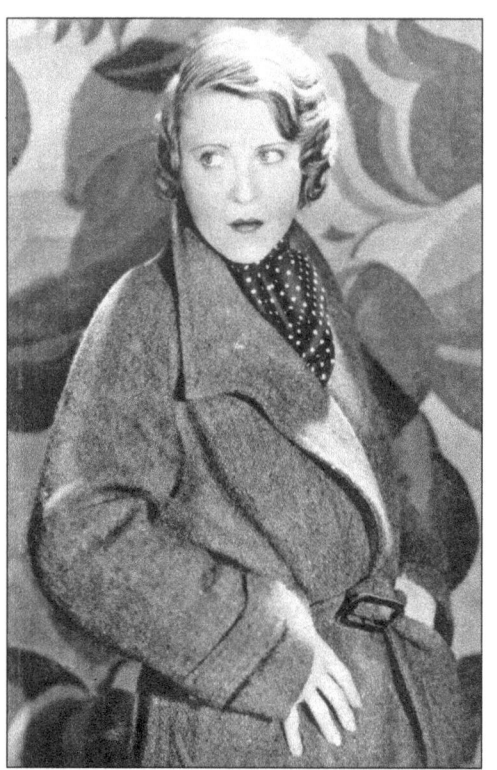

RUTH CHATTERTON. Actress and aviatrix Ruth Chatterton (1892–1961) made the leap from the New York stage to movie stardom without any trouble at all. She gave acclaimed performances in *Madame X*, *Sarah and Son*, *Anybody's Woman*, *The Magnificent Lie*, *The Rich Are Always with Us*, and *Dodsworth*. For years, even during her failed marriages to actors Ralph Forbes and George Brent, Chatterton lived at 704 North Palm Drive, Beverly Hills.

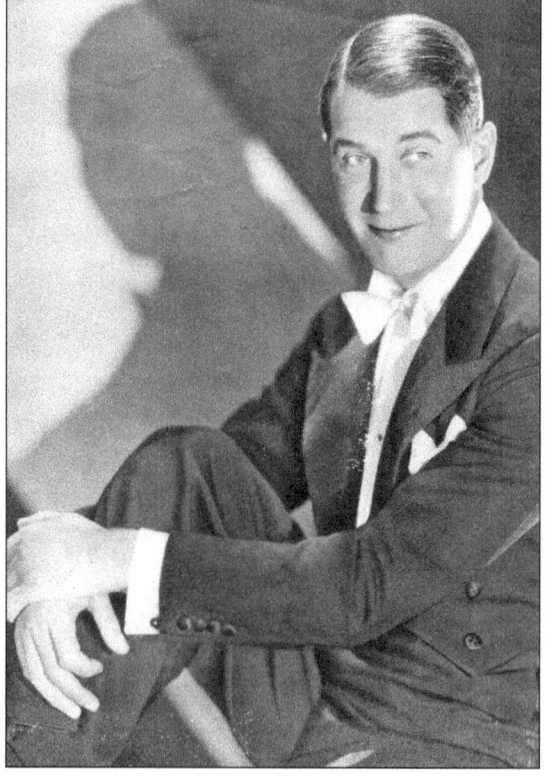

MAURICE CHEVALIER. During his first years in Hollywood, Maurice Chevalier (1888–1972) lived in a Mediterranean-style house at 6680 Whitley Terrace, Hollywood. The unforgettable Frenchman with the straw hat charmed millions with such films as *Innocents of Paris*, *The Love Parade*, *The Smiling Lieutenant*, *One Hour with You*, *Love Me Tonight*, *The Merry Widow*, *Gigi*, and *I'd Rather Be Rich*. From 1952 until his death, he lived at his French estate, La Louque.

LEW CODY. Ever the womanizer of the silent screen, the fascinating actor Lew Cody (1884–1934) delighted fans with his "male vamp" tricks. His pictures include *Don't Change Your Husband*, *Three Women*, *Exchange of Wives*, and *His Secretary*. Among his talkies are *What a Widow!* and *X Marks the Spot*. His wife was comedienne Mabel Normand (1892–1930). In 1934, Cody died suddenly in his mansion at 609 North Maple Drive, Beverly Hills.

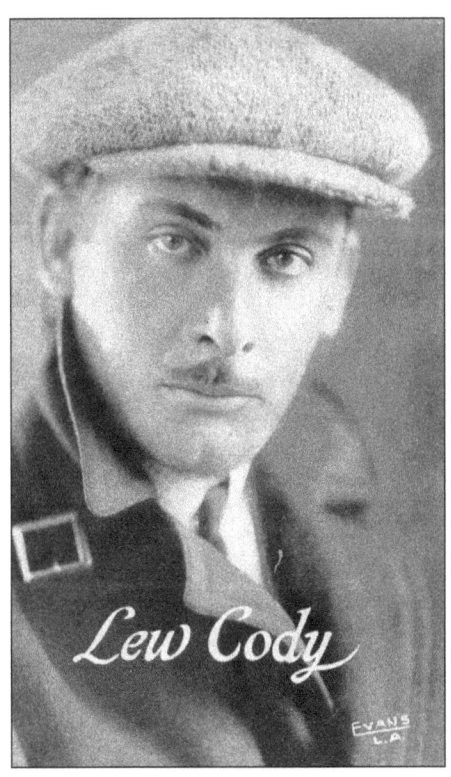

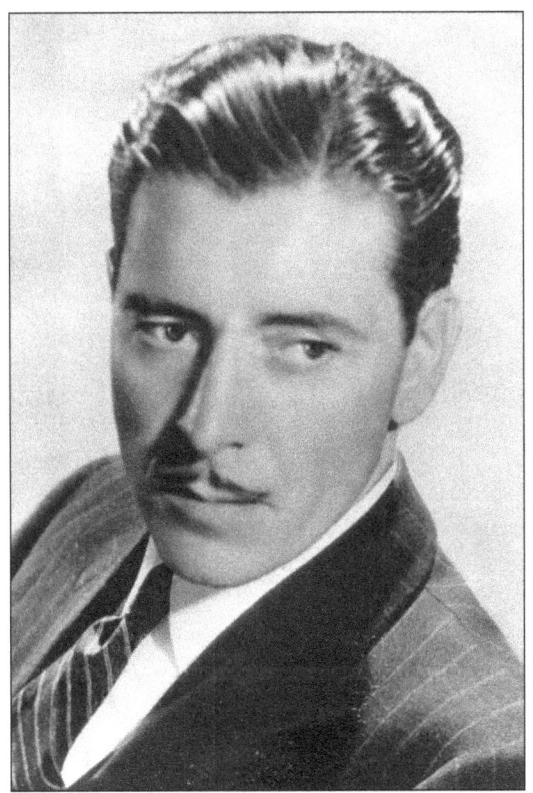

RONALD COLMAN PORTRAIT. Born in Richmond, Surrey, Ronald Colman (1891–1958) acted on the English stage and served in the British army before coming to the United States in 1920. On the stage, he was seen in popular plays, such as *The Dauntless Three*, *East Is West*, and *The Green Goddess*. In 1923, he made his screen debut as the leading man in *The White Sister*, opposite Lillian Gish.

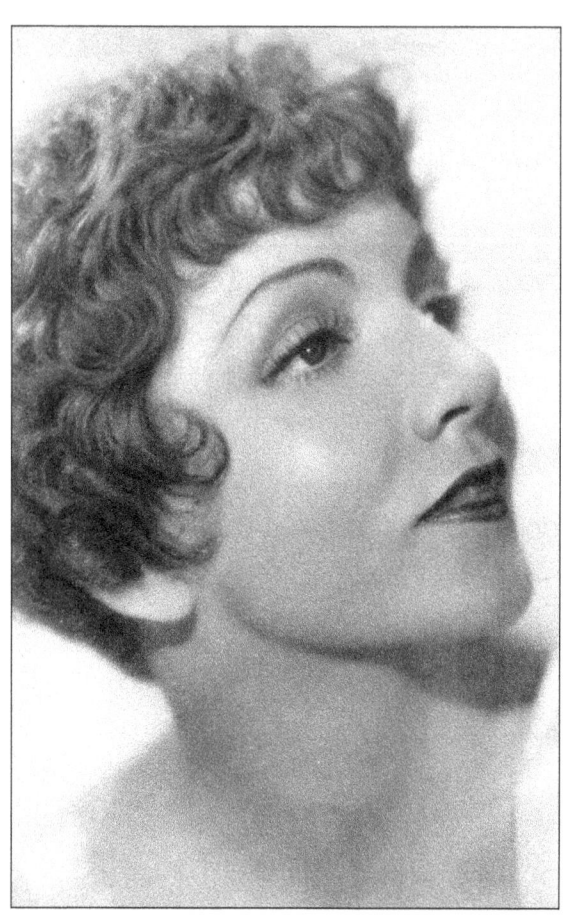

CLAUDETTE COLBERT PORTRAIT.
This photograph, taken at the height of her early career in the 1930s, shows Claudette Colbert, who rapidly rose to stardom thanks to her musical voice, acting skills, charm, and beauty. Her first films included *For the Love of Mike*, *A Hole in the Wall*, *The Lady Lies*, *Young Man of Manhattan*, *The Big Pond*, *Manslaughter*, *The Mysterious Mr. Parkes*, *The Smiling Lieutenant*, and *The Secrets of a Secretary*.

CLAUDETTE COLBERT. French-born Claudette Colbert (1903–1993) and her husband, Dr. Joel Pressman, lived in this Moderne and English Colonial mansion at 615 North Faring Road, Holmby Hills. In 1935, she commissioned architect Lloyd Wright to design it; she named it Bellerive. Colbert won an Oscar for her role in *It Happened One Night* (1934). She also starred in *Tonight Is Ours*, *Cleopatra*, *Imitation of Life*, *Remember the Day*, and *The Palm Beach Story*.

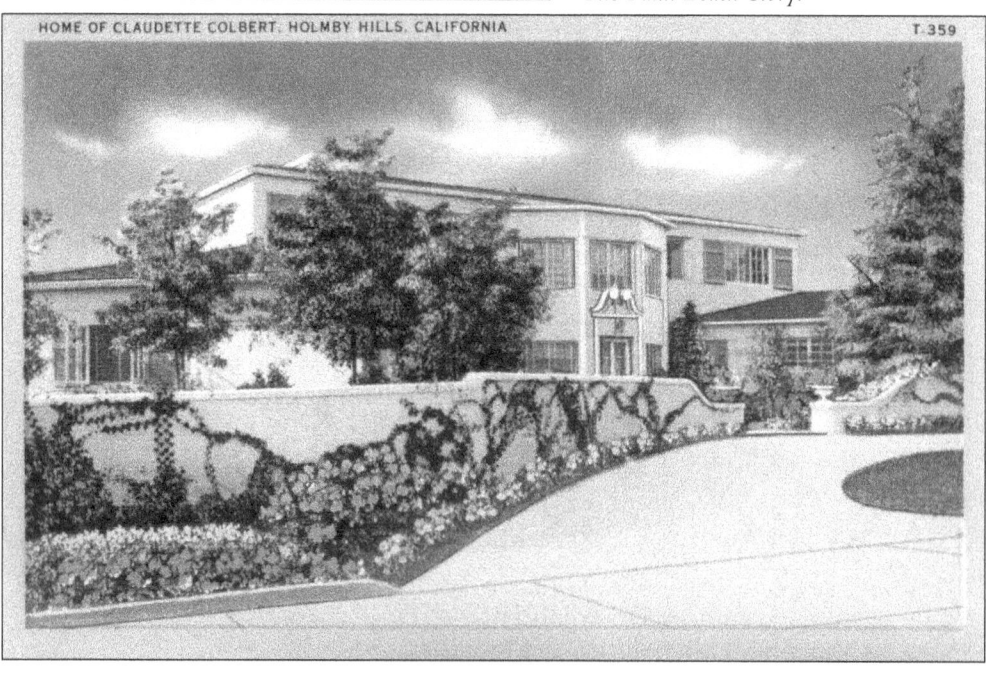

HOME OF CLAUDETTE COLBERT, HOLMBY HILLS, CALIFORNIA   T-359

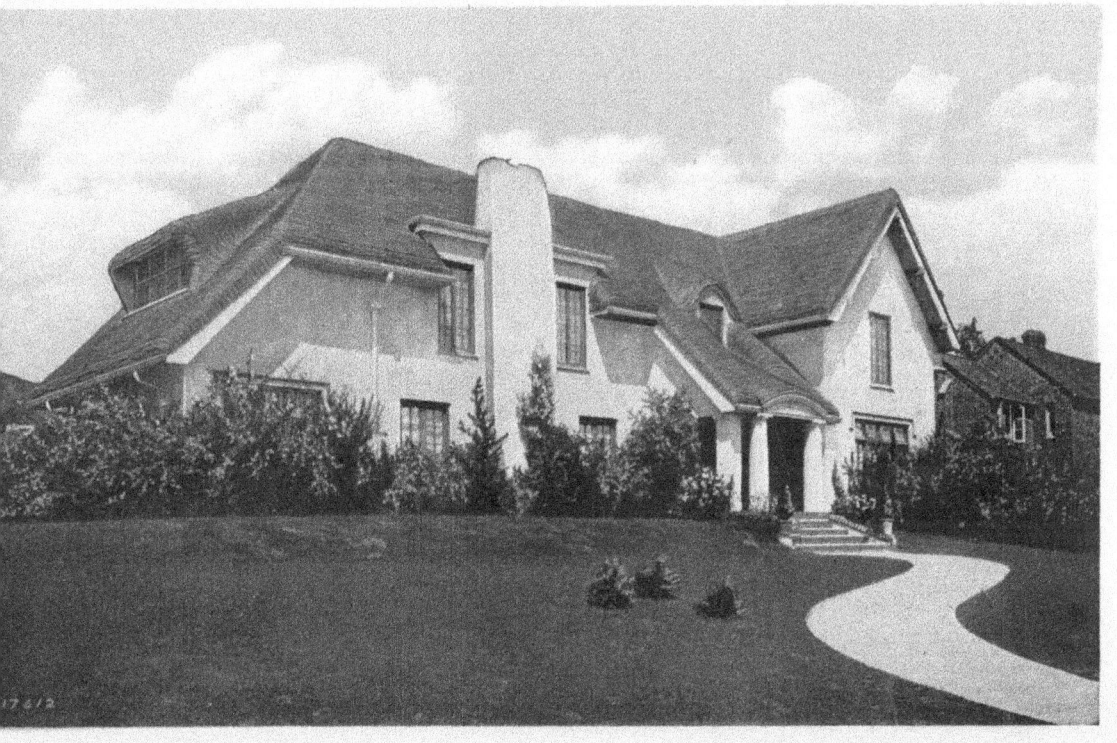

BETTY COMPSON. Screen favorite Betty Compson (1897–1974) lived in this house at 7315 Hollywood Boulevard in 1923. The daughter of a Utah grocer, she found success in vaudeville and on screen. Her silent films include *The Miracle Man, Ladies Must Live, The Fast Set, Miami,* and *The Docks of New York,* and her sound films are *The Barker, The Great Gabbo* (opposite Erich von Stroheim), and *Street Girl.*

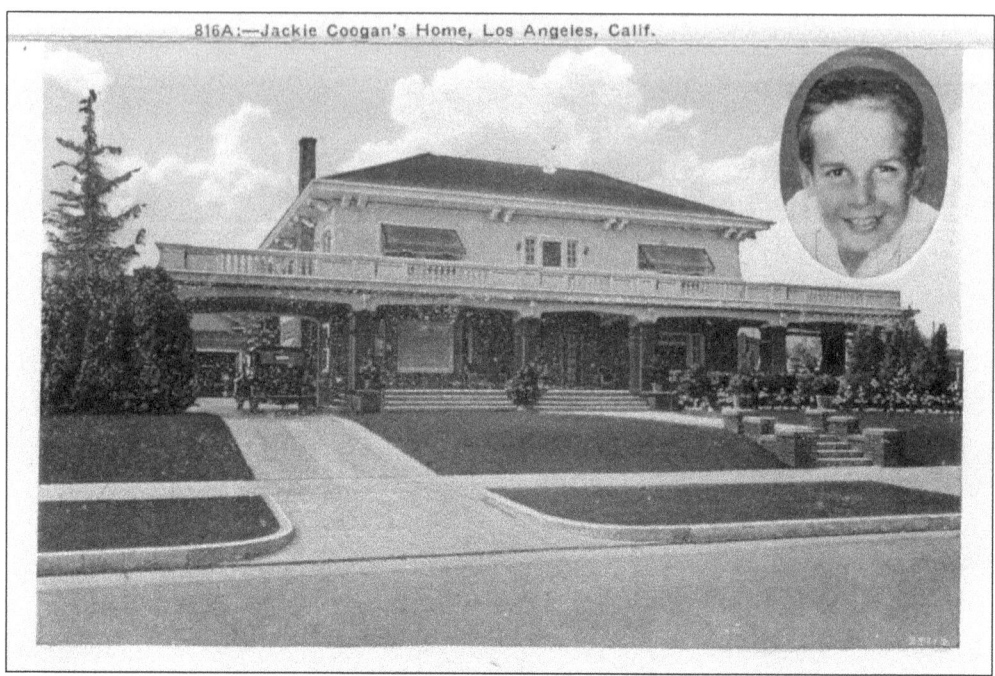

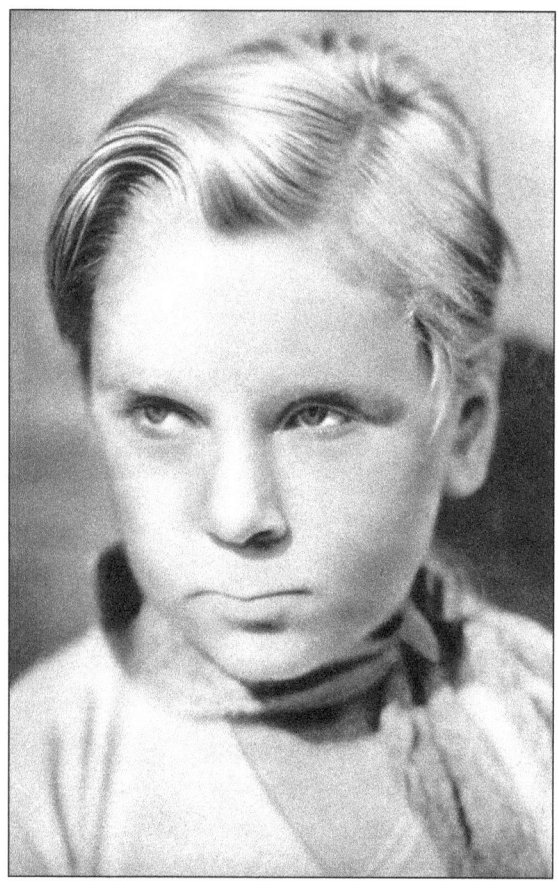

JACKIE COOGAN. In January 1922, child star Jackie Coogan (1914–1984) bought this house at 673 South Oxford Street, Los Angeles, formerly owned by silent film star Bessie Barriscale. Jackie lived there with his parents, John and Lillian Coogan, and his brother. Among his films are *The Kid*, *My Boy*, *Oliver Twist*, *Little Robinson Crusoe*, *Tom Sawyer*, and *Huckleberry Finn*. On television, he was Uncle Fester on *The Addams Family* (1964–1966).

JACKIE COOPER PORTRAIT. The first major child star of the Great Depression, Jackie Cooper (1922–2011) was the tough kid of popular tearjerker melodramas. After he grew up, his future in Hollywood looked bleak, but his perseverance eventually paid off with television stardom in two sitcoms, *The People's Choice* (NBC, 1955–1958) and the more dramatic *Hennesey* (CBS, 1959–1962). He found renewed fame as Perry White in *Superman* (1978).

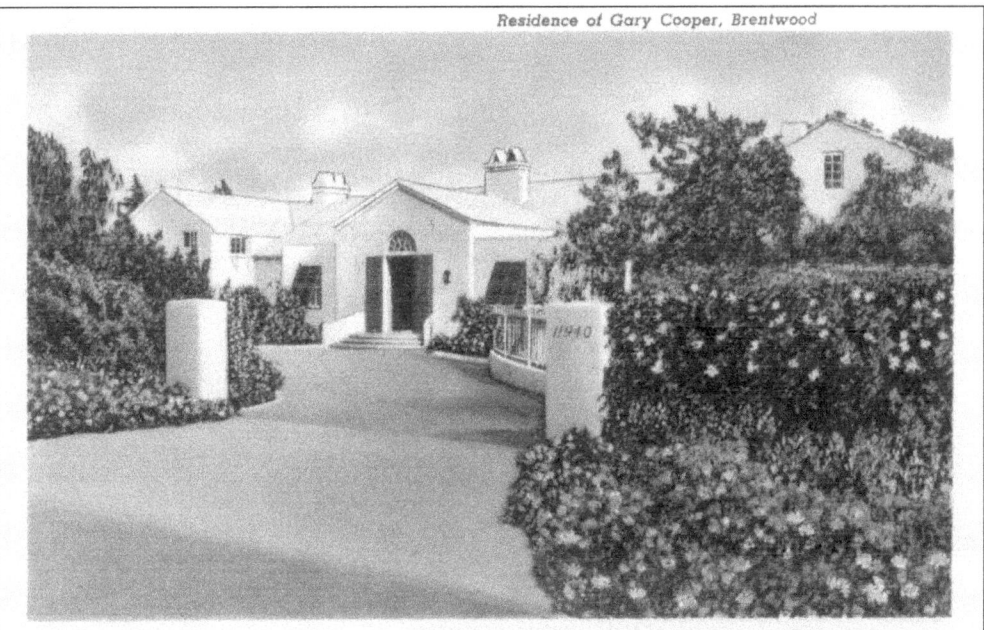

GARY COOPER. In 1936, Gary Cooper (1901–1961) and his wife built this Bermuda-style house at 11940 Chaparal Street, Brentwood; he lived there until their separation in 1951. The estate included an avocado orchard, a citrus grove, and tennis courts. Truly an immortal of the screen, Cooper was in *A Farewell to Arms*, *Mr. Deeds Goes to Town*, *Meet Joe Doe*, *Sergeant York* (Oscar, 1941), *The Pride of the Yankees*, and *High Noon* (Oscar, 1952).

GARY COOPER PORTRAIT. The son of prosperous English immigrants, the future movie star was born Frank James Cooper in Montana. His parents, Judge Charles and Alice Cooper, sent their sons, Arthur (1895–1982) and Frank (1901–1961), to England for their education. Young Cooper became an actor unintentionally when he accepted work as a film extra in Westerns for $5 a day in 1925. His first starring role was in *Arizona Bound* (1927).

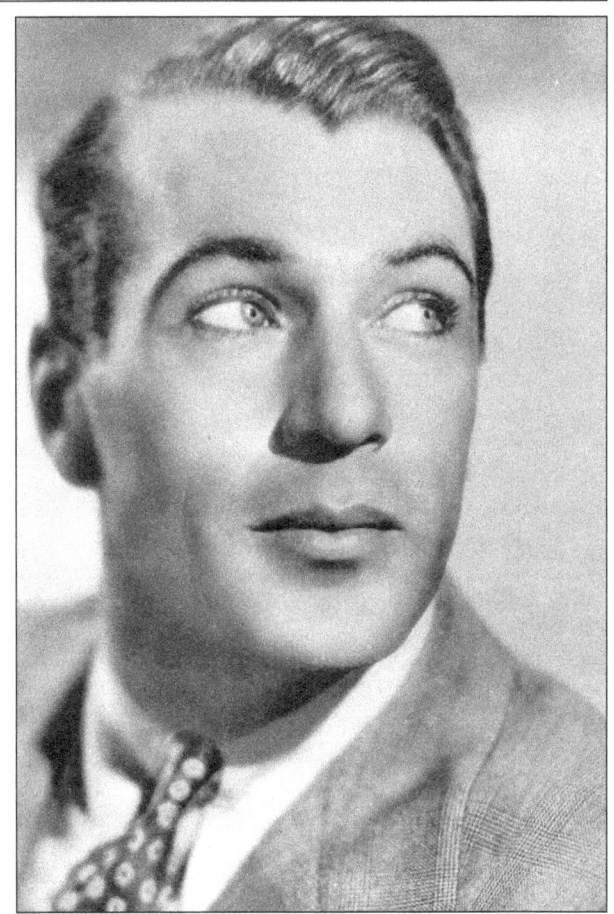

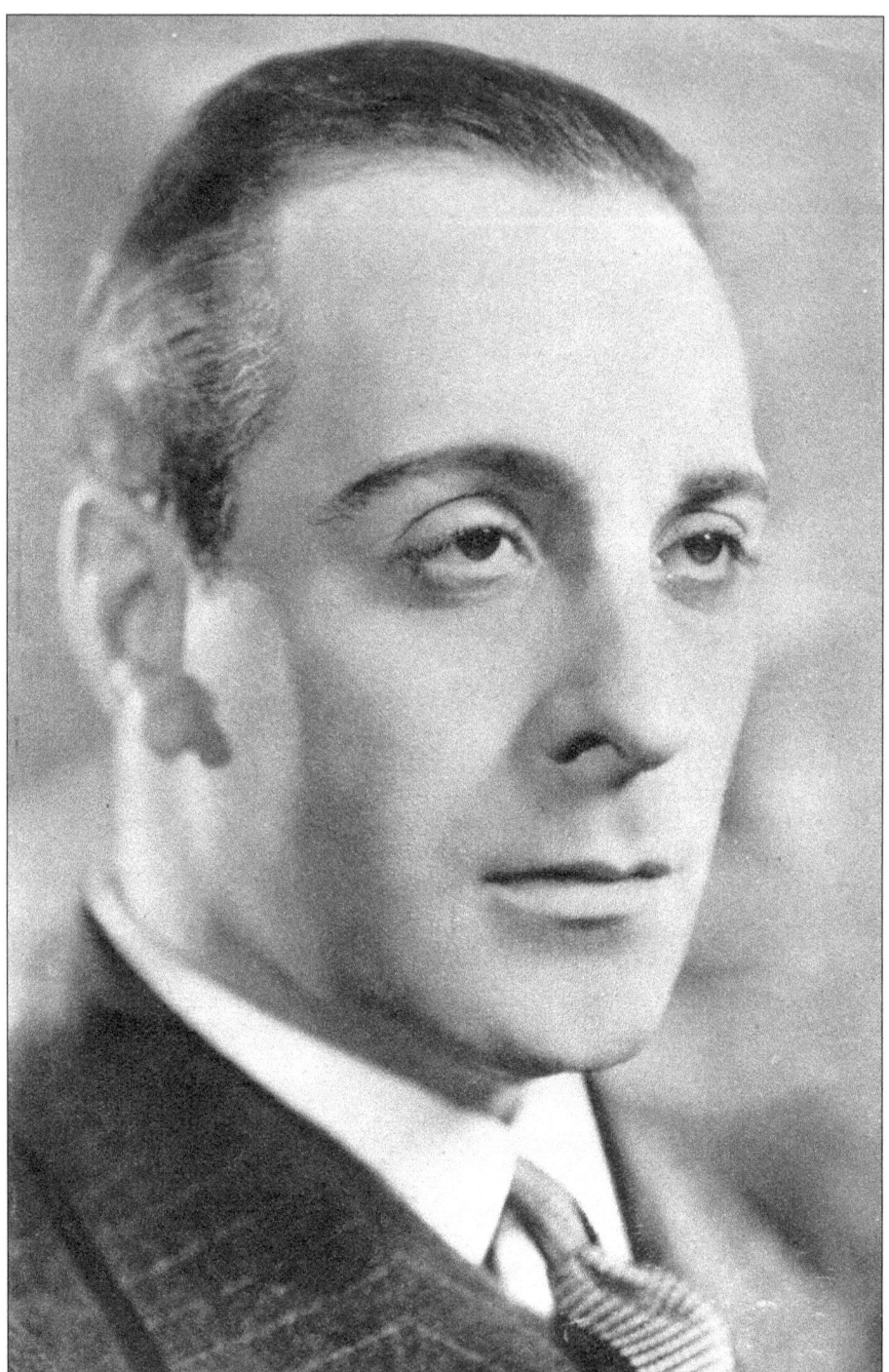

RICARDO CORTEZ. A popular romantic "Latin Lover" of the silent screen, Cortez's streetwise New York accent made him an effective villain in talkies. In 1936, Ricardo Cortez (1900–1977) and his wife, Christine, lived at 1707 Tropical Avenue, Beverly Hills. Cortez was born Jake Krantz on September 19, 1900. Cortez's films include *Torrent* (with Greta Garbo), *Argentine Love*, *The Sorrows of Satan*, and *Midnight Mary*. In 1931, he was Sam Spade in *The Maltese Falcon*.

JOAN CRAWFORD PORTRAIT. Born Lucille LeSeuer, Joan Crawford was given her stage name by MGM Studios, and she transformed herself into a star. Though silent films, such as *Four Walls* (with John Gilbert) and *The Unknown* (with Lon Chaney and Norman Kerry), made her famous, talkies, like *Rain, Dancing Lady, The Gorgeous Hussy, Mildred Pierce* (Oscar, 1945), and *Daisy Kenyon* (with Dana Andrews and Henry Fonda), transformed her into an even bigger star. She is pictured at home with her adopted children Christopher and Christina.

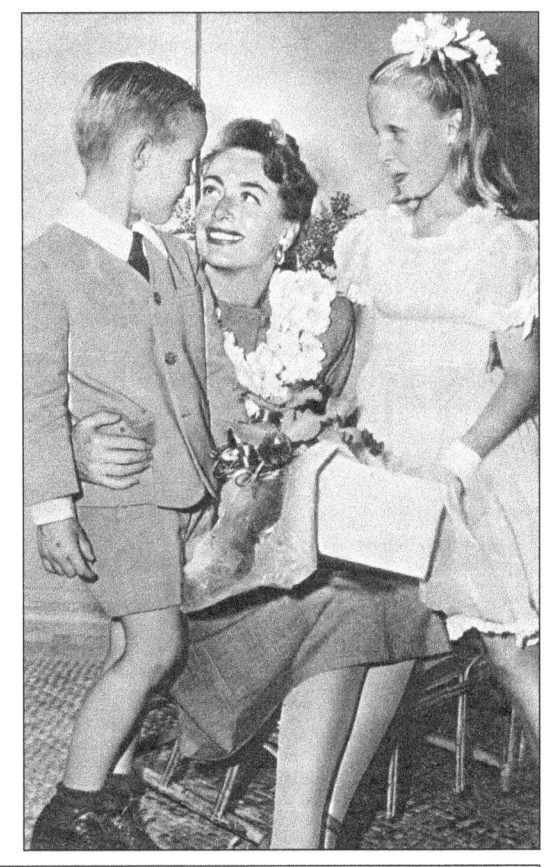

JOAN CRAWFORD. In 1928, Joan Crawford (1905–1977) bought this Brentwood Heights house at 426 North Bristol Avenue. In 1929, she married Douglas Fairbanks Jr. and had the house remodeled and redecorated. They divorced in 1933, and later, she shared it with subsequent husbands, Franchot Tone and Phillip Terry. The estate grew through additions and enlargements. After her fourth and last marriage to the chief executive officer of Pepsi, Alfred Steele (1955), she sold it to Donald O'Connor.

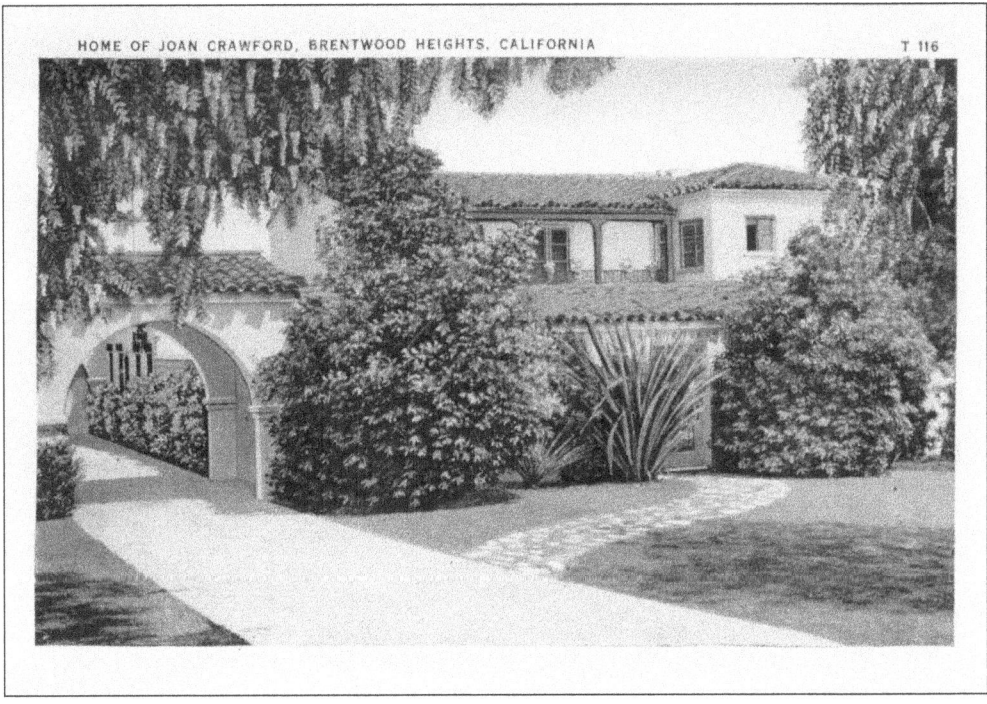

HOME OF JOAN CRAWFORD, BRENTWOOD HEIGHTS, CALIFORNIA   T 116

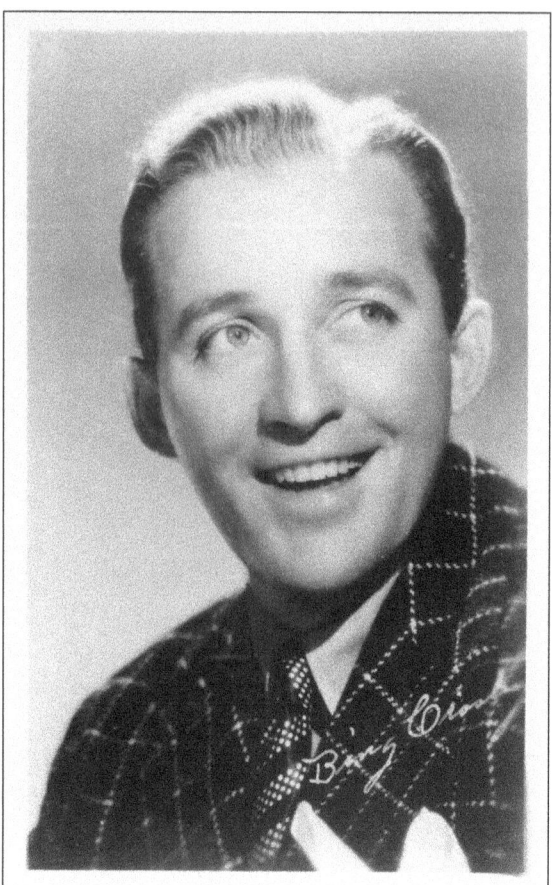

BING CROSBY PICTURE POSTCARD. The legendary Bing Crosby was born Harry Lillis Crosby in Tacoma, Washington. His father was of English descent, and his mother was Irish. In 1923, he formed a band with friends and then a singing trio called The Three Harmony Aces. They were discovered by the immensely popular Paul Whiteman Orchestra and were dubbed "The Rhythm Boys." Crosby became a recording and radio star, and Hollywood soon beckoned.

BING CROSBY. The best-selling recording artist of the 20th century, Bing Crosby (1903–1977) built this Colonial mansion at 10500 Camarillo Street, Toluca Lake (1935). It had 23 rooms, tennis courts, and servants' quarters. With his wife and sons, Crosby lived there until flames destroyed it (1943). Crosby's films include *We're Not Dressing, Mississippi, Anything Goes, Sing You Sinners, Going My Way* (Oscar, 1944), and *The Country Girl* (with Grace Kelly and William Holden).

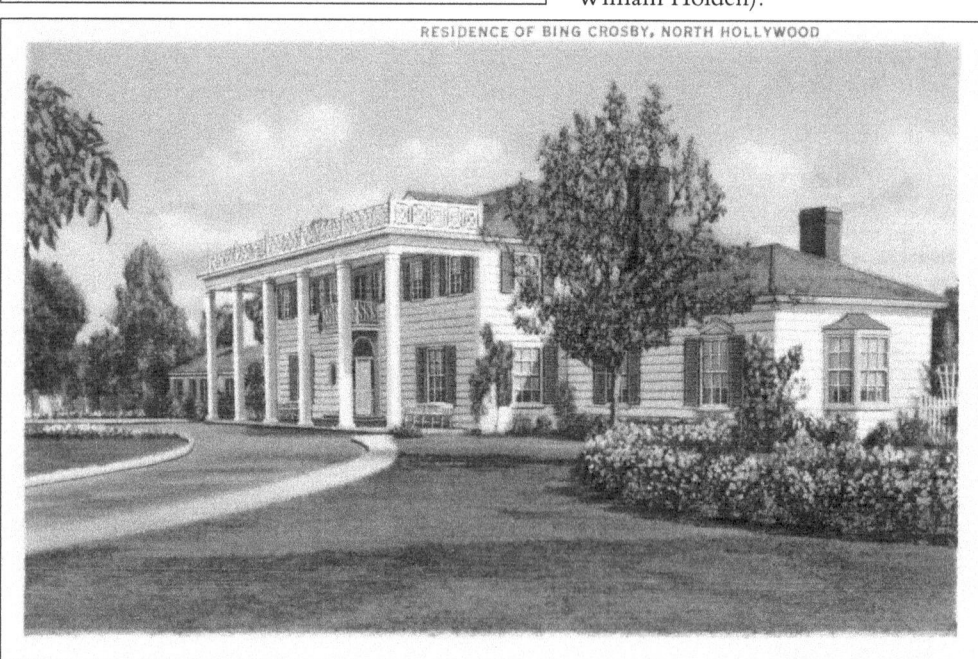

RESIDENCE OF BING CROSBY, NORTH HOLLYWOOD

DAN DAILEY PICTURE POSTCARD.
Vaudevillian turned Broadway musical
star Dan Dailey made an even more
lasting mark on Hollywood. The native
Irish New Yorker starred in musicals,
such as *You Were Meant for Me*, *Give My
Regards to Broadway*, and *When My Baby
Smiles at Me*, all in 1948, and *You're My
Everything* and *My Blue Heaven* in 1949.
He did a baseball biopic, *The Pride of St
Louis*, in 1951. Dan Dailey (1915–1978)
lived in North Hollywood.

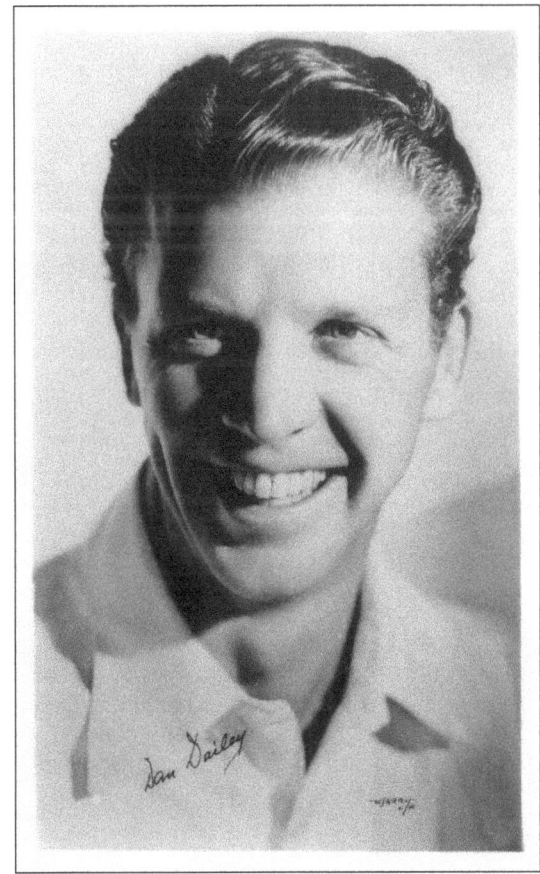

MARION DAVIES. In the 1920s, screen
star Marion Davies (1897–1961) lived in
this mansion at 1700 Lexington Road,
Beverly Hills. The longtime mistress
of tycoon William Randolph Hearst,
Davies was very popular in movies. Her
films include *April Folly*, *Little Old New
York*, *Tillie the Toiler*, *Quality Street*, and
The Patsy. Her successful talkies include
Polly of the Circus, *Peg O' My Heart*,
Operator 13, *Page Miss Glory*, and *Ever
Since Eve*.

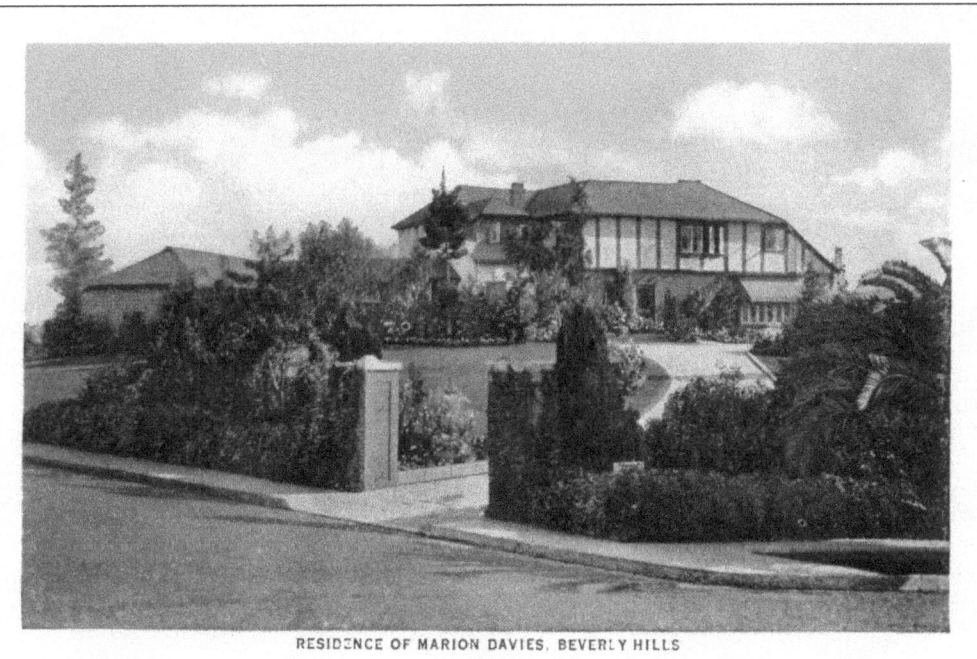

RESIDENCE OF MARION DAVIES, BEVERLY HILLS

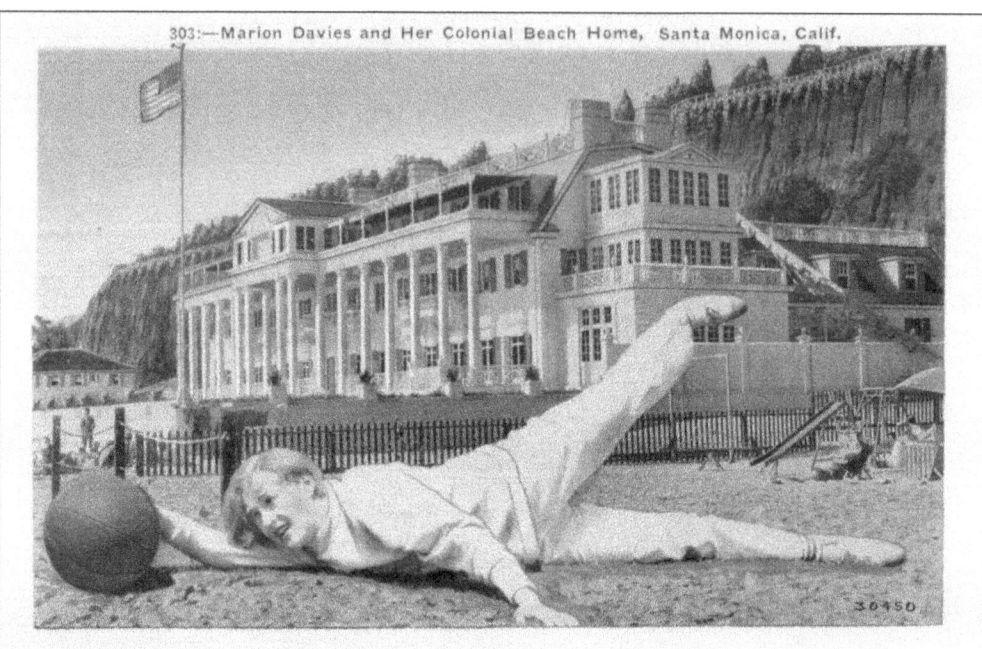

MARION DAVIES. Marion Davies received this beachfront Georgian Revival mansion as a present from tycoon William Randolph Hearst. Called Ocean House and located in Santa Monica, it had 118 rooms. Its extravagant grandeur was stunning. Aside from the expected tennis courts, swimming pool, and guest cottages, it even had a banqueting hall and a ballroom. Davies sold the estate for $600,000 in 1945.

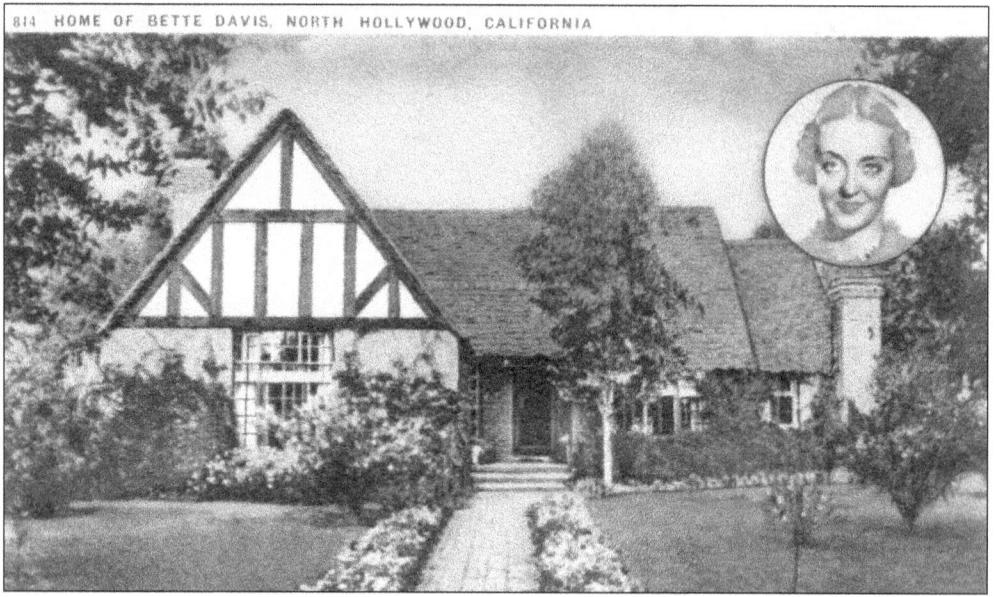

BETTE DAVIS. From April to June 1932, Bette Davis rented actor Charles Farrell's Tudor-style house at 9918 Toluca Lake Avenue. It was within walking distance of her studio, Warner Bros. One of the screen's greatest iconic stars, Bette Davis's films include *Dangerous* (Oscar, 1935), *Marked Woman, Jezebel* (Oscar, 1938), *Dark Victory, The Little Foxes, A Stolen Life, All About Eve, Whatever Happened to Baby Jane?*, and *Dead Ringer*.

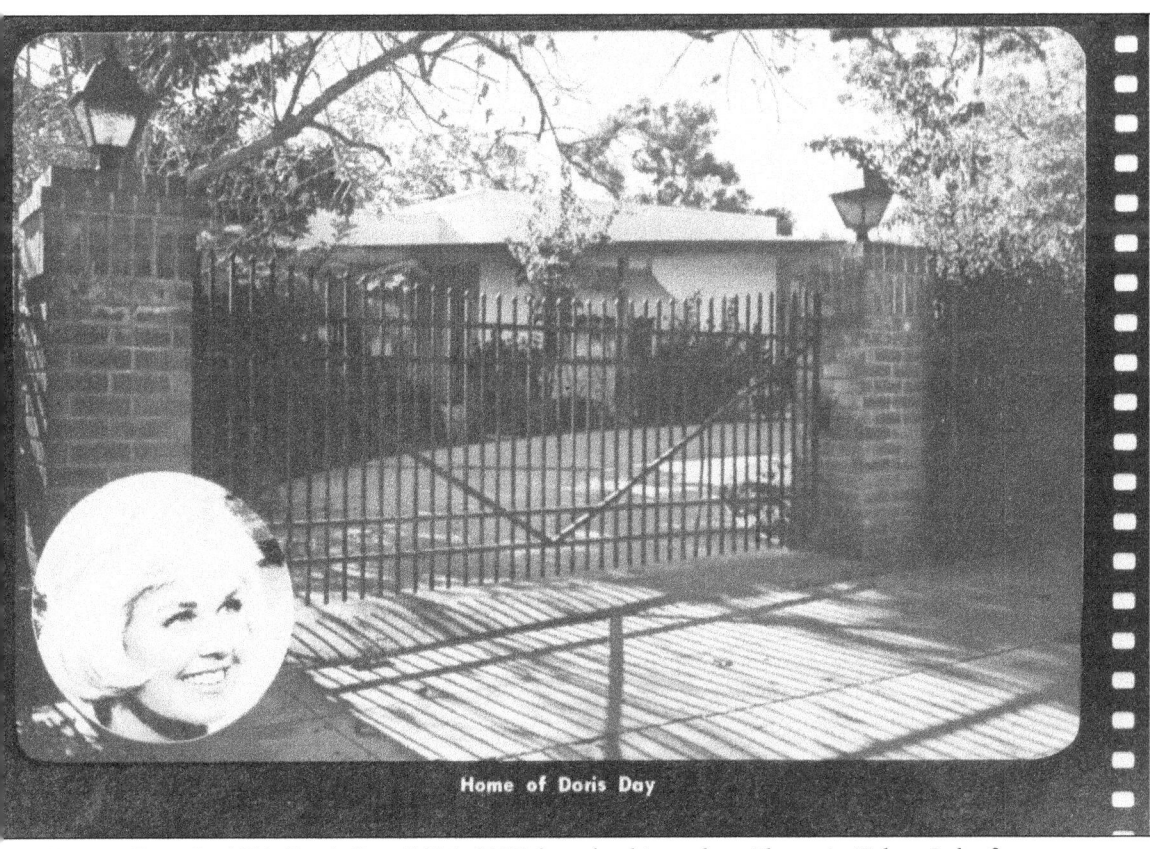

Home of Doris Day

DORIS DAY. In 1951, Doris Day (1924–2019) bought this posh residence in Toluca Lake from comedienne Martha Raye and lived there until 1955. Doris Day rose from band singer to movie star within only a few years. Her films include *Romance on the High Seas, On Moonlight Bay, By the Light of the Silvery Moon, Love Me or Leave Me, I'll See You in My Dreams, Calamity Jane,* and *Julie.*

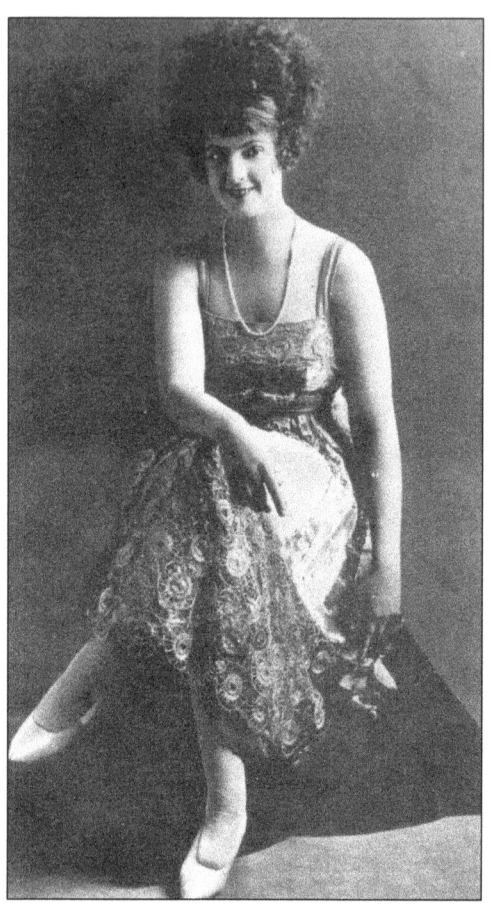

PRISCILLA DEAN PORTRAIT. Recognized by her mysterious yet enchanting smile, her flashing eyes, and her hair tightly held in place with a French-style hairnet, the fiery Priscilla Dean was one of Hollywood's most formidable female stars. At Universal Pictures, she thrilled fans with films, like *The Exquisite Thief*, *Kiss or Kill*, and *Pretty Smooth*. She acted in more than 90 films, including five talkies.

PRISCILLA DEAN. Located at 5611 Hollywood Boulevard, Beverly Hills, this Colonial-style house was the residence of film star Priscilla Dean (1896–1987) and her first husband, actor Wheeler Oakman (1890–1949). Priscilla Dean divorced Oakman to marry aviator Leslie Arnold and, eventually, retired from the screen and settled in Leonia, New Jersey. Her films include *The Wicked Darling*, *Outside the Law* (with Oakman and Lon Chaney), *Under Two Flags*, *White Tiger*, and *Slipping Wives.*

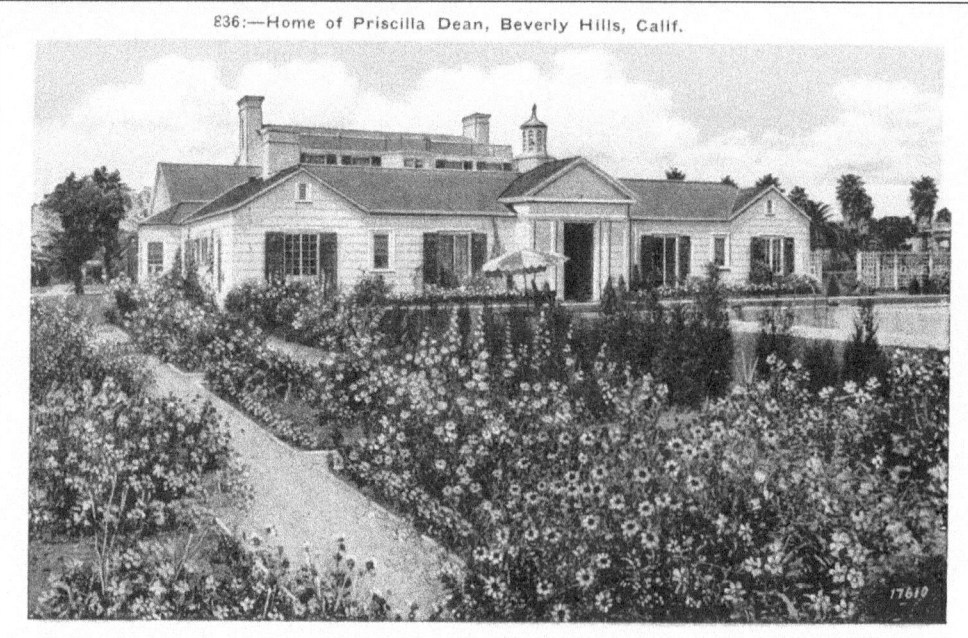

836:—Home of Priscilla Dean, Beverly Hills, Calif.

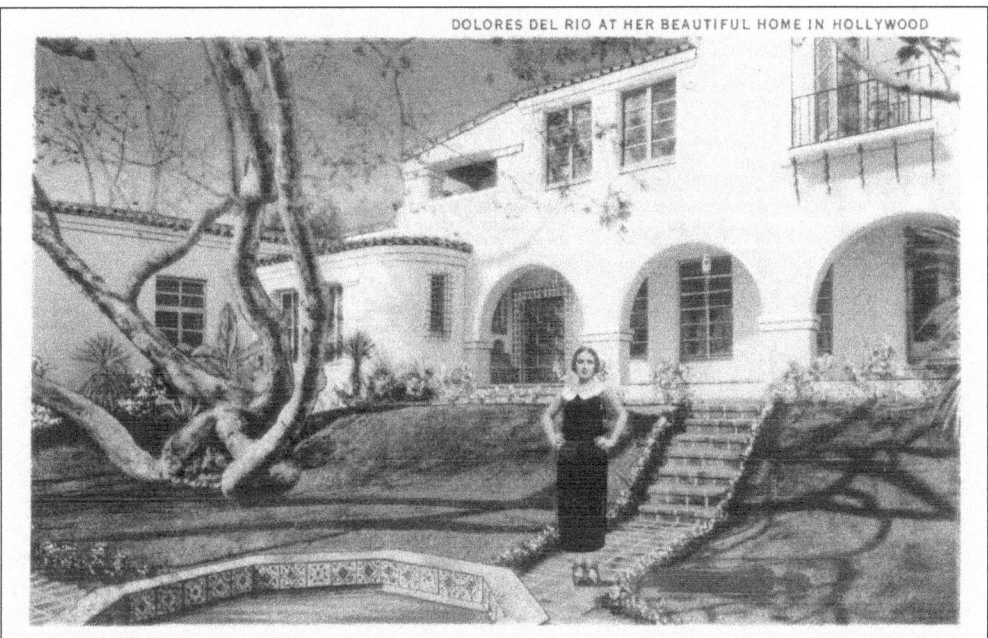

DOLORES DEL RIO. This postcard shows Dolores del Rio (1904–1983) in front of her magnificent Spanish Baroque mansion in Outpost Estates. Located at 1903 Outpost Drive, Hollywood Hills, it was built for her in 1926–1927. The Mexican beauty with the classic face reigned in Hollywood in films, such as *What Price Glory, The Loves of Carmen, Ramona, Evangeline, The Bad One, Bird of Paradise, The Devil's Playground*, and *Journey into Fear*.

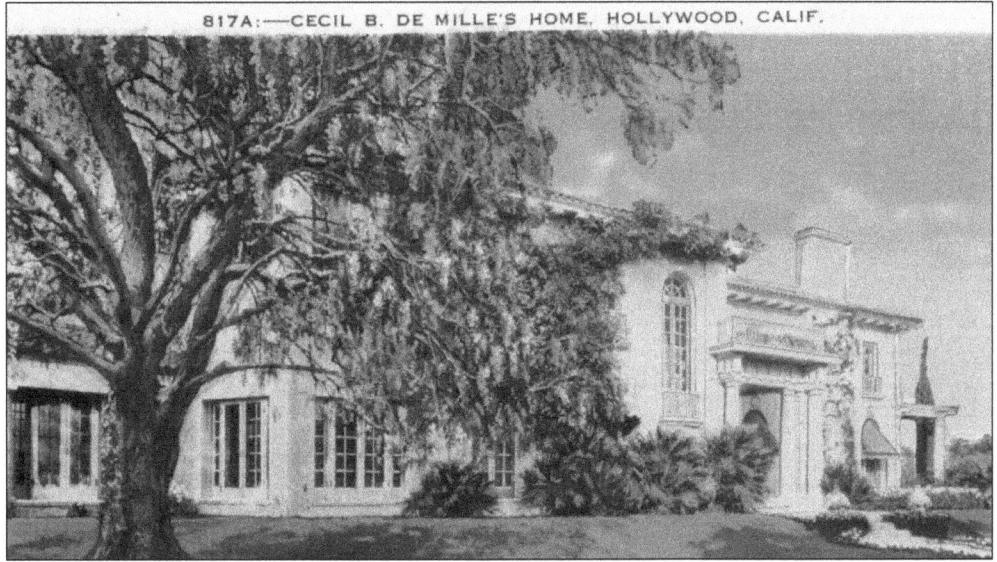

CECIL B. DEMILLE. Located in exclusive Laughlin Park, Cecil B. DeMille's massive Beaux-Arts mansion at 4 Laughlin Park (renamed 2000 DeMille Drive in the 1920s), Hollywood, was built in 1913–1914. Pioneer producer-director DeMille (1881–1959) of Paramount Pictures was famous for his motion picture epics *King of Kings, The Sign of the Cross, Cleopatra, Samson and Delilah, The Greatest Show on Earth* (Oscar, 1952), and both his 1923 and 1956 versions of *The Ten Commandments*.

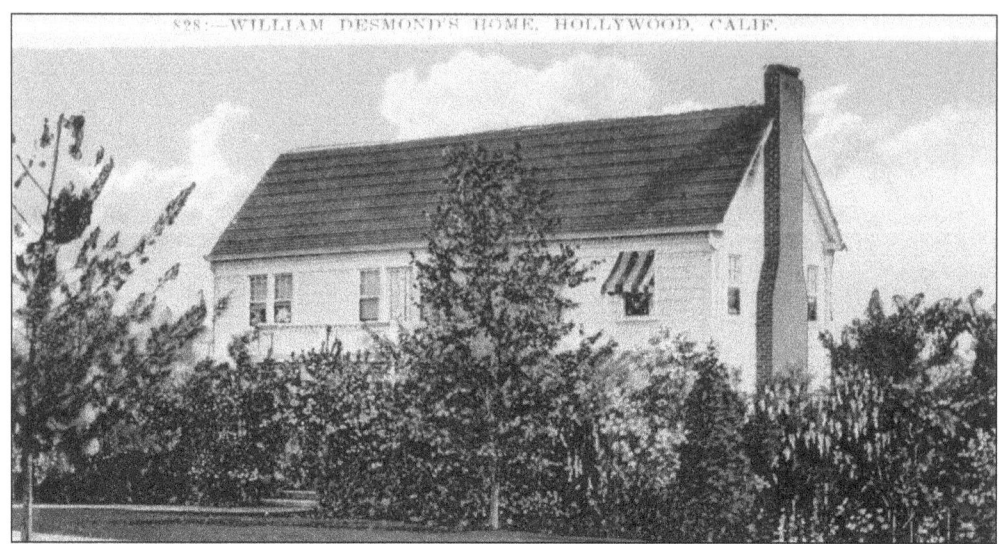

WILLIAM DESMOND. Irish-born William Desmond (1878–1949) made a name as a dramatic actor, first on stage and then on screen. In the 1920s, he became a star of Westerns. His credits include *White-Washed Walls*, *McGuire of the Mounted*, *Outwitted*, *The Breathless Moment*, *Shadows of the North*, *The Winking Idol*, and *Red Clay*. Pictured is his home at 340 DeLongpre Avenue, Hollywood.

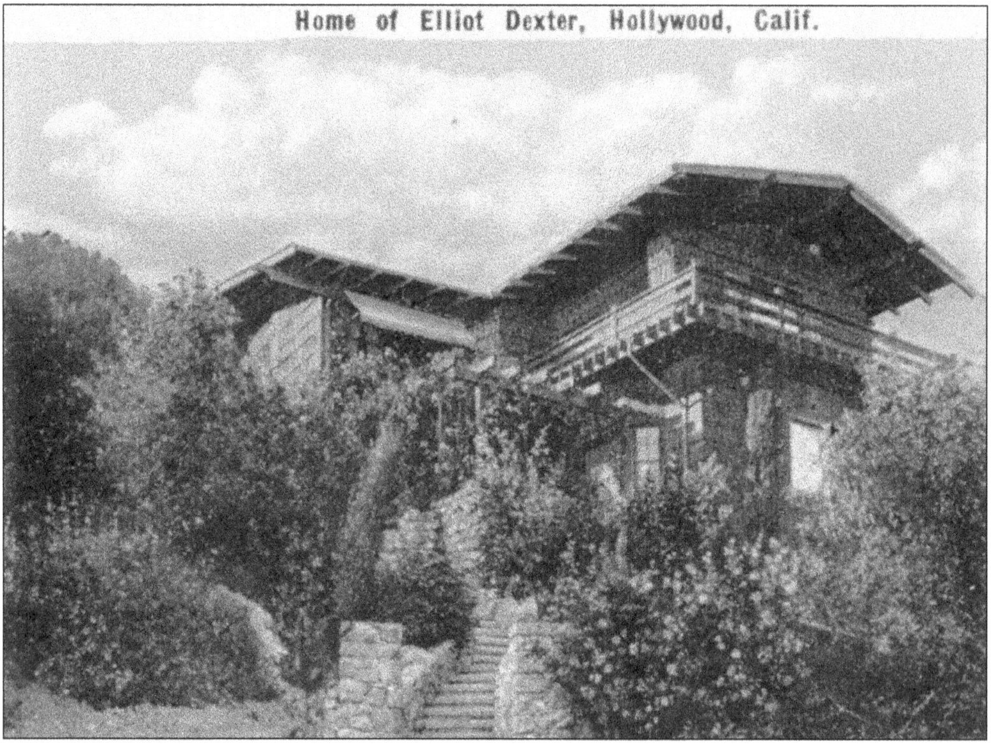

Home of Elliot Dexter, Hollywood, Calif.

ELLIOTT DEXTER. A leading character actor of stage and screen, Elliott Dexter (1870–1941) did not switch from vaudeville to Hollywood until 1915. When his screen career faded in 1924, back to the stage he went. Dexter's memorable films were *A Romance of the Redwoods*, *The Inner Shrine*, *The Rise of Jennie Cushing*, *The Eternal Temptress*, and *Something to Think About*, with Gloria Swanson.

MARLENE DIETRICH PORTRAIT.
The daughter of Ludwig and
Wilhelmina Josefina Dietrich,
the future actress was born Maria
Magdalene Dietrich in Berlin.
After the international success
of her film *The Blue Angel*, in
which she sang her signature
tune, "Falling in Love Again,"
Paramount Pictures persuaded
her to come to Hollywood, so
she sailed to New York on the SS
Bremen in April 1930.

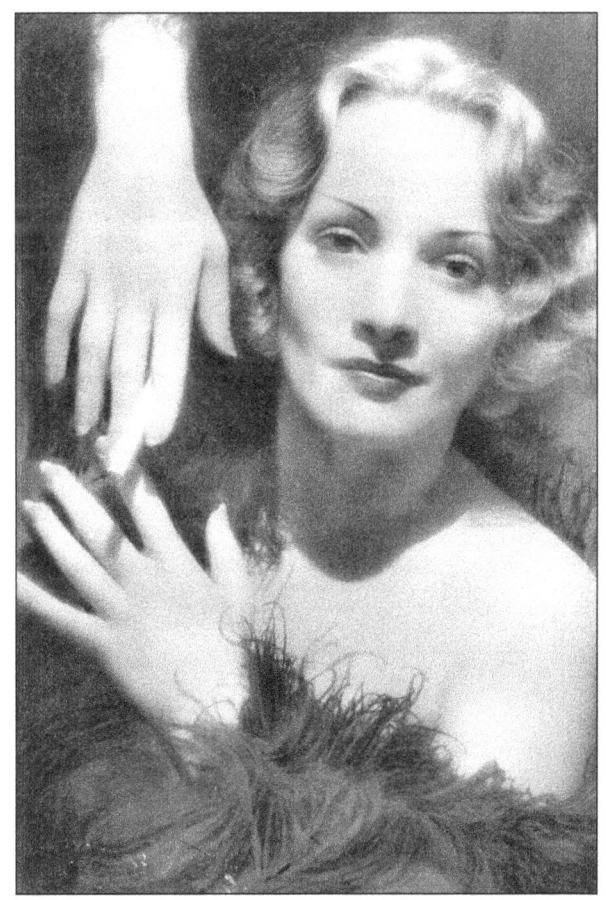

MARLENE DIETRICH. In 1931,
German film star Marlene Dietrich
(1901–1992) moved into this Art
Deco Mediterranean-style house
at 822 North Roxbury, Beverly
Hills—her first American home!
She lived there only a few months.
One of Hollywood's iconic stars,
Dietrich was in *Blonde Venus*,
Shanghai Express, *The Scarlet
Empress*, *The Devil Is a Woman*,
Destry Rides Again, *The Spoilers*,
Stage Fright, *No Highway in the Sky*,
and *Judgement at Nuremburg*.

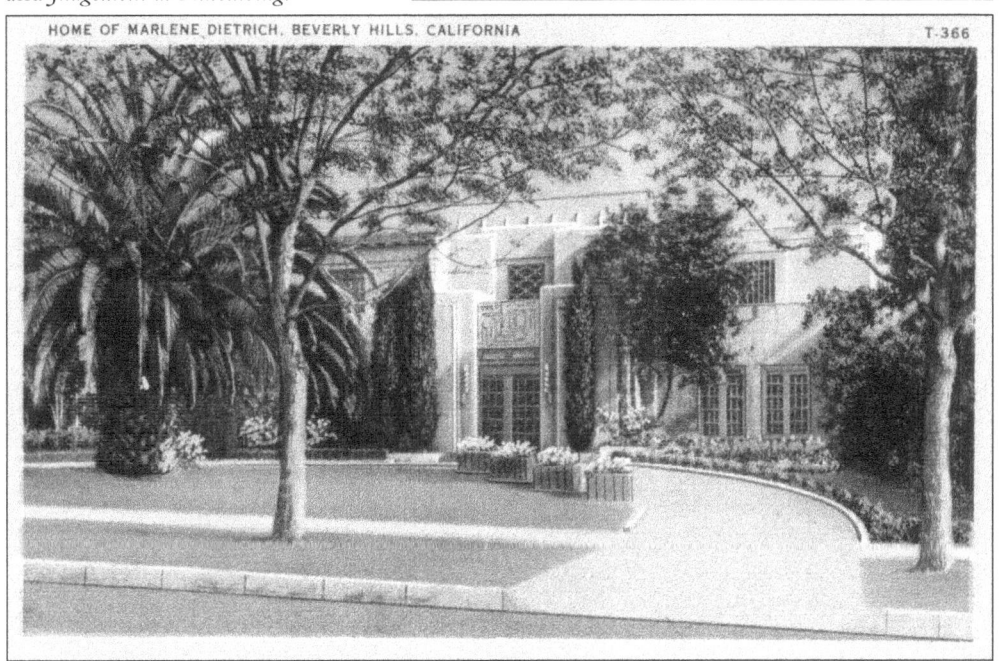

HOME OF MARLENE DIETRICH. BEVERLY HILLS. CALIFORNIA   T-366

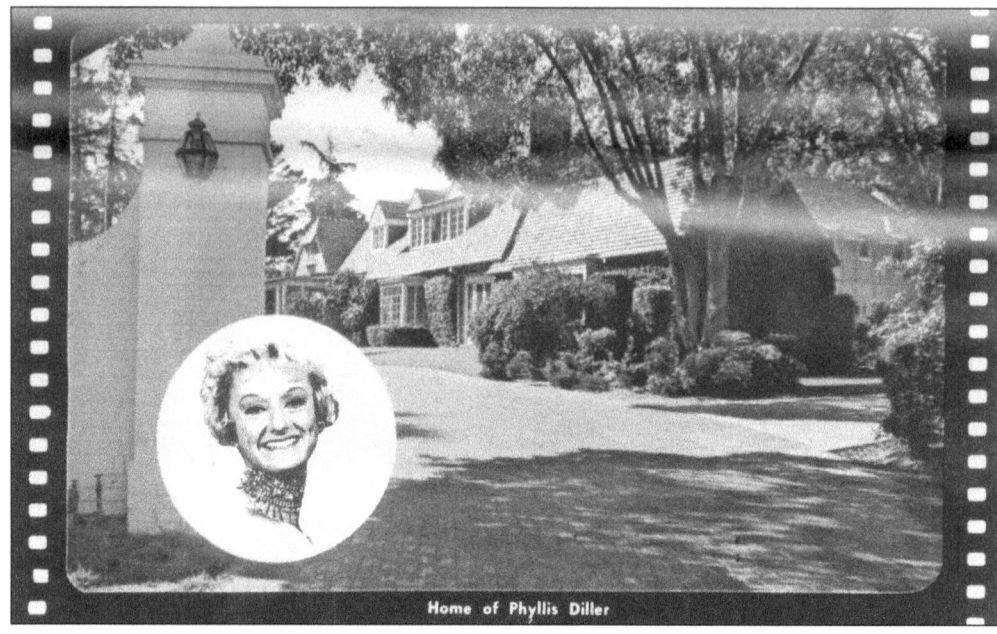

Home of Phyllis Diller

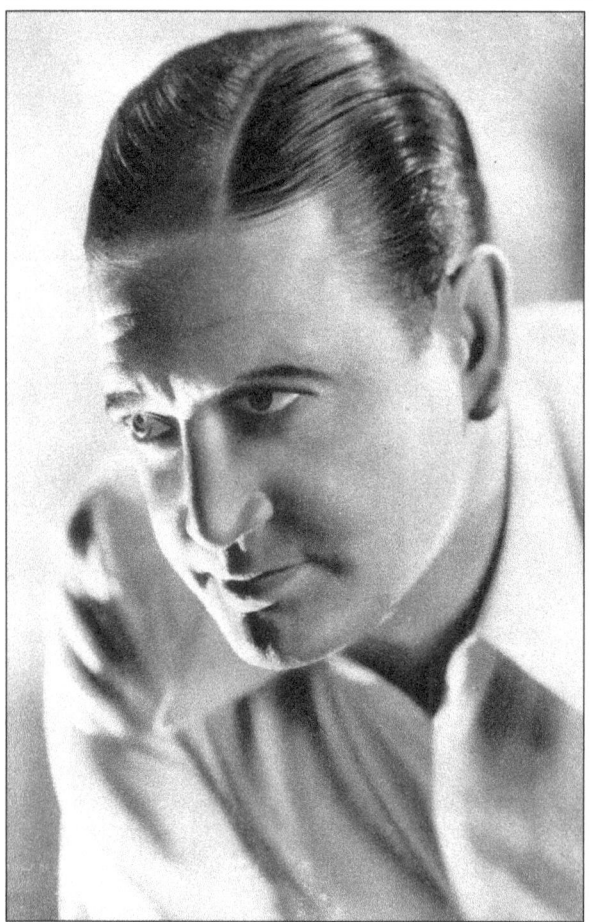

PHYLLIS DILLER. The zany comedienne Phyllis Diller (1917–2012) lived in this mansion at 163 Rockingham Road, Brentwood, for 50 years. In her kitchen, she concocted her notorious "garbage soup." As a housewife with five children, she first drew national attention as a contestant on Groucho Marx's game show *You Bet Your Life.* Her credits include *The Pruitts of Southampton* (ABC-TV) and the movie *Did You Hear the One About the Traveling Saleslady?*

RICHARD DIX. Dramatic star Richard Dix (1893–1949) and his family lived at 1119 Calle Vista Drive, Beverly Hills. The six-bedroom, $200,000 mansion was built in 1930 and renovated in 1938. The tall, rugged actor starred in 52 sound films, including *Nothing but the Truth, Seven Keys to Baldpate, The Lost Squadron, Cimarron* (Oscar, 1931), *Stingaree, The Ghost Ship,* and seven Whistler film noir mysteries beginning with *The Whistler* (1944).

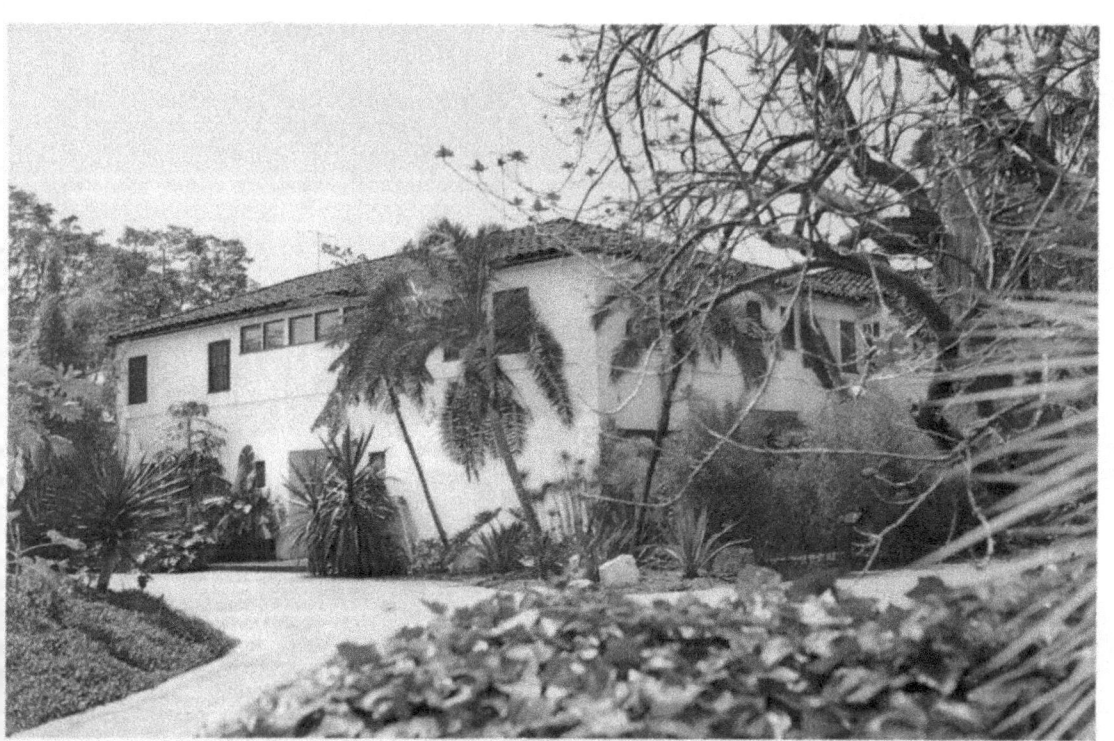

HOME OF KIRK DOUGLAS LOCATED IN HOLLYWOOD

KIRK DOUGLAS. Movie legend Kirk Douglas (born 1916) launched his career in 1946 and was hailed for his performances in *Mourning Becomes Electra*, *A Letter to Three Wives*, and *Champion*. In the 1950s and 1960s, he was at the pinnacle of stardom with *Young Man with a Horn*, *The Bad and the Beautiful*, *Lust for Life*, *Spartacus*, and *Seven Days in May*. He lived at 707 North Canon Drive, Beverly Hills.

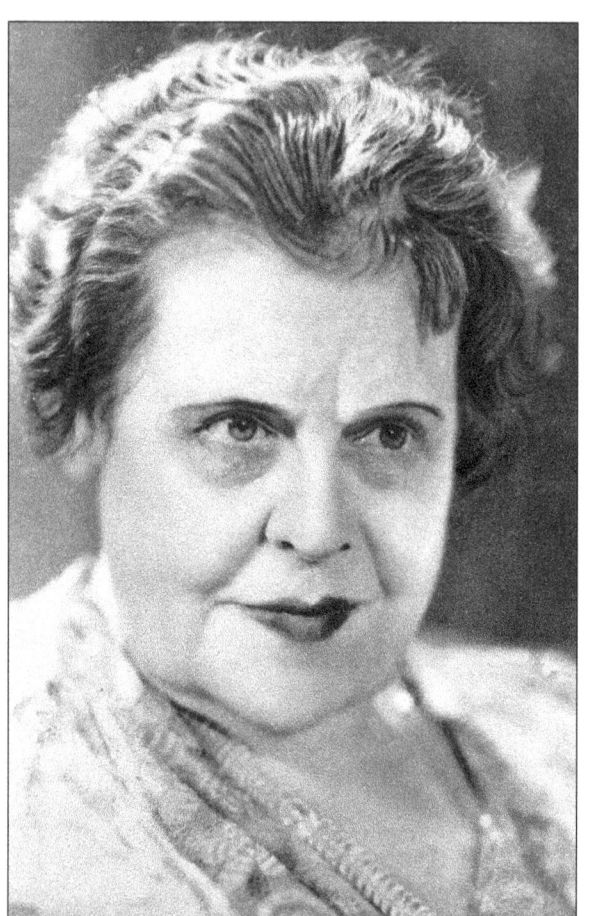

MARIE DRESSLER PORTRAIT. Marie Dressler's dramatic life made a fascinating story filled with her struggles and rise to fame in vaudeville, her work in silent pictures, and then her decline into obscurity; however, at long last, a reversal in fortune made her a top star in Hollywood. At the time of her death in 1934, her home and furnishings on Alpine Drive were valued at $100,000.

MARIE DRESSLER. A Canadian, Marie Dressler was born in this house, in Coburg, Ontario. A washed-up vaudeville star, Dressler (1868–1934) returned to pictures in 1927 and went on to win greater acclaim than ever thanks to her extraordinary charisma. In 1932, she bought a house at 801 North Alpine Drive, Beverly Hills. Her films include *Anna Christie, Chasing Rainbows, Min and Bill* (Oscar, 1931), *Emma, Dinner at Eight*, and *Tugboat Annie.*

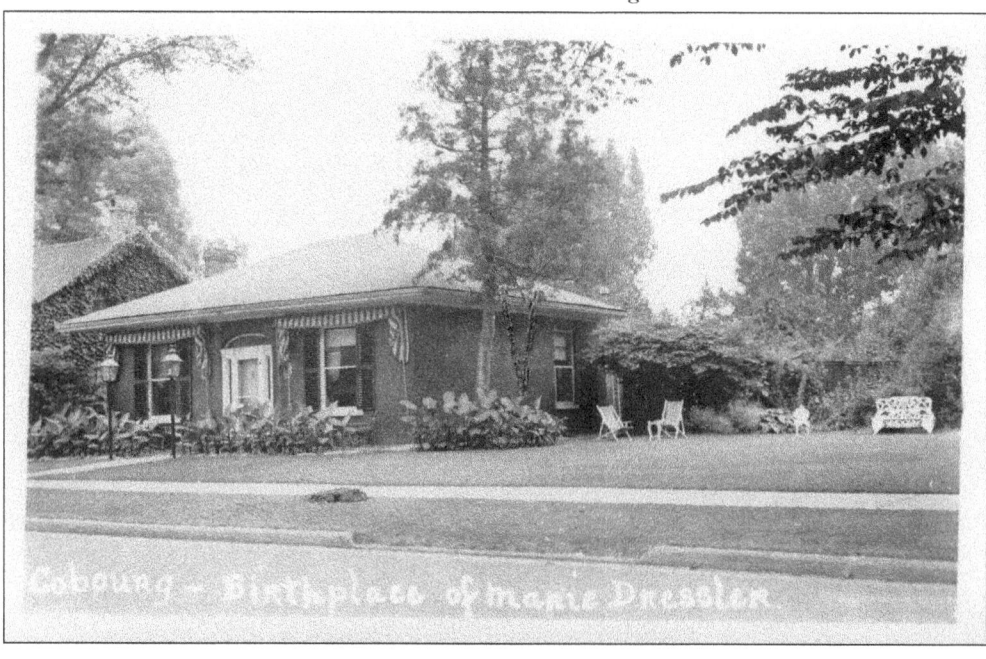

HOWARD DUFF PICTURE POSTCARD. Known for both having a hot temper and being a practical actor, Howard Duff excelled in dramas. He made his first impression as radio's *Sam Spade* (1946–1950). His films include *The Naked City*, *Illegal Entry*, *Red Canyon*, *Johnny Stool Pigeon*, and *Woman in Hiding* opposite English actress Ida Lupino, whom he eventually married (1951). In 1950, Duff lived at 1555 North Hayworth Avenue, Hollywood.

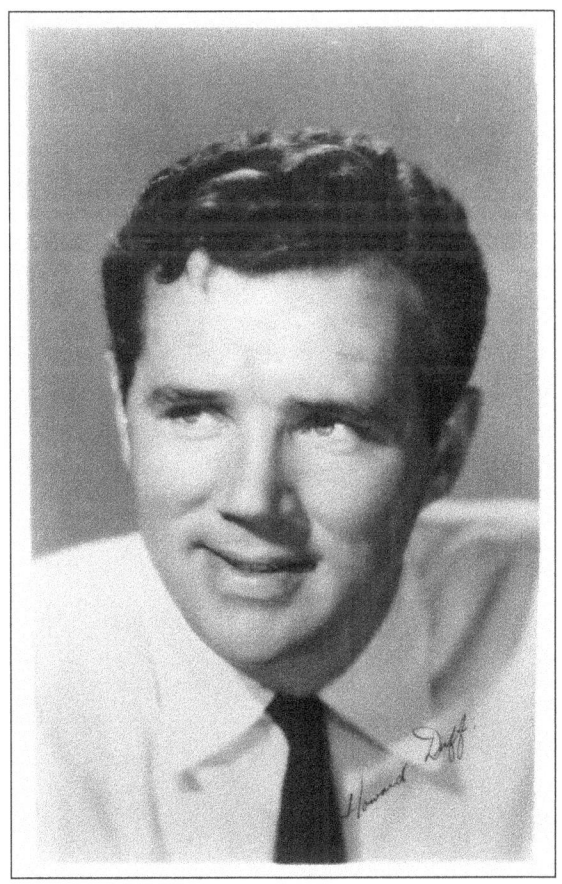

DEANNA DURBIN. In the 1930s and 1940s, teenaged singing sensation Deanna Durbin lived with her parents in this mansion at 5526 Linwood Drive, in exclusive Laughlin Park, Los Feliz, Hollywood. Built in 1922, it has six bedrooms and five bathrooms. Canadian-born Deanna Durbin (1921–2013) scored high in *Three Smart Girls*, *First Love*, *Spring Parade*, *Nice Girl?*, *It Started with Eve*, and *Something in the Wind*.

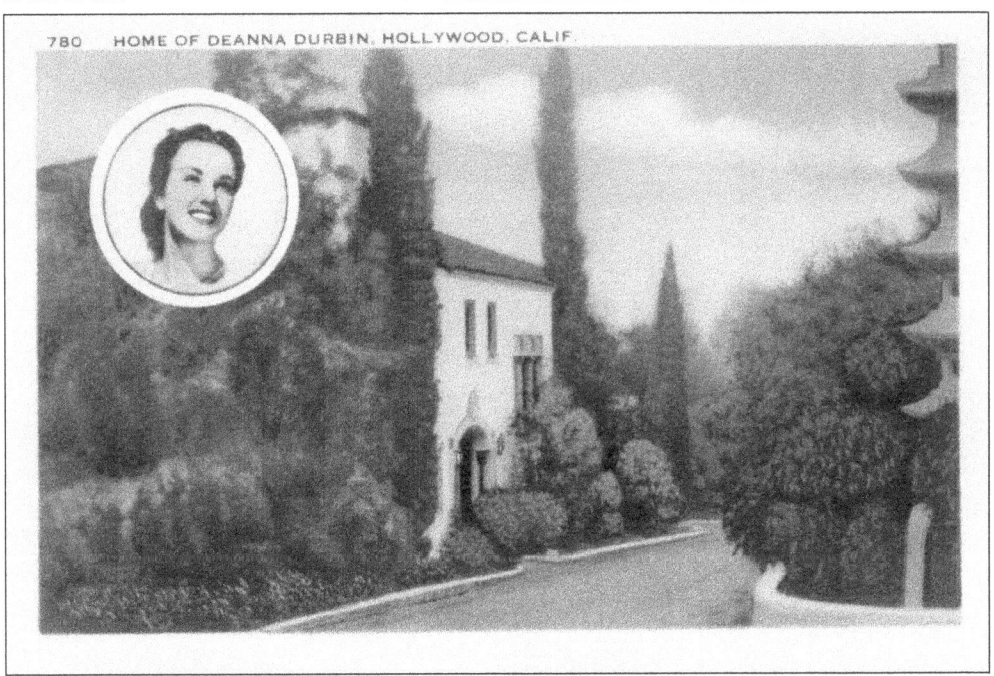

780   HOME OF DEANNA DURBIN, HOLLYWOOD, CALIF.

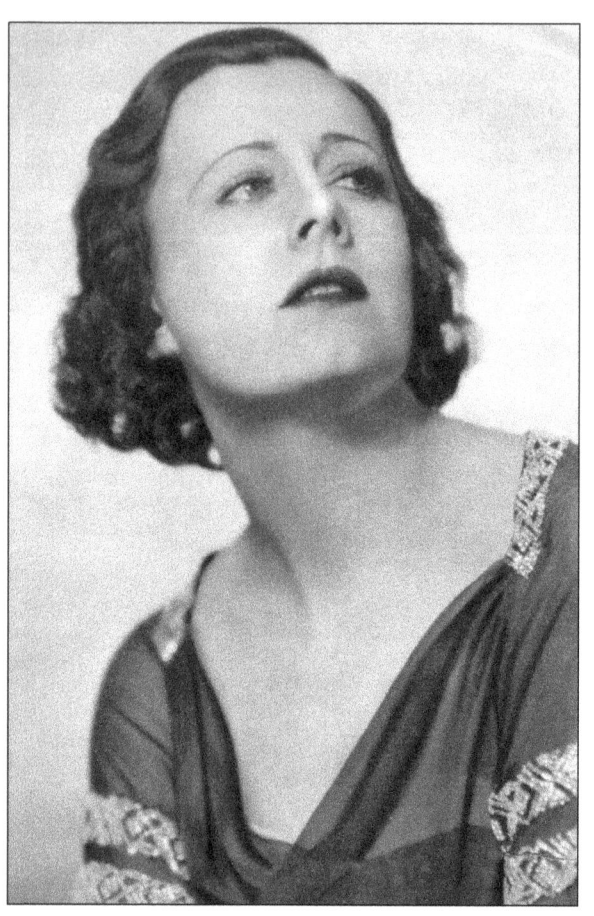

IRENE DUNNE PORTRAIT. Irene Dunne first won acclaim in the theater with *Show Boat* in 1929. This led to a film contract with RKO Pictures, and she became a leading lady. She was the daughter of US steamboat inspector Joseph Dunne (1863–1913) and Adelaide Dunne (1871–1936). In 1936, her mother, who had just returned home from doing Christmas shopping, suddenly died of apoplexy at her daughter's Holmby Hills residence.

IRENE DUNNE. The home of film great Irene Dunne (1898–1990) and her husband, Dr. Francis Griffin, at 461 North Faring Road, Holmby Hills, was designed by Spaulding Sumner in 1935. It had breathtaking views of the Pacific Ocean and the Santa Monica Mountains. Irene Dunne's film credits include *Cimarron, Roberta, Magnificent Obsession, Show Boat, Theodora Goes Wild, Anna and the King of Siam, Life with Father, I Remember Mama,* and *The Mudlark.*

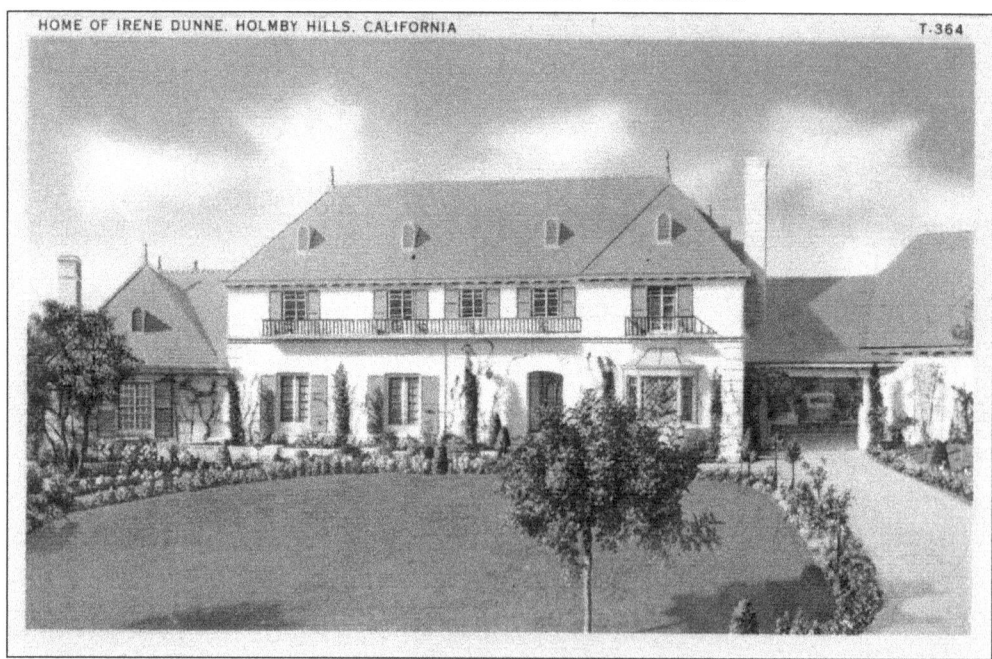

HOME OF IRENE DUNNE. HOLMBY HILLS. CALIFORNIA   T-364

JIMMY DURANTE PICTURE POSTCARD. A son of Italian immigrants from Salerno, Italy, comedian Jimmy Durante (1893–1980) made his start in show business as a ragtime pianist in his native New York. Nicknamed "Ragtime Jimmy," he soon jumped into the new wave of pop music—jazz. In the Roaring Twenties, he became popular in vaudeville, speakeasies, and radio. In 1930, he opened on Broadway in *The New Yorkers* and provided comic relief in the movie *Roadhouse Nights*.

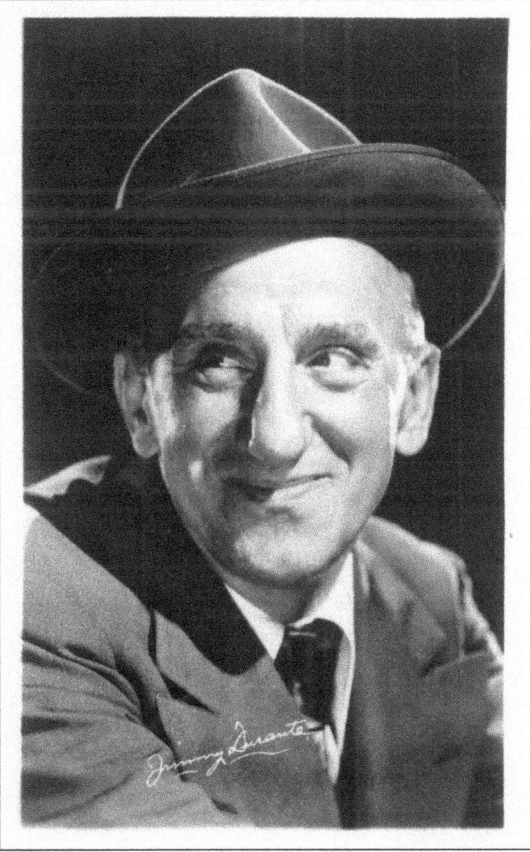

JIMMY DURANTE. This postcard from the 1950s shows Jimmy Durante's house at 511 North Beverly Drive, Beverly Hills. Durante was a very popular entertainer. The exuberant Italian American comedian was in movies, including *Speak Easily*, *The Man Who Came to Dinner*, *It Happened in Brooklyn*, *The Milkman*, and *Billy Rose's Jumbo*, and on television with shows such as *The Jimmy Durante Show* and *The Hollywood Palace*. He recorded his theme song, "Inka Dinka Doo," in 1934.

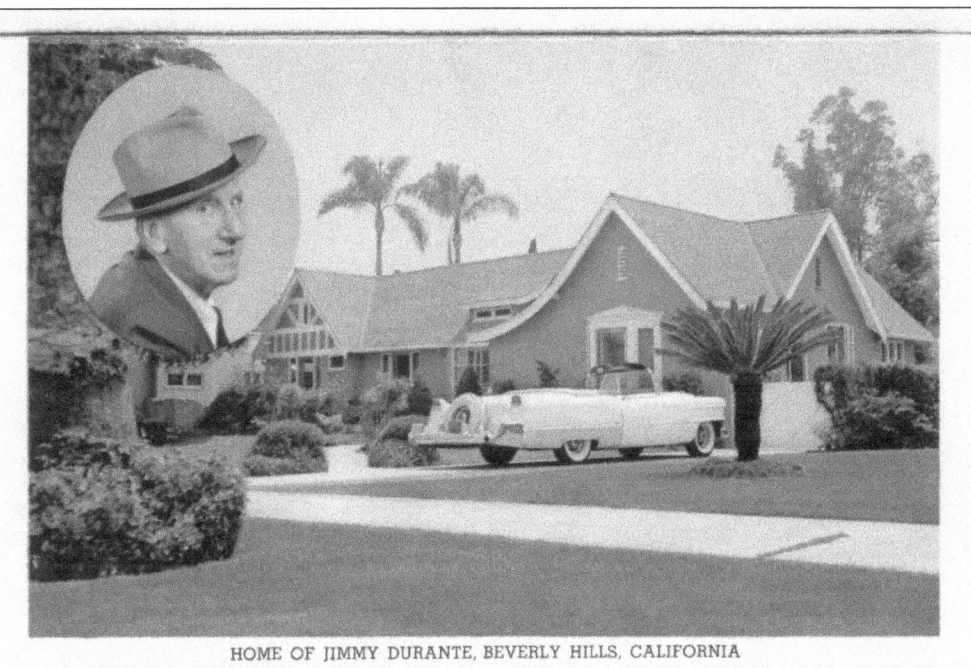

HOME OF JIMMY DURANTE, BEVERLY HILLS, CALIFORNIA

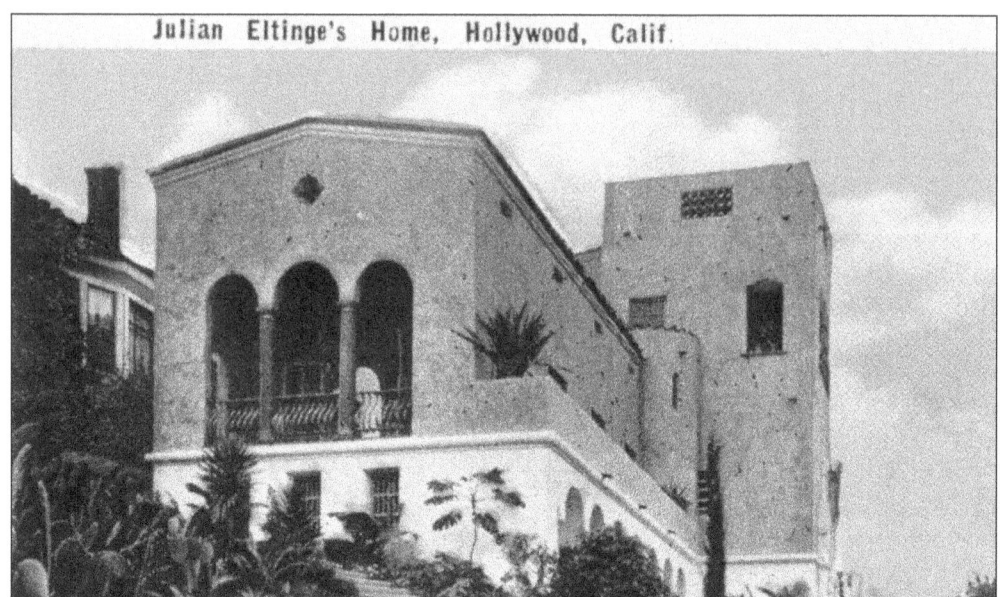

Julian Eltinge's Home, Hollywood, Calif.

JULIAN ELTINGE. Vaudeville headliner turned Broadway and Hollywood star Julian Eltinge (1881–1941) lived in this mansion at 2328 Baxter Street, Silver Lake. The celebrated female impersonator's lavish home was exquisitely landscaped and richly decorated. Eltinge's films (1914–1925) include *The Crinoline Girl, Cousin Lucy, The Widow's Mite, The Countess Charming, The Isle of Love, Madame Behave!,* and *The Fascinating Widow.* The comedy *Maid to Order* (1931) is one of just a few talking films he did.

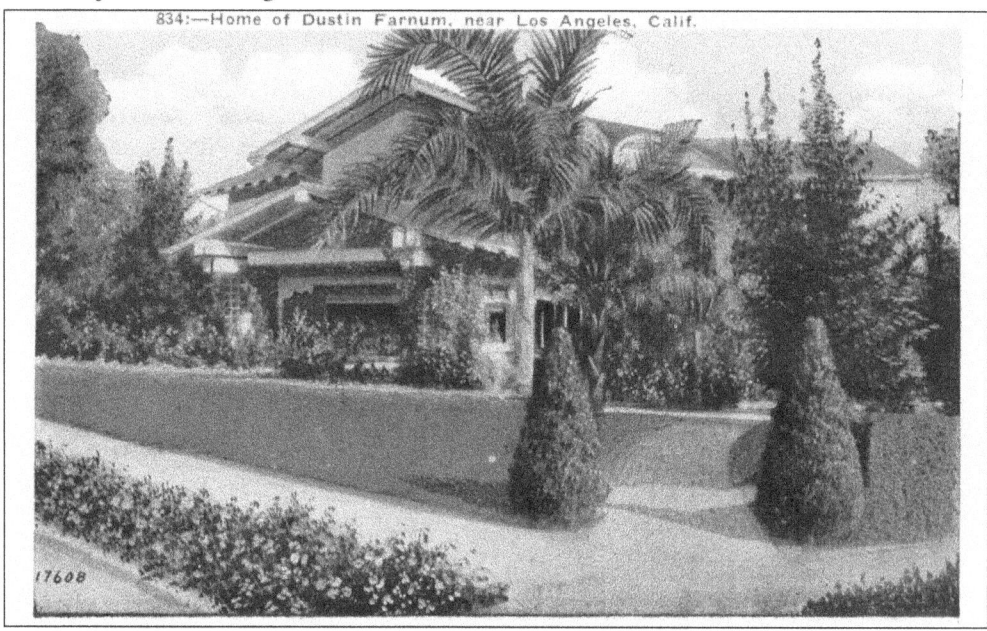

834:—Home of Dustin Farnum, near Los Angeles, Calif.

DUSTIN FARNUM. In the 1910s and early 1920s, this very popular star of silent screen Westerns lived at 1284 North Crescent Heights Boulevard, Hollywood. Dustin Farnum (1874–1929), already admired as a stage actor, began making silent dramas for Famous Players-Lasky in 1914, and among them were *The Squaw Man, Davy Crockett, The Virginian, Cameo Kirby, The Gentleman from Indiana,* and *The Parson of Panamint.* His last film was *The Flaming Frontier* (1926).

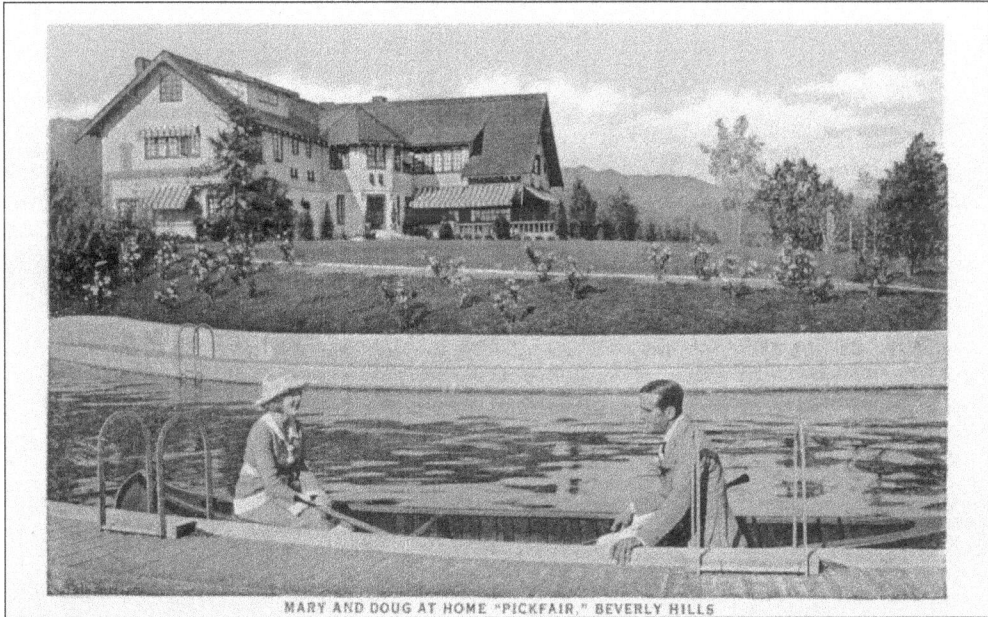

MARY AND DOUG AT HOME "PICKFAIR," BEVERLY HILLS

DOUGLAS FAIRBANKS AND MARY PICKFORD. Architect Wallace Neff designed the mock Tudor–style estate dubbed Pickfair. Purchased in 1919 by Douglas Fairbanks (1883–1939) and Mary Pickford (1893–1979) at 1143 Summit Drive, it became the most famous estate in Beverly Hills. Fairbanks's films include *Intolerance*, *The Mark of Zorro*, *Robin Hood*, and *The Gaucho*, while Pickford starred in *A Good Little Devil*, *Hearts Adrift*, *Pollyanna*, and *Secrets*.

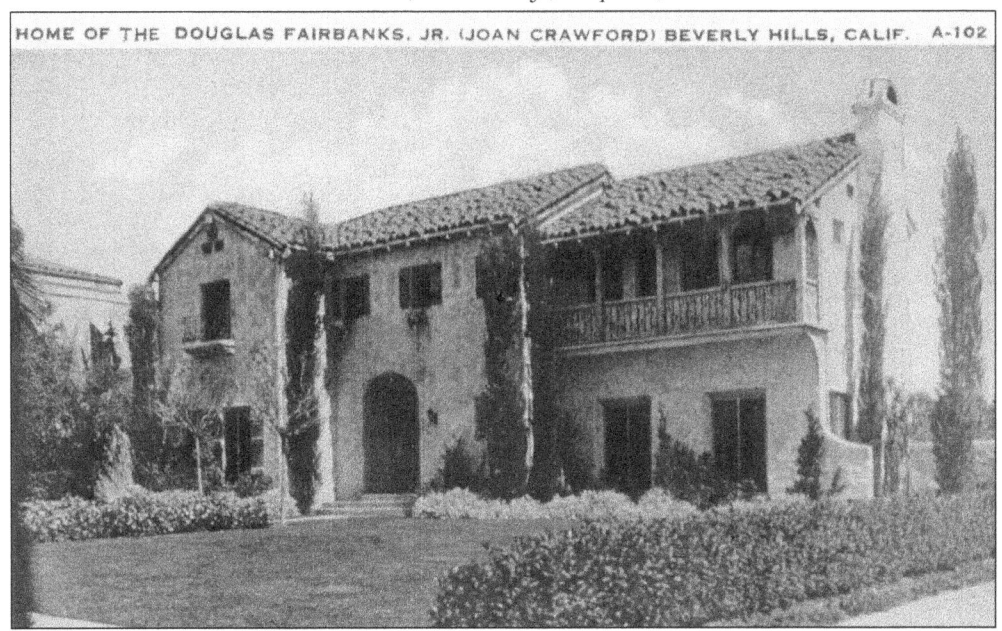

HOME OF THE DOUGLAS FAIRBANKS, JR. (JOAN CRAWFORD) BEVERLY HILLS, CALIF.   A-102

DOUGLAS FAIRBANKS JR. As a young star in the late 1920s, Douglas Fairbanks Jr. (1909–2000) and his first wife, Joan Crawford, lived in Brentwood Heights, Beverly Hills, pictured. Although he pursued his career in the shadow of his celebrated father, Fairbanks achieved genuine stardom in his own right. His many films include *The Dawn Patrol*, *Little Caesar*, *The Prisoner of Zenda*, *Gunga Din*, *The Corsican Brothers*, and *State Secret*, an espionage thriller.

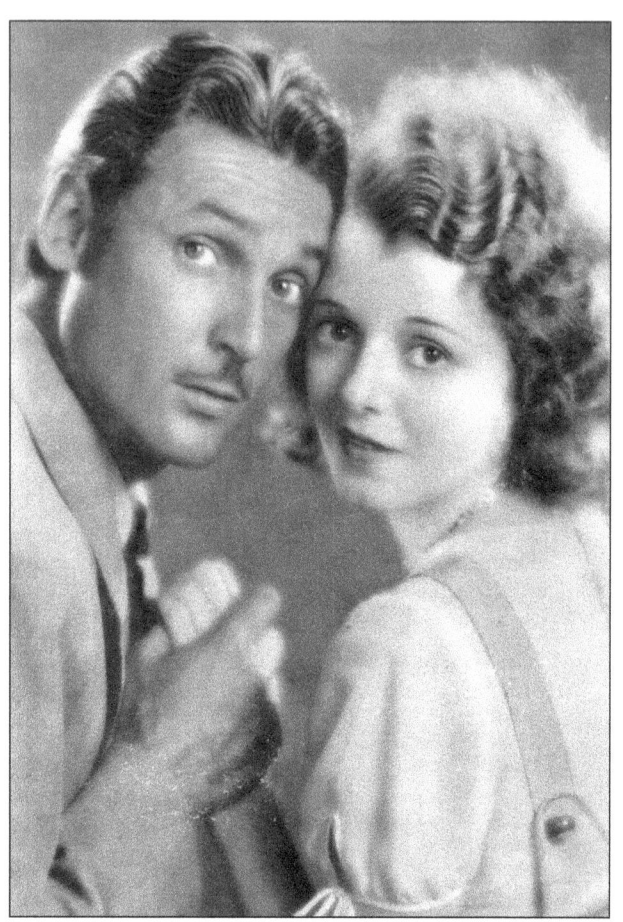

CHARLES FARRELL AND JANET GAYNOR. Screen favorites Charles Farrell and Janet Gaynor enchanted fans with romantic films, such as *Seventh Heaven*, *Street Angel*, *Lucky Star*, and *Sunny Side Up*. In 1930, Farrell (1900–1990) lived with his parents at 9918 Toluca Lake Avenue, North Hollywood, and Janet Gaynor (1906–1984) lived with her husband, writer Jesse Lydell Peck (1899–1957), at 504 North Palm Drive, Beverly Hills. The Pecks were married from 1929 to 1933.

ALICE FAYE. Film star Alice Faye (1915–1998) lived in Beverly Hills at 705 North Rexford Drive in 1937–1938 and 1100 Benedict Canyon Drive in 1939; she also had a home in Encino. Groomed as a successor to Jean Harlow, she became one of the biggest romantic and musical stars. Her top-grossing films include *In Old Chicago*, *Alexander's Ragtime Band*, *Rose of Washington Square*, *Tin Pan Alley*, and *Hello, Frisco, Hello*.

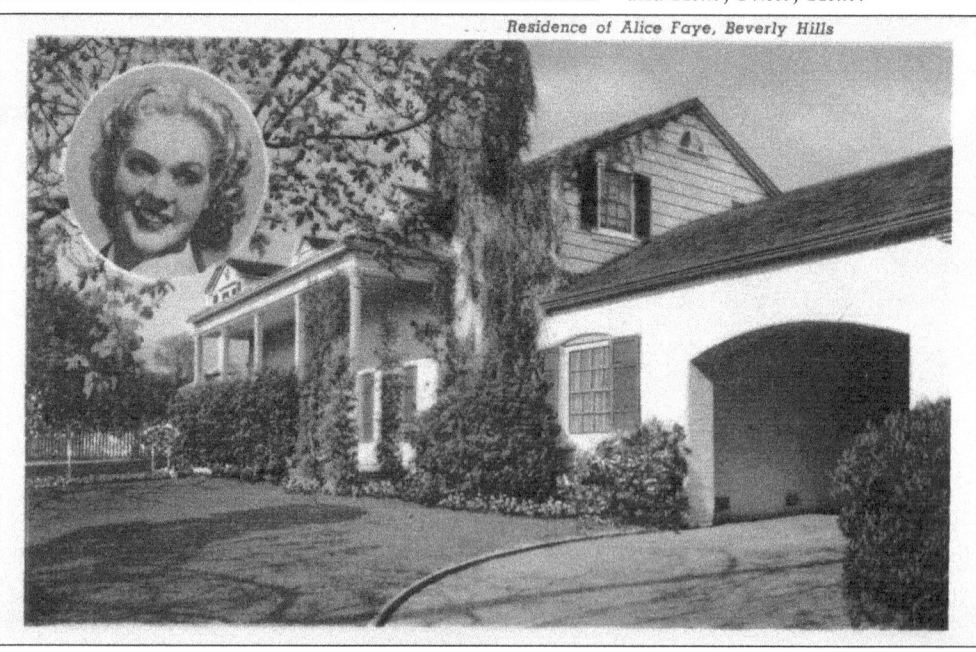

Residence of Alice Faye, Beverly Hills

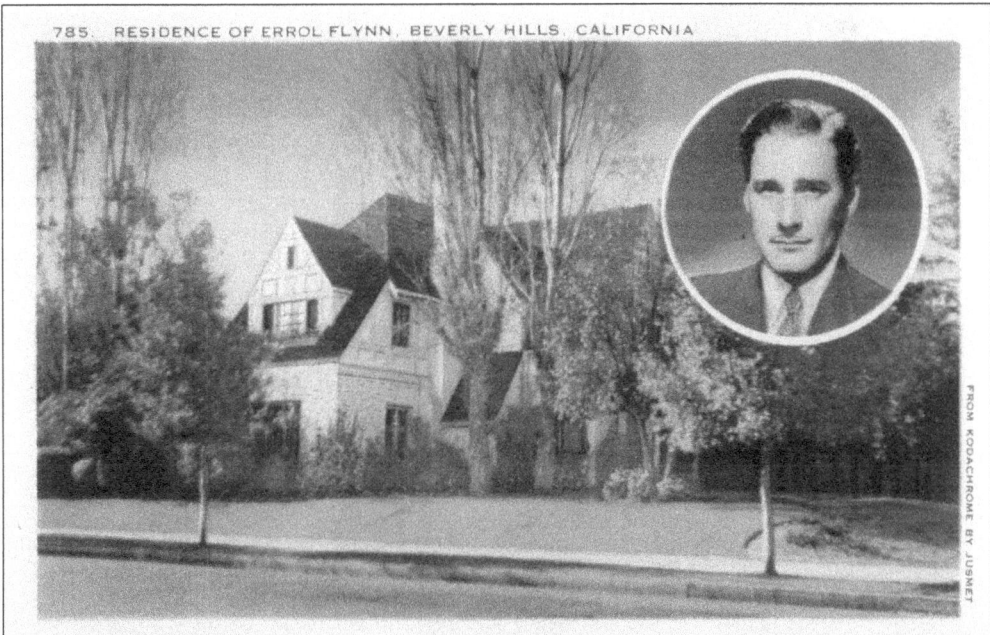

785. RESIDENCE OF ERROL FLYNN, BEVERLY HILLS, CALIFORNIA

FROM KODACHROME BY JUSMET

ERROL FLYNN. From 1938 to 1940, Errol Flynn (1909–1959) and his pal David Niven rented this house at 601 North Linden Drive, Beverly Hills, as a bachelor pad. Their wild parties there were notorious. After Niven left, Flynn lived there with his first wife, actress Lili Damita. A great star, Flynn was in *Captain Blood*, *The Adventures of Robin Hood*, *Dodge City*, *The Sea Hawk*, and *Footsteps in the Dark*.

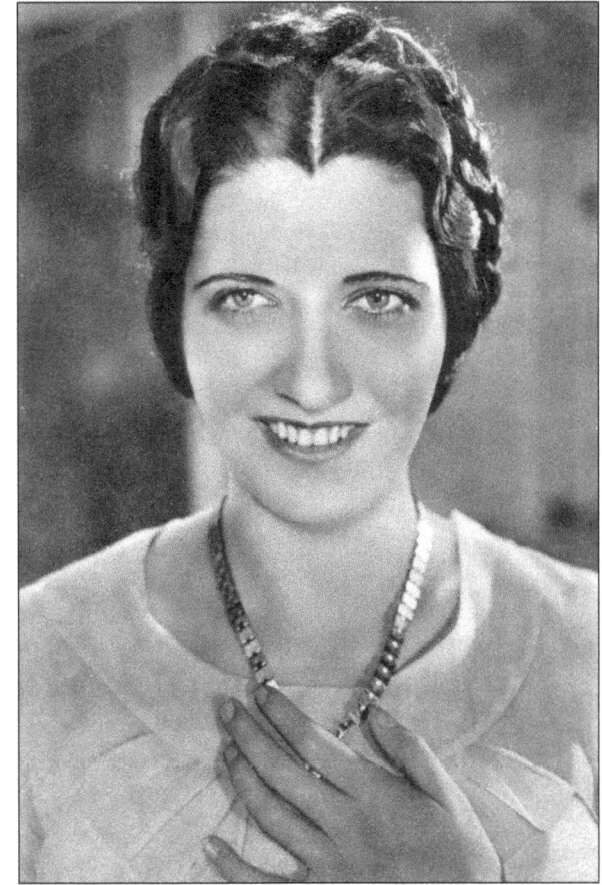

KAY FRANCIS. A screen favorite in the 1930s, Kay Francis had several residences in Hollywood and Beverly Hills. Francis (1905–1968) was one of the many stage actresses that made it big in Hollywood thanks to the advent of the talkies. Her movies include *For the Defense*, *Transgression*, *One-Way Passage*, *Trouble in Paradise*, *Wonder Bar*, *Dr. Monica*, *First Lady*, and *Charley's Aunt*. In 1948, she retired from show business.

57

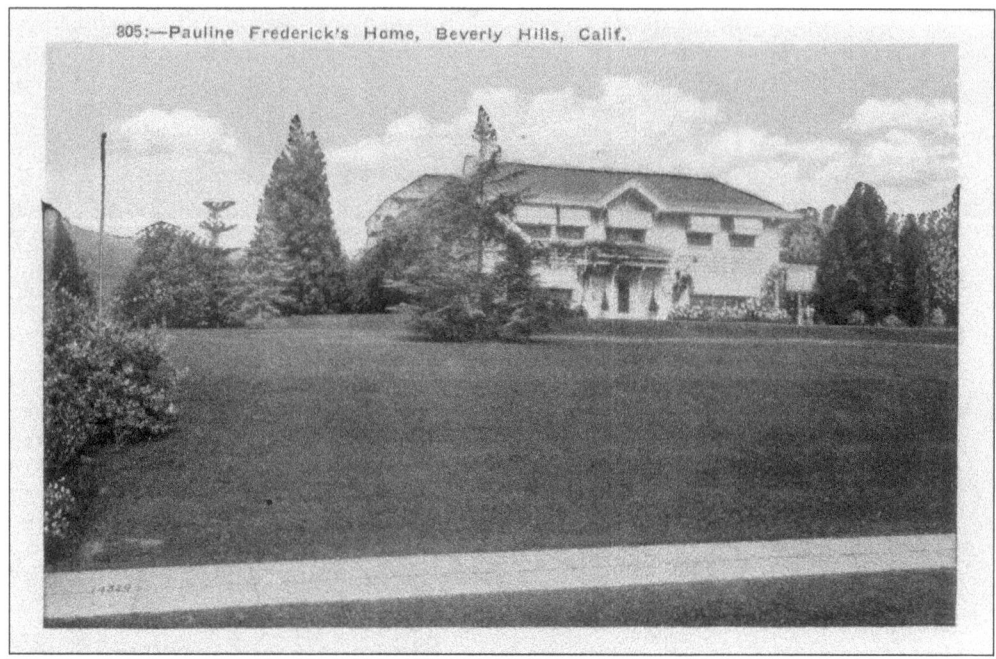

805:—Pauline Frederick's Home, Beverly Hills, Calif.

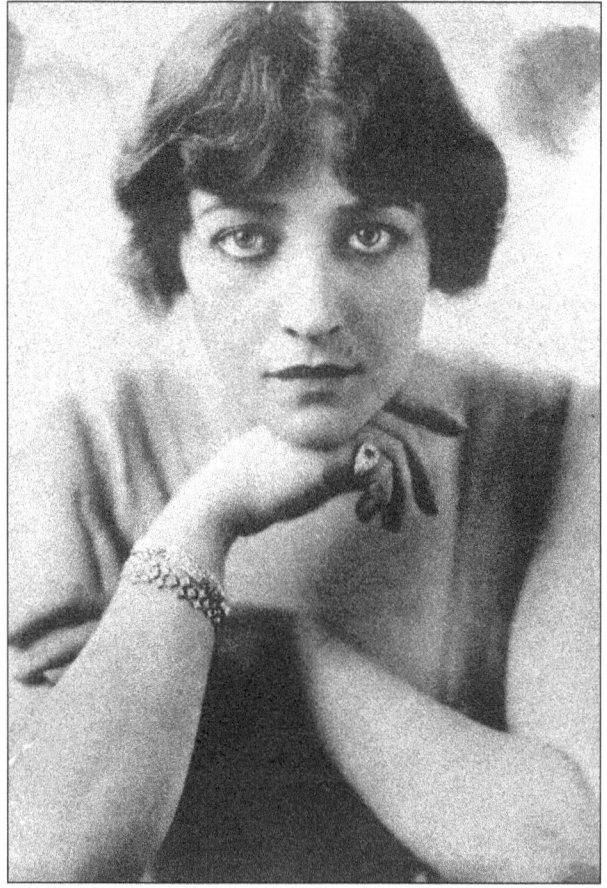

PAULINE FREDERICK. In 1918, actress Pauline Frederick (1883–1938) settled in Beverly Hills, making her one of the first stars to do so. Located at 503 Sunset Boulevard, the elegant cream-tinted mansion was widely admired. Among her greatest silent film triumphs are *Zaza*, *Ashes of Embers*, *The Woman in the Case*, *Resurrection*, *Madame X*, and *Smouldering Fires*. At the age of 53, she died of asthma in her aunt's Beverly Hills home.

PAULINE FREDERICK PORTRAIT. The future tragedienne of the silent screen was born Pauline Beatrice Libbey on August 12, 1883, in Boston. She was the daughter of railroad yardmaster Richard Libbey and his wife, Loretta (1859–1938), who following her husband's death lived with Pauline in Beverly Hills. Much admired, Pauline Frederick returned to the screen to star with Joan Crawford and Neil Hamilton in *This Modern Age* (1931).

Three

CLARK GABLE TO RAMÓN NOVARRO

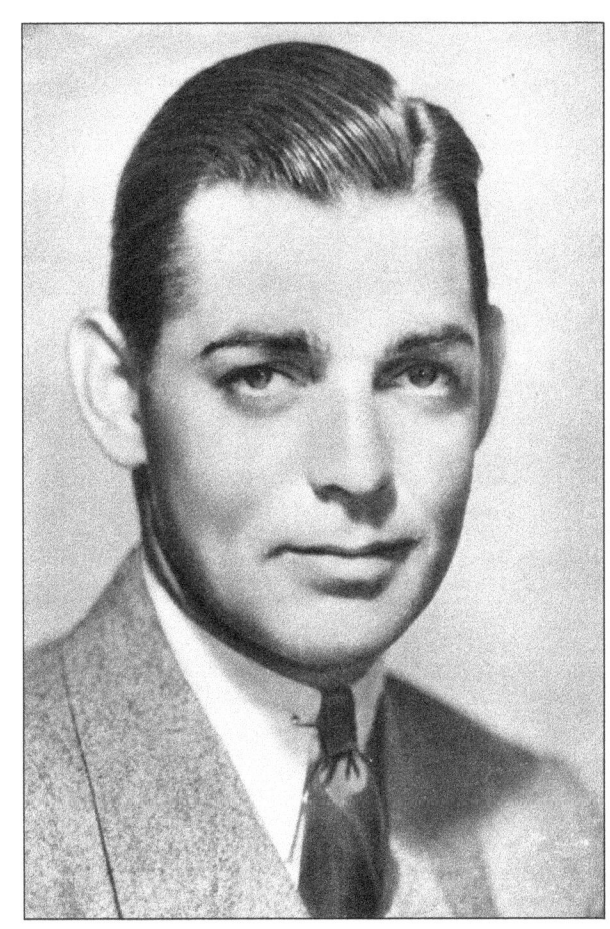

CLARK GABLE PORTRAIT. The son of William Gable, an itinerant oil field worker, Clark drifted into acting, a field that seemed to offer more opportunities than common labor. Throughout the 1920s, Gable acted in traveling stock companies, and on Broadway, he appeared in *Machinal* (1928) and *The Last Mile* (1930), and the latter helped him break into pictures.

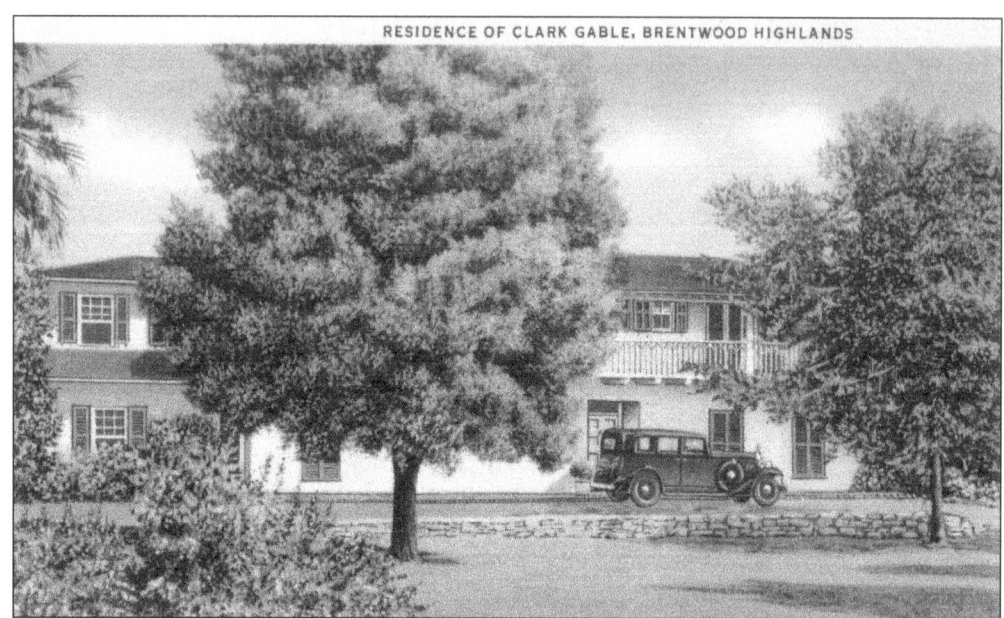

CLARK GABLE. The celebrated "King of Hollywood," Clark Gable (1901–1960) lived in this Brentwood Heights residence during his marriage to his second wife, Maria Langham Gable (1884–1966). One of Hollywood's top money-making stars, Clark Gable was in *Red Dust*, *It Happened One Night*, *Manhattan Melodrama*, *Wife vs. Secretary*, *The Call of the Wild*, *Mutiny on the Bounty*, *Idiot's Delight*, *Gone with the Wind*, *Mogambo*, and *The Misfits* to name a few.

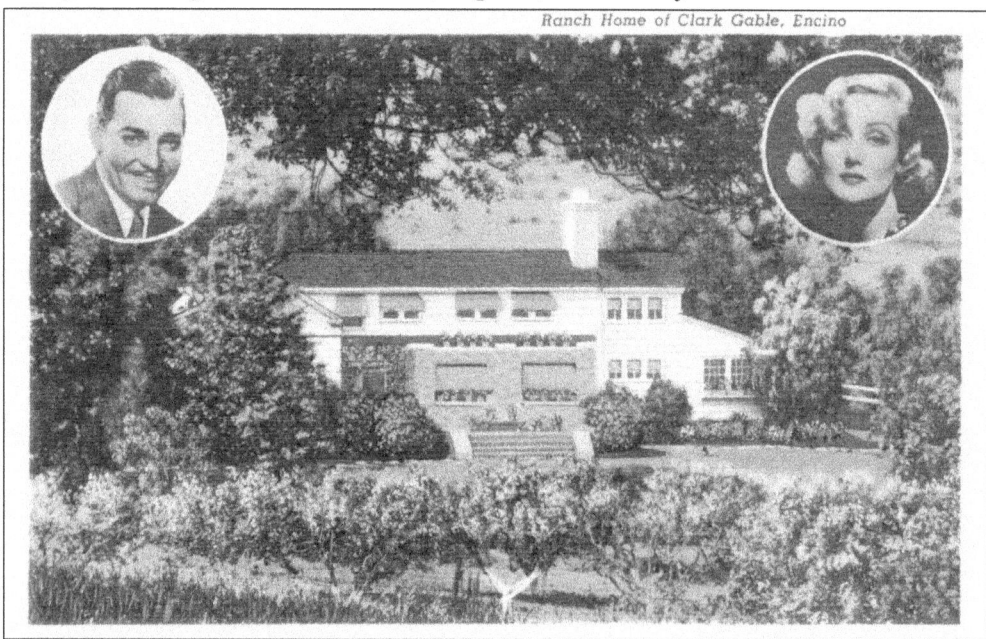

Ranch Home of Clark Gable, Encino

CLARK GABLE AND CAROLE LOMBARD. In 1939, newlyweds Clark Gable and Carole Lombard (1909–1942) moved to this 20-acre ranch in Encino. The wholesome rural life they found there was far more appealing than Tinseltown. But their marriage ended in tragedy—Lombard died in an airplane crash. Lombard's credits include *Twentieth Century*, *My Man Godfrey*, *Nothing Scared*, *Mr. and Mrs. Smith*, and *To Be or Not to Be*.

GRETA GARBO PORTRAIT. Perhaps the greatest beauty of the screen, the legendary Greta Garbo also had a striking screen presence as an actress. Among her most admired films are *The Temptress, Flesh and the Devil, A Woman of Affairs, Anna Christie, Mata Hari, Grand Hotel, Queen Christina,* and *Anna Karenina.* For years, Garbo (1905–1990) lived in Santa Monica, but by 1948, her address was 904 North Bedford Drive, Beverly Hills.

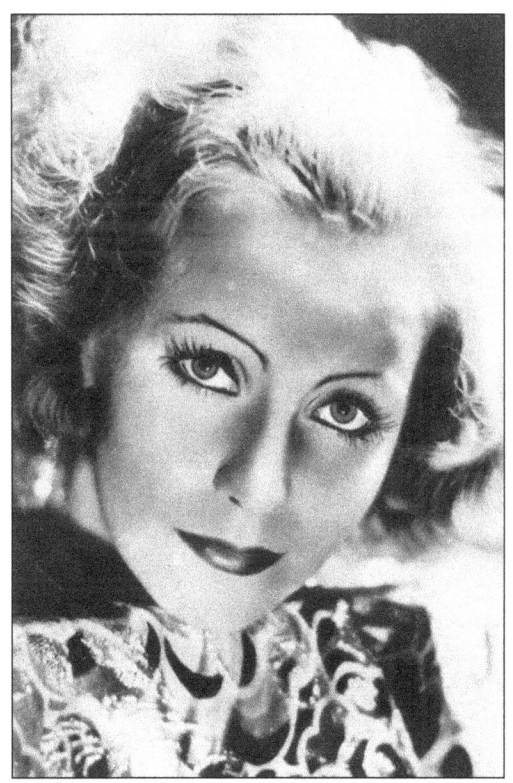

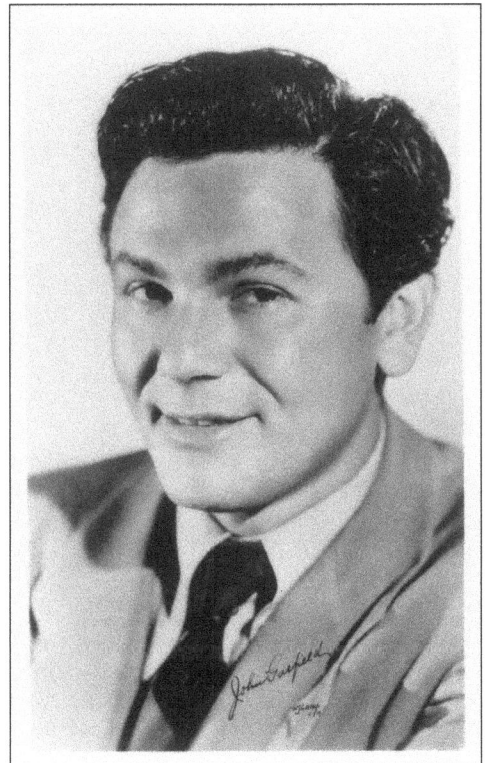

JOHN GARFIELD PICTURE POSTCARD. A fine dramatic actor, John Garfield was born Jacob Garfinkle on New York City's Lower East Side. Originally a stage actor, he found success in Hollywood films, including *Four Daughters, Pride of the Marines, The Postman Always Rings Twice,* and *Body and Soul.* Garfield and his wife lived at 1712 North Stanley Avenue, Hollywood Hills, formerly the home of William Haines and Tallulah Bankhead.

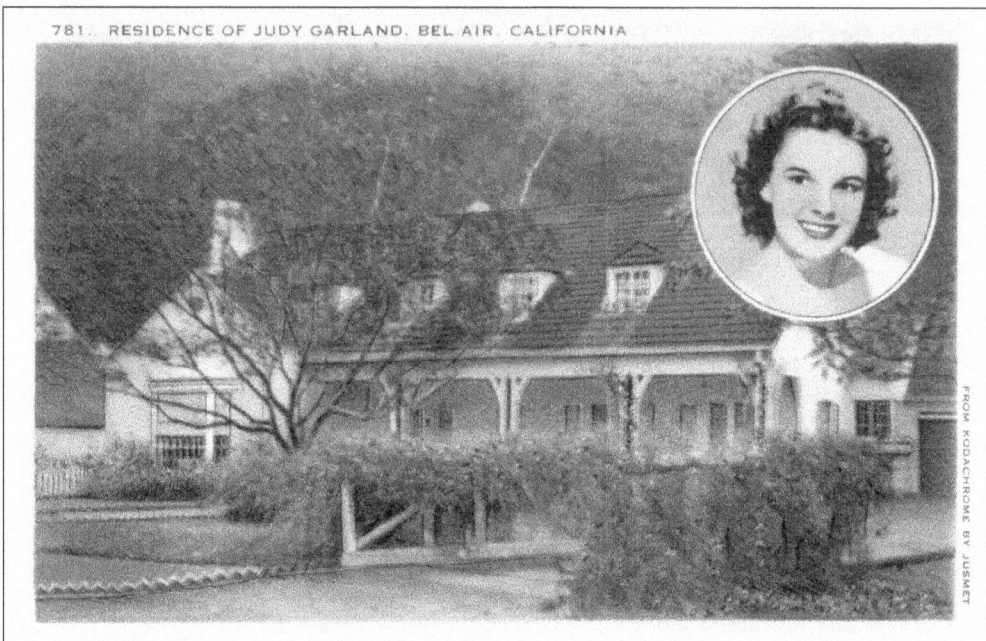

FROM KODACHROME BY JUSMET

JUDY GARLAND'S BEL AIR HOUSE. Before she married David Rose in 1941, Judy Garland (1922–1969) lived in this lovely house at 1231 Stone Canyon Road, Bel Air, from 1939 to 1941, with her mother, Ethel Garland, and her older sister Sue. The multitalented actress had a slew of hit films, including *The Wizard of Oz*, *Presenting Lily Mars*, *Meet Me in St. Louis*, *The Harvey Girls*, *Easter Parade*, and *A Star Is Born*.

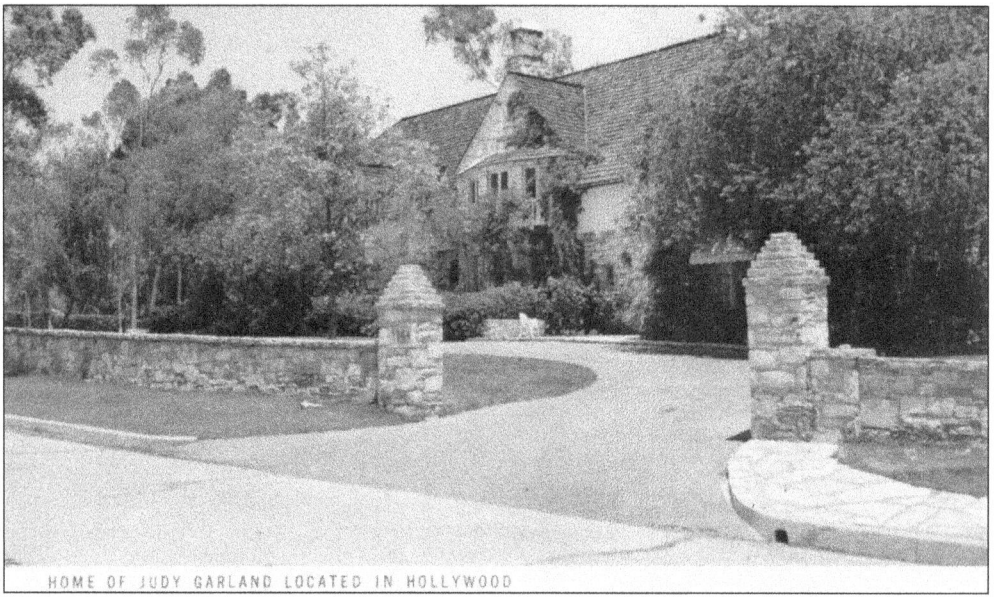

HOME OF JUDY GARLAND LOCATED IN HOLLYWOOD

JUDY GARLAND'S HOLMBY HILLS HOUSE. Superstar Judy Garland lived here—144 South Mapleton Drive, Holmby Hills—with her third husband, talent agent and sometime theatrical producer Sidney "Sid" Luft (1915–2005), from about 1953 to the early 1960s. The Lufts married in 1952 and had two children, Lorna and Joseph; they divorced in 1965. Sid produced Judy Garland's comeback hit film *A Star Is Born* (1954).

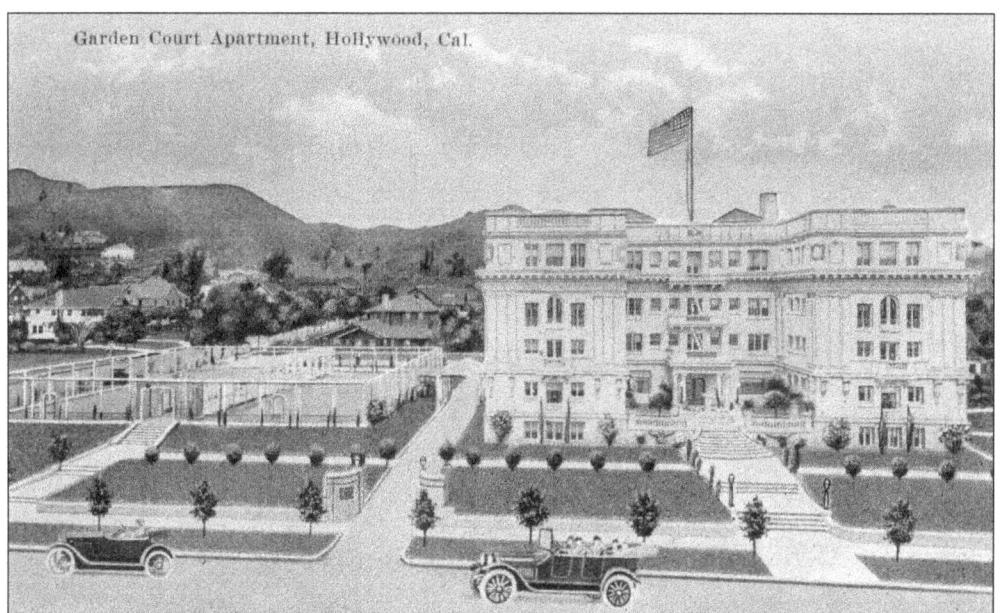

GARDEN COURT APARTMENT. Designed by Frank Meline (1875–1944) and opened in 1917, the Garden Court Apartment building was located at 7021 Hollywood Boulevard. Among its film colony guests were Bessie Love, Virginia Valli, May Allison, Louis B. Mayer, Mack Sennett, and Laurel and Hardy. In its heyday, guests enjoyed its air of charm, exquisite appointments, and tennis courts. Vacated in 1980, it was demolished in 1984.

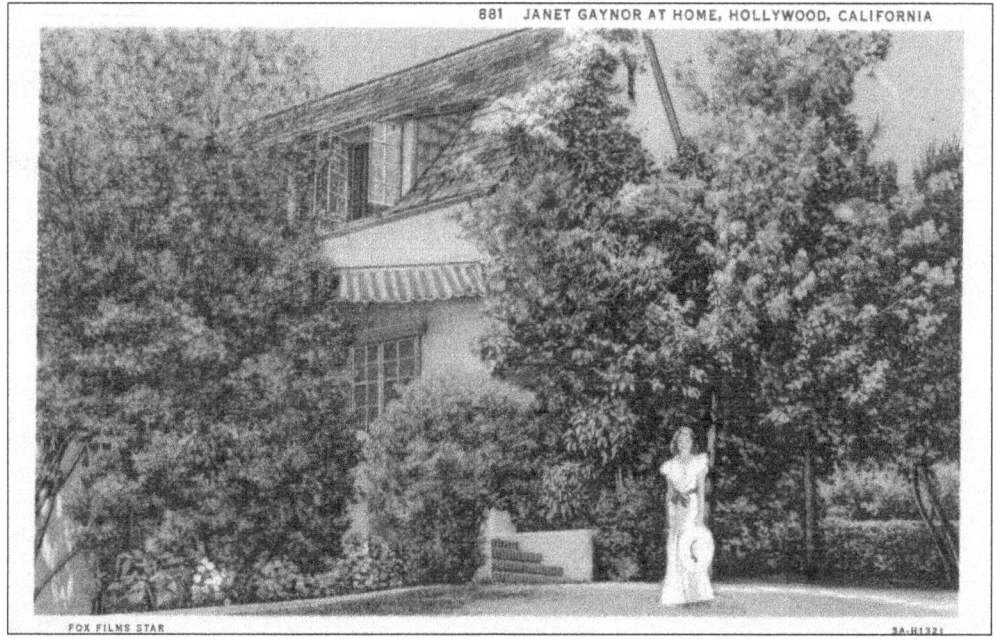

881   JANET GAYNOR AT HOME, HOLLYWOOD, CALIFORNIA

FOX FILMS STAR

JANET GAYNOR. In the 1930s, silent and sound film star Janet Gaynor (1906–1984) and her husband lived at 2074 Watsonia Terrace, Hollywood. Janet Gaynor's credits include *Seventh Heaven, Sunrise, Street Angel* (Oscar for all three, 1929), *Daddy Long Legs, State Fair, The Farmer Takes a Wife, A Star Is Born* (1937), and *The Young in Heart*. Although she retired in 1939, she returned, once more, for *Bernardine* (1957).

63

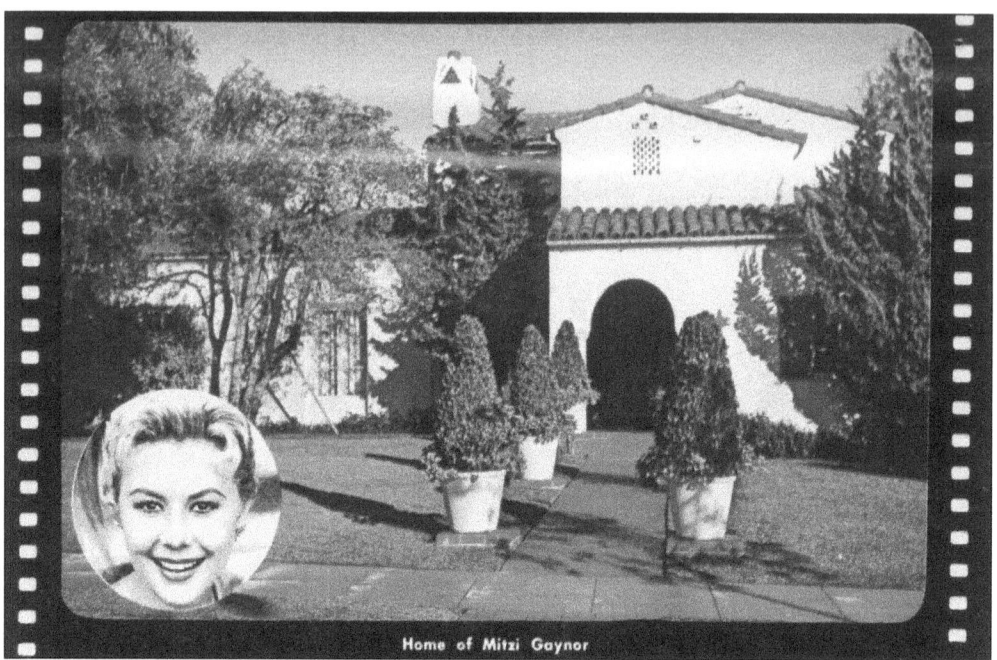

Home of Mitzi Gaynor

MITZI GAYNOR. The Spanish Colonial villa of legendary star Mitzi Gaynor (born 1931) is at 610 North Arden Drive, Beverly Hills. The effervescent actress, singer, and dancer made a splash in movies, like *Golden Girl*, *The I Don't Care Girl*, *There's No Business Like Show Business*, *The Birds and the Bees*, *The Joker Is Wild*, *South Pacific*, and *Surprise Package*. From 1968 through the 1970s, her television specials kept her popular.

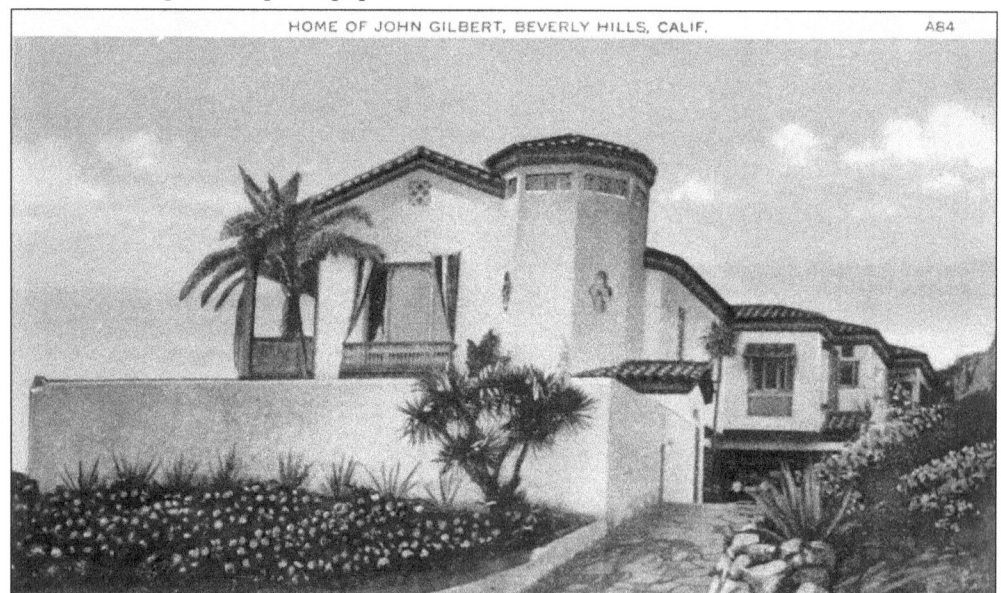

HOME OF JOHN GILBERT, BEVERLY HILLS, CALIF.   A84

JOHN GILBERT. Silent screen star John Gilbert built this mansion at 1400 Tower Road, Beverly Hills, in the mid-1920s. He lived there during his brief marriages to Broadway star Ina Claire and film actress Virginia Bruce. After his death, Miriam Hopkins bought it. Gilbert graced silent films, like *He Who Gets Slapped*, *The Merry Widow*, *The Big Parade*, and *La Bohème*; his talkies include *The Phantom of Paris*, *Fast Workers*, and *Queen Christina*.

HOOT GIBSON PORTRAIT. This movie star collectors' card from the 1920s highlights one of Universal Pictures' most popular Western stars, Hoot Gibson. Carl Laemmle of Universal put Gibson in action-packed two-reelers, like *The Night Riders* (1916). Throughout the 1920s, Gibson was one of the most popular heroes of the silver screen.

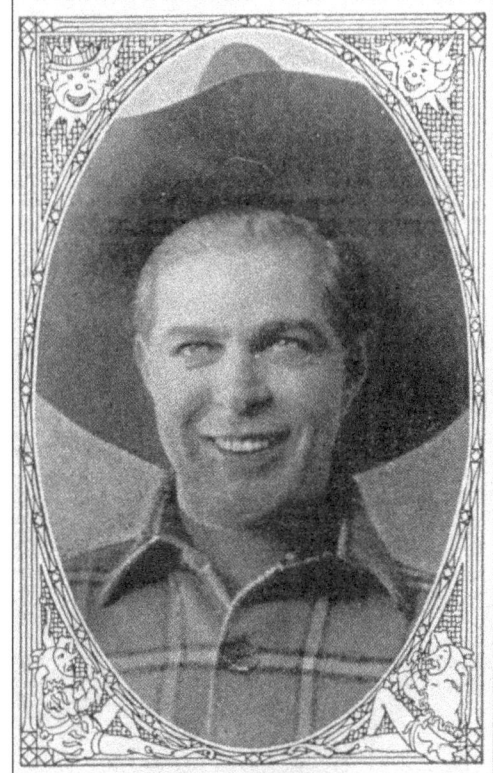

HOOT GIBSON. On view here is Western star Hoot Gibson's home at 814 North Bedford Drive, Beverly Hills. In the 1920s, Nebraska-born Edmund "Hoot" Gibson (1892–1962) was one of Hollywood's top Western stars. A rodeo champion and stuntman before entering the pictures, Gibson later ran a rodeo-ranch in nearby Bouquet Canyon. His best-loved films include *Sure Fire*, *The Ramblin' Kid*, *Flaming Frontier*, *Trigger Tricks*, *Danger Ahead*, and *Long, Long Trail*.

HOOT GIBSON
Starring in Universal Pictures
47

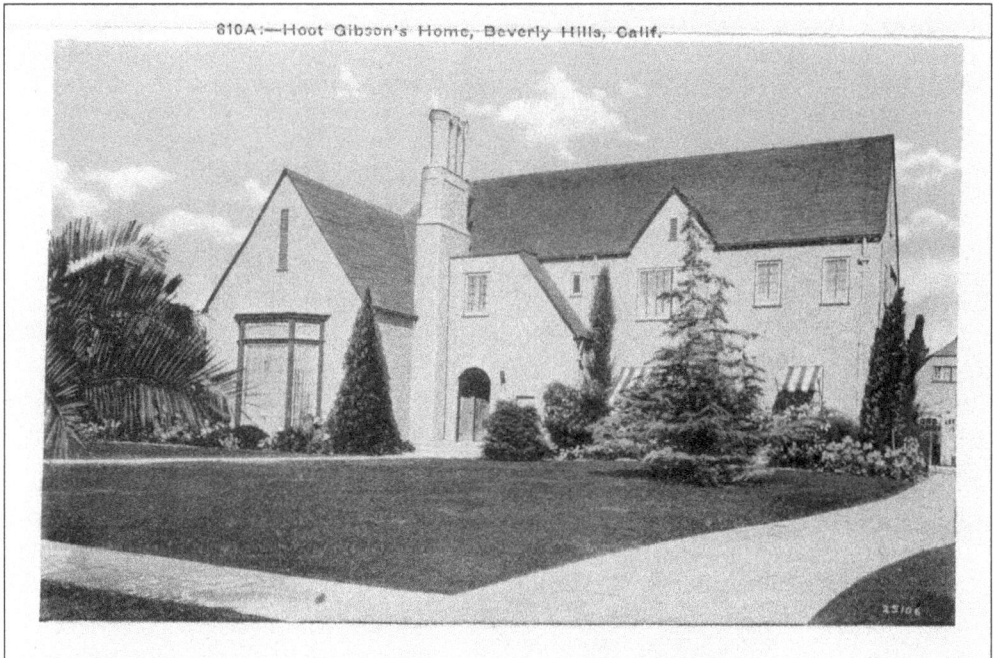

810A:—Hoot Gibson's Home, Beverly Hills, Calif.

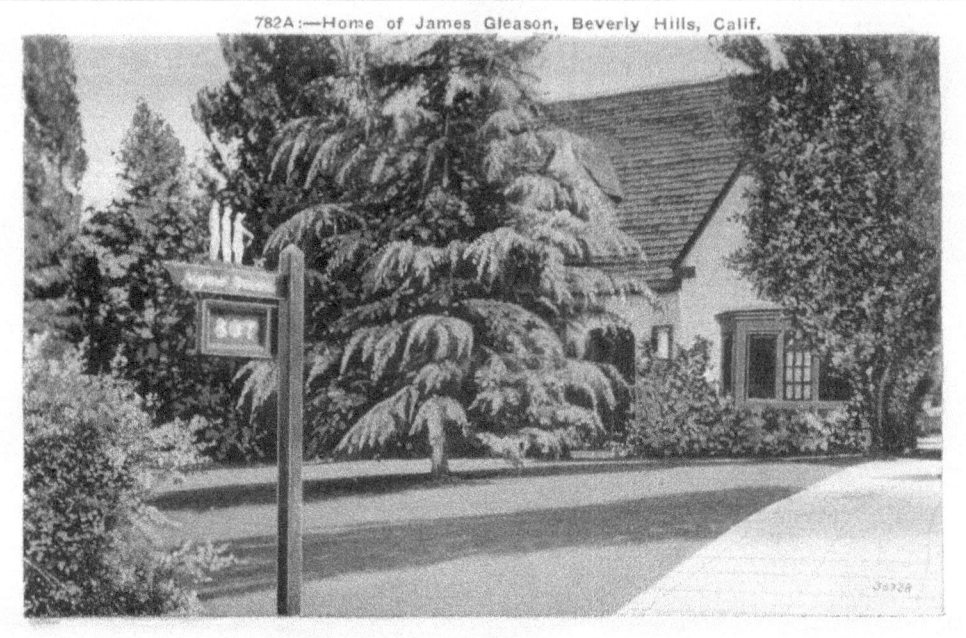

782A:—Home of James Gleason, Beverly Hills, Calif.

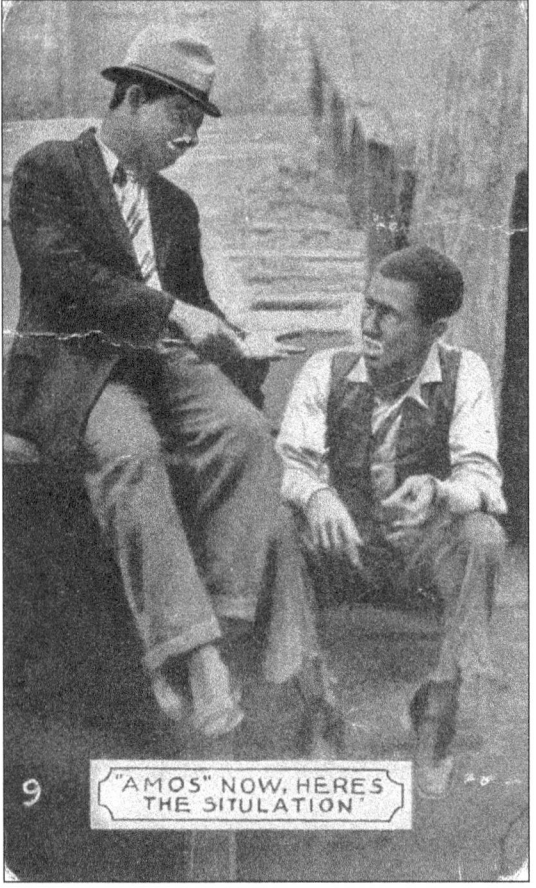

"AMOS" NOW, HERES THE SITUATION"

JAMES GLEASON. Vaudeville and Hollywood actors James and Lucile Gleason lived in this house at 807 North Alpine Drive, Beverly Hills. A master character comedian, James Gleason (1882–1959) excelled in playing tart, sarcastic detectives and tough New Yorkers. James and Lucile Gleason (1888–1947) costarred in two films, *The Shannons of Broadway* and *Money to Burn*. Among James's other films are *The Penguin Pool Murders*, *Here Comes Mr. Jordan*, and *The Last Hurrah*.

GOSDEN AND CORRELL. Perhaps the greatest comedy duo of old-time radio were the gifted voice actors Freeman Gosden (1899–1982) and Charles Correll (1890–1972). Their character portrayals on *Amos 'n' Andy* (1928–1960) made that series the nation's favorite during the Great Depression. For years, Gosden lived at 900 North Alpine Drive, and Correll lived at 10250 West Sunset Boulevard, Holmby Hills.

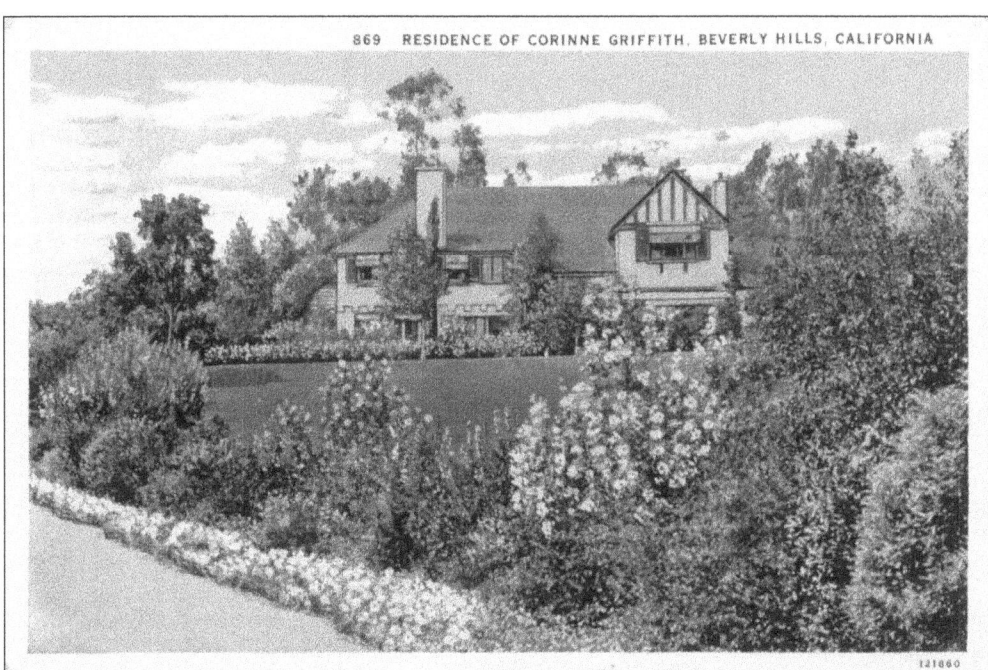

CORINNE GRIFFITH. Screen beauty Corinne Griffith (1894–1979), one of the greatest silent film stars, lived in this Tudor-style estate in the 1920s. Located at 1003 Summit Drive, Beverly Hills, it was furnished with antiques and was exquisitely landscaped. In 1927, she sold it for $186,000. Corinne Griffith's films include *The Climbers, Babs, Thin Ice, The Broadway Bubble, Déclassé, The Garden of Eden*, and *The Divine Lady*. Her sound films include *Back Pay* and *Paradise Alley*.

CORINNE GRIFFITH PICTURE POSTCARD. Proving her status as an international favorite, this postcard bearing the photograph of Hollywood star Corinne Griffith was published in the Netherlands. It was postmarked in Hoorn, a Dutch town, and addressed to a *Mejuffrouw T. Bloem, van Deventerlaan, Voorburg, Holland* (Miss T. Bloem, Van Deventer Lane, Voorburg, Holland).

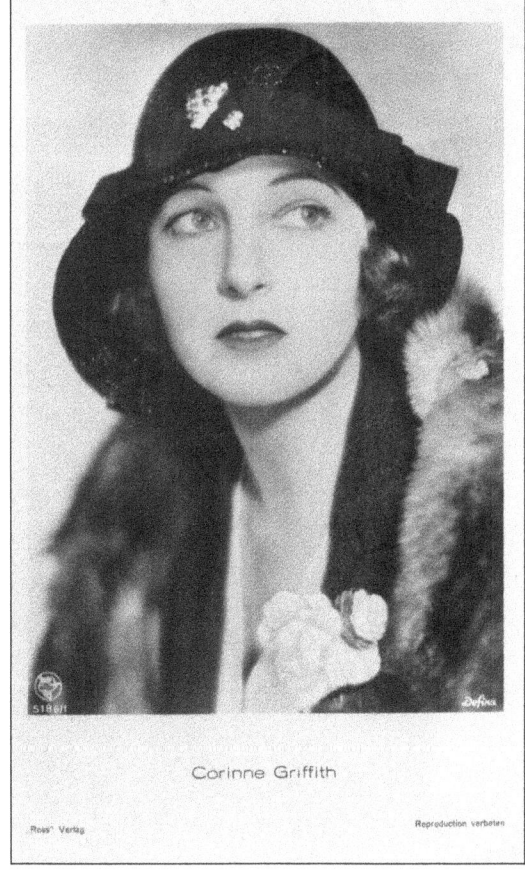

Corinne Griffith

67

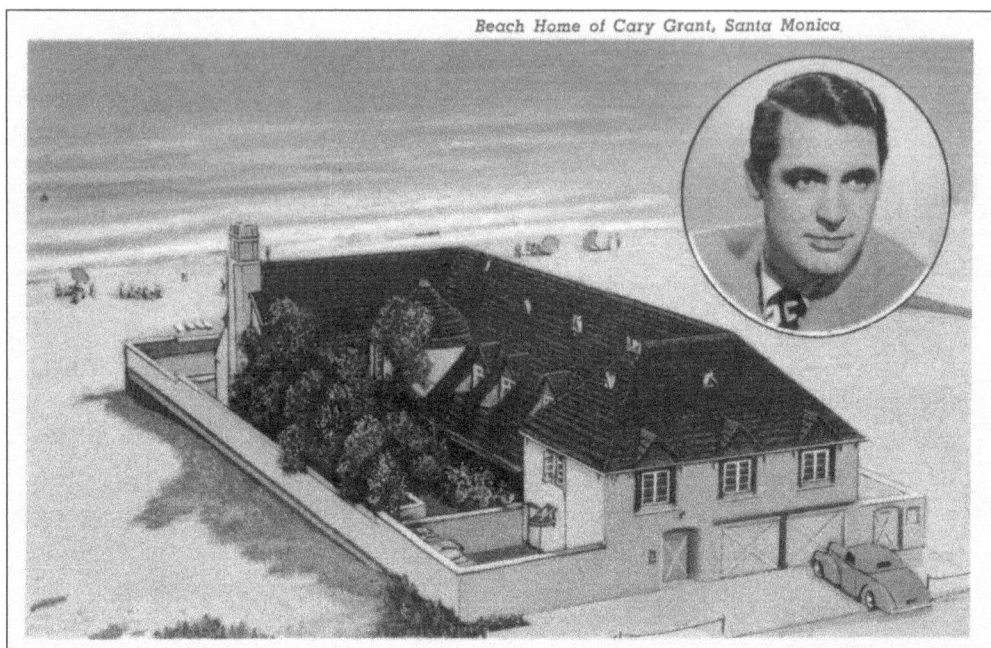

CARY GRANT AND RANDOLPH SCOTT. Shown here is the Santa Monica beach house Cary Grant (1904–1986) shared with actor Randolph Scott. Grant, one of Hollywood's most sophisticated stars, began as an English acrobat. His films include *Bringing Up Baby, Holiday, His Girl Friday, The Philadelphia Story, None but the Lonely Heart, To Catch a Thief,* and *North by Northwest.* Western star Randolph Scott (1898–1987) later lived at 156 Copley Place, Beverly Hills.

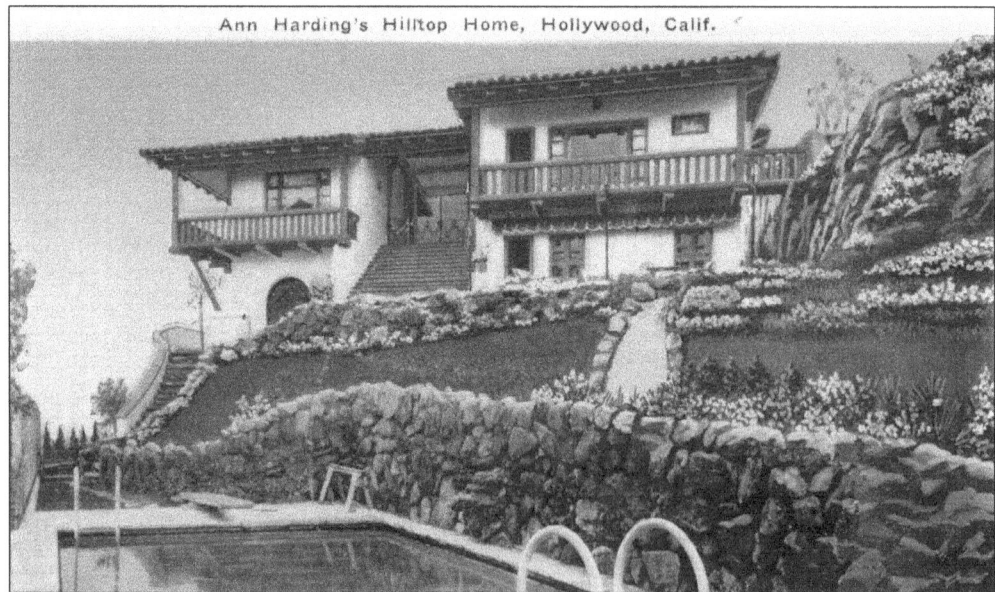

ANN HARDING. In the 1930s, Ann Harding (1902–1981) lived in this mansion at 7430 Pyramid Place, Hollywood Hills. Built for Harding and her first husband in 1930, it featured five bedrooms and six bathrooms. The actress continued living there until the early 1940s. It was eventually sold to crooner Rudy Vallée. Ann Harding's films include *Holiday, East Lynne, Westward Passage, When Ladies Meet, Enchanted April,* and *Love from a Stranger.*

JEAN HARLOW PORTRAIT.
Hollywood superstar Jean Harlow
was an exceptional young woman.
She was born Harlean Carpenter in
Kansas City, Missouri, a dentist's
daughter. At 16, she eloped and
married banker Charles McGrew,
who took her to Beverly Hills.
Bored, she soon divorced him
and found work as an extra.
Her celluloid possibilities were
appreciated by Howard Hughes who
cast her in the picture the made her
a star, *Hell's Angels*.

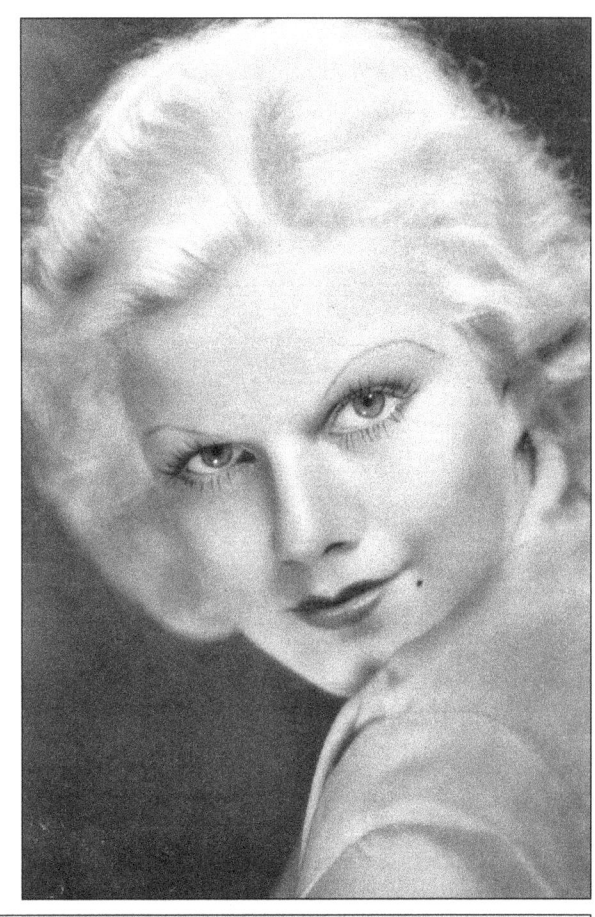

JEAN HARLOW. In 1932, platinum
blonde superstar Jean Harlow (1911–
1937) and her husband, Paul Bern,
lived in this brick mansion painted
white. The address is reportedly
1353 Club View Drive, Bel Air.
Harlow's hit films include *Platinum
Blonde*, *The Beast of the City*, *Dinner
at Eight*, *Hold Your Man*, *Bombshell*,
The Girl from Missouri, *China Seas*,
Reckless, and *Libeled Lady*. Before her
tragic death, she even wrote a novel,
Today Is Tonight.

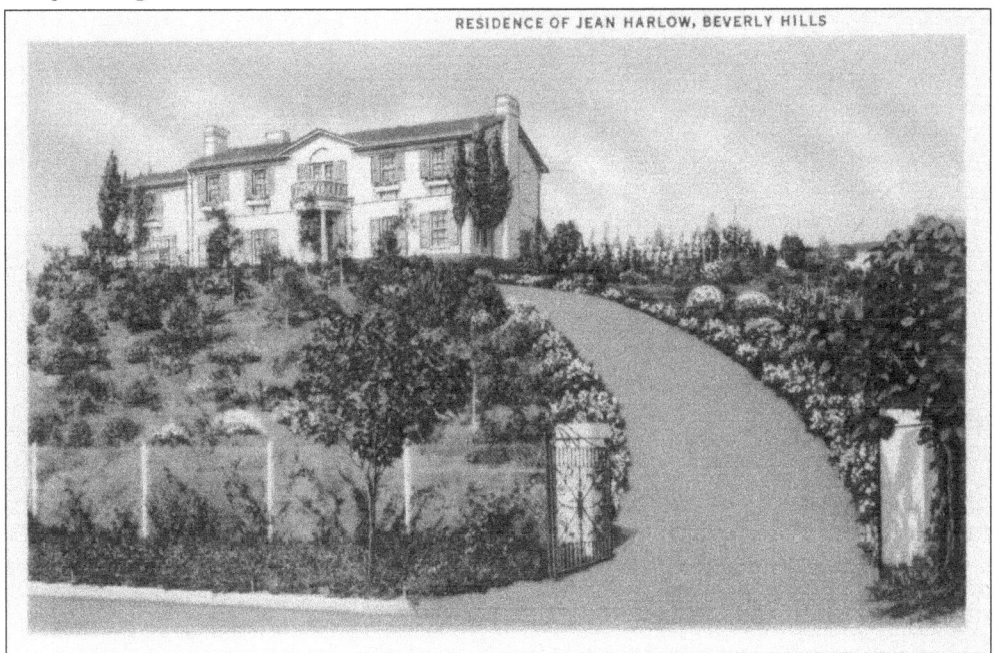

RESIDENCE OF JEAN HARLOW, BEVERLY HILLS

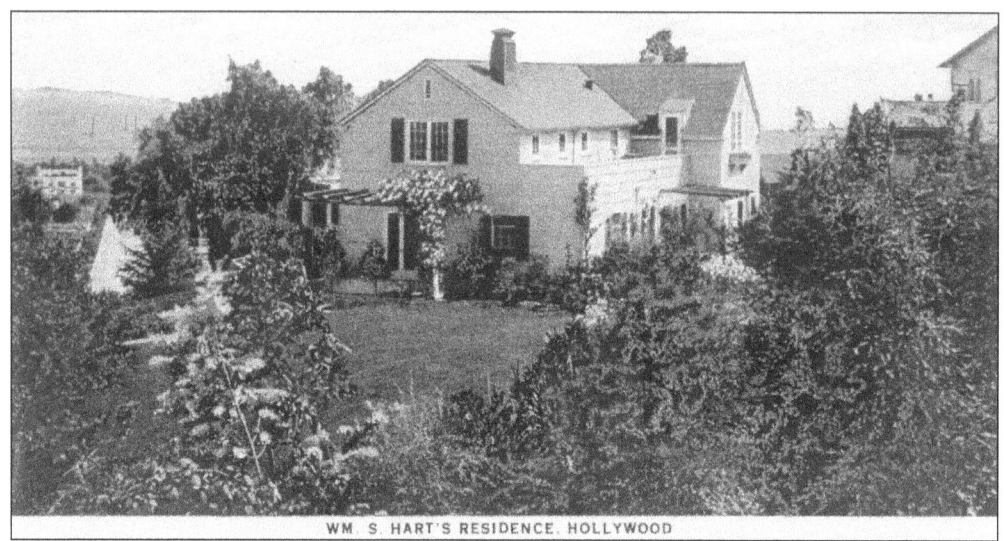

WM. S. HART'S RESIDENCE, HOLLYWOOD

WILLIAM S. HART. In the early 1920s, William S. Hart (1864–1946) lived in this house, presumably at 149 Orange Street, Hollywood. From 1914 to 1925, classical stage actor turned silent screen star Hart dominated Westerns. Bringing a rugged authenticity to the genre, his films include *The Bargain*, *The Scourge of the Desert*, *On the Night Stage*, *The Border Wireless*, *O'Malley of the Mounted*, and *Tumbleweeds*. He died at his magnificent ranch in Newhall.

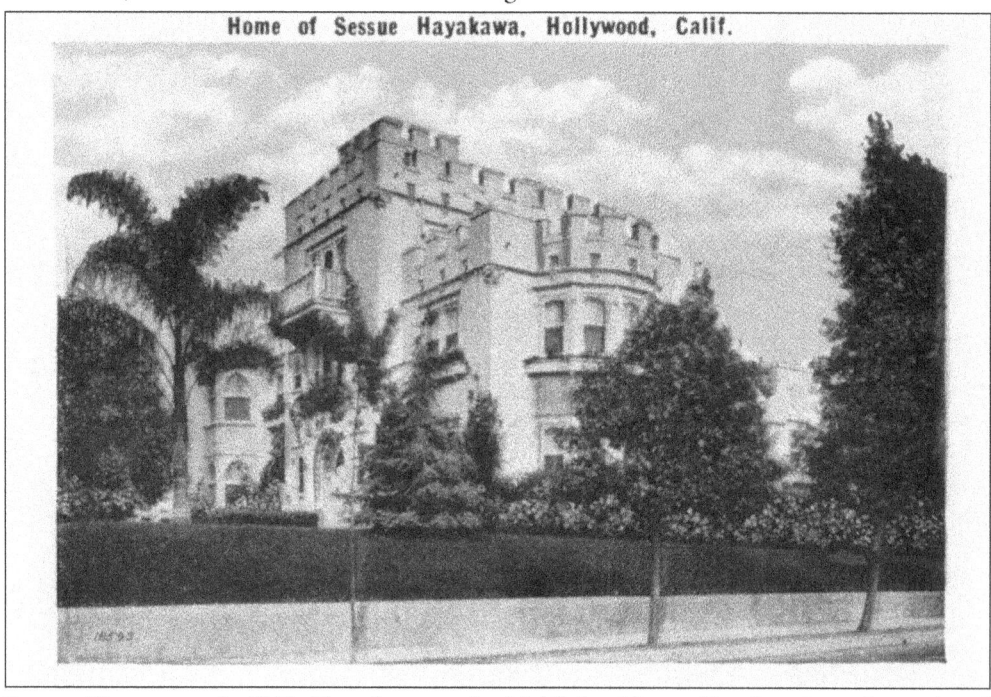

Home of Sessue Hayakawa, Hollywood, Calif.

SESSUE HAYAKAWA. In 1920, *Photoplay* magazine highlighted Sessue Hayakawa's newly purchased mansion Glengarry Castle. Built in 1909 by Alfred Schloesser (1851–1933), it stood at 1908 Argyle Avenue, Hollywood. Hayakawa and his wife, actress Tsuru Aoki, filled it with fine period furniture. They sold it in 1923. Handsome Sessue Hayakawa (1889–1973) was a popular film star and appeared in *The Temple of Dusk*, *The Dragon Painter*, *The Cheat*, *The Great Prince Shahn*, and *Tokyo Joe*, among others.

DICK HAYMES. Popular crooner Dick Haymes (1916–1980) had several homes, including a ranch in Van Nuys with his second wife, actress Joanne Dru, and later a residence on Canon Drive, Beverly Hills, with third wife, Nora Eddington, who was Errol Flynn's ex-wife. Haymes also had a whirlwind marriage to Rita Hayworth, wife number four. The Argentine singer's films include *Diamond Horseshoe*, *State Fair*, *Do You Love Me*, and *One Touch of Venus*.

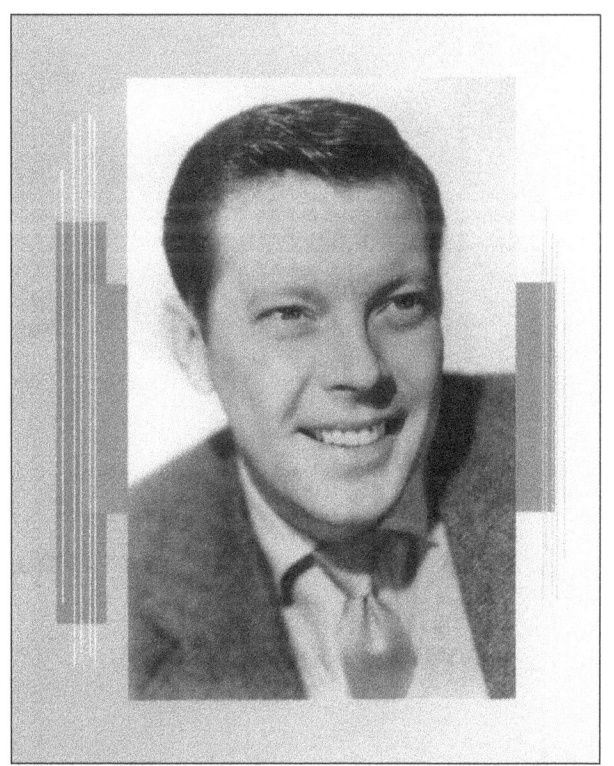

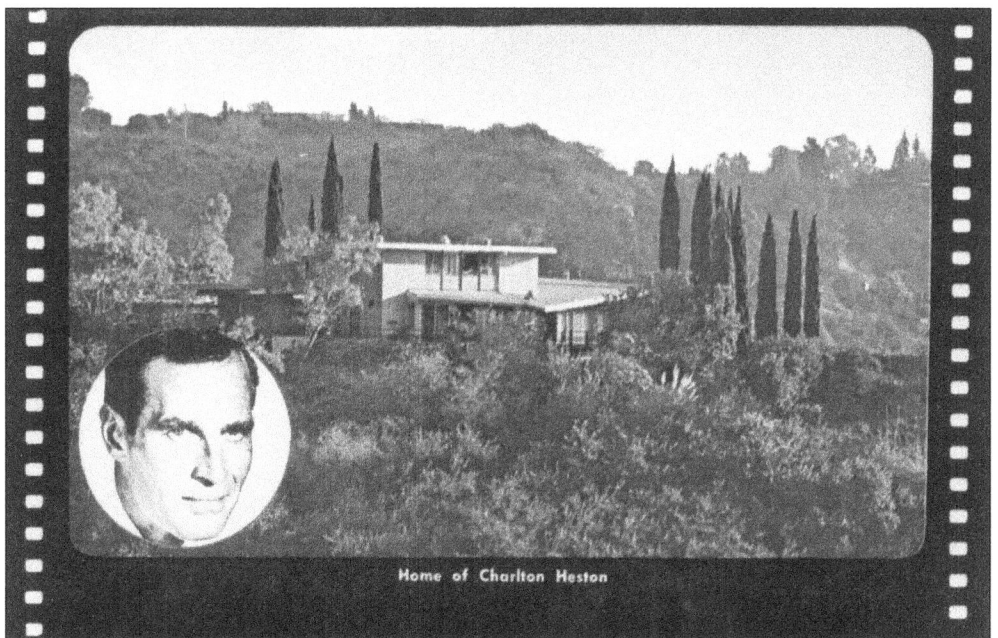

Home of Charlton Heston

CHARLTON HESTON. Perched high on a hill, Charlton Heston's estate commanded an enchanting mountain view on every side. Located at 2859 Coldwater Canyon Drive, Beverly Hills, it boasted a two-story library, a screening room, and a three-story art studio. One of Hollywood's greats, Heston (1923–2008) starred in *Dark City*, *The Greatest Show on Earth*, *Ben-Hur* (Oscar, 1959), *The Agony and the Ecstasy*, and *Planet of the Apes*.

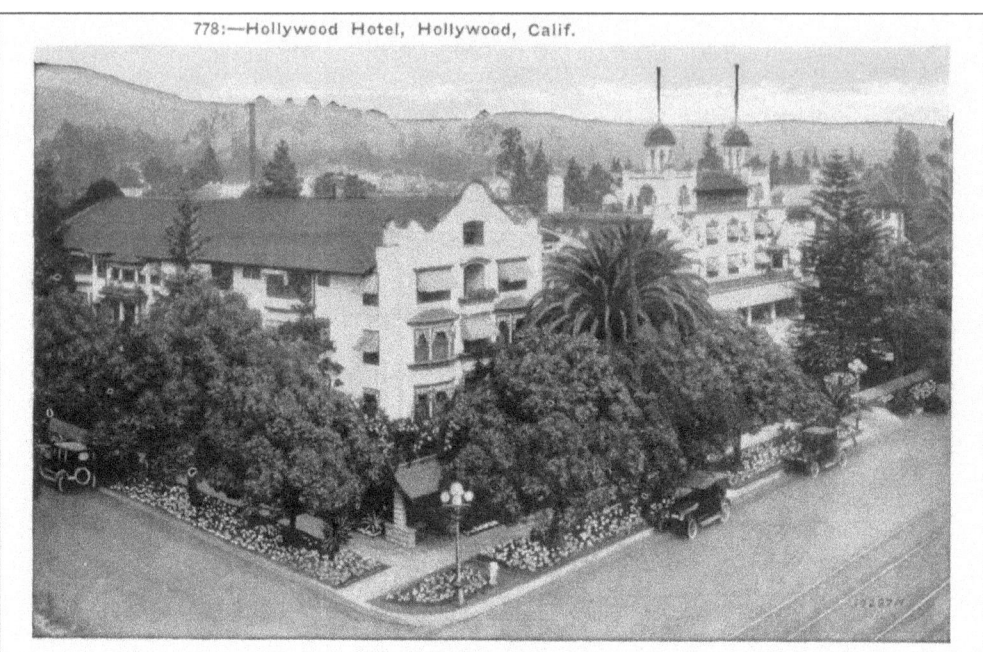

HOLLYWOOD HOTEL. Located at 1755 Highland Avenue, the Hollywood Hotel opened in December 1902. Enlarged several times, it was finally demolished in 1956. The hotel was a mecca for thespians and, at one time or another, housed Ethel Barrymore, Betty Blythe, Hobart Bosworth, Viola Dana, Madge Evans, Ian Keith, Thomas Meighan, Owen Moore, Nazimova, Herbert Rawlinson, Milton Sills, H.B. Warner, and Rudolph Valentino as well as producers Carl Laemmle, Jesse Lasky, and Harry Warner.

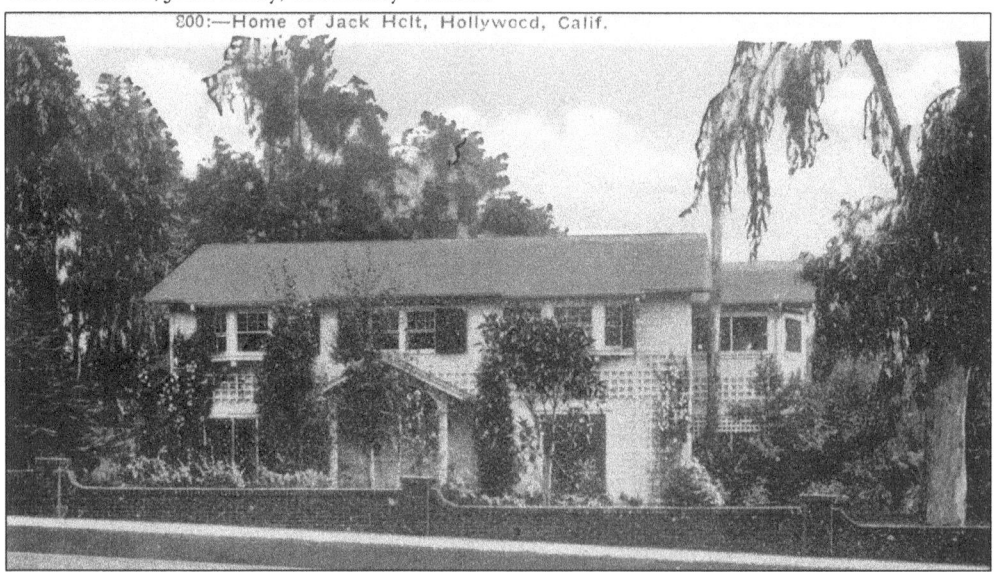

JACK HOLT. For years, leading man Jack Holt (1888–1951) and his family—including his son, future Western star Tim Holt (1919–1973)—lived at 1632 North Laurel Avenue, Hollywood. It was big, rambling, and surrounded by a brick wall. Jack Holt was in silent films, such as *The Little American, Crooked Street,* and *The Lone Wolf,* as well as talkies, like *Behind the Mask, Whirlpool, The Littlest Rebel, Storm over the Andes,* and *End of the Trail.*

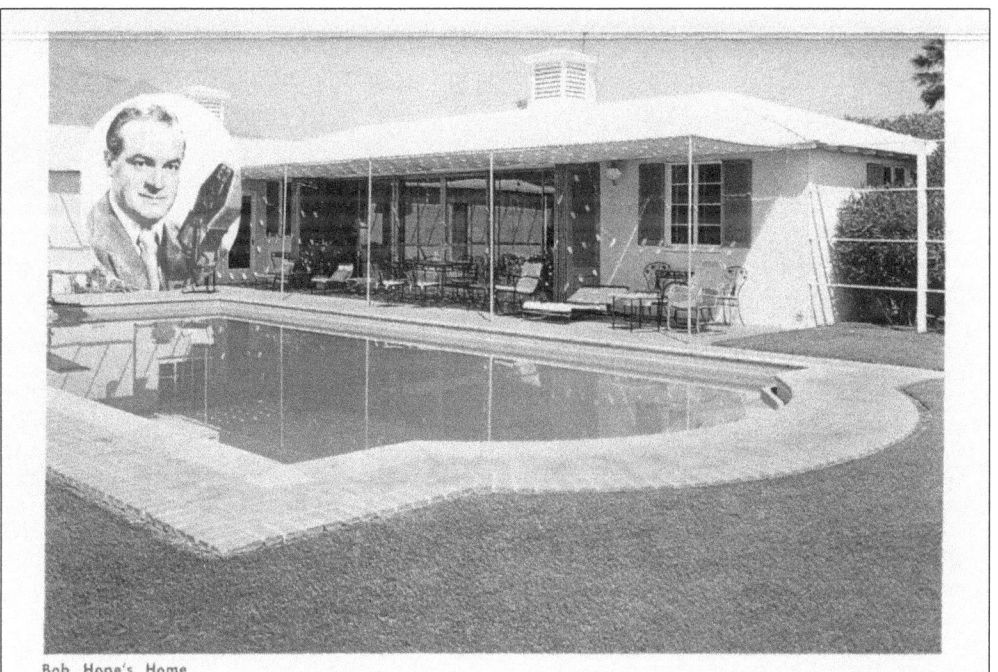

Bob Hope's Home

BOB HOPE. In 1946, Bob Hope and his wife, Dolores (1909–2011), bought this five-bedroom house at 1188 East Alameda, Palm Springs. Its lush, secluded grounds included a swimming pool. They already owned a house at 1014 East Buena Vista Drive, which they had bought in 1941. The third Hope property was the Modernist estate at 2466 Southridge Drive, designed by John Lautner in 1979.

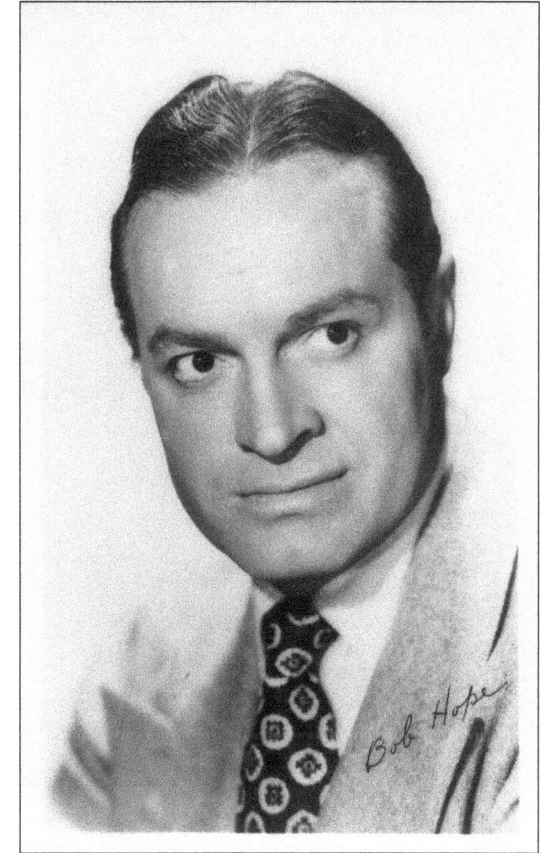

BOB HOPE PICTURE POSTCARD. Actor Bob Hope (1903–2003) was born Leslie Townes Hope in Eltham, England, to a stonemason and his wife, and his family emigrated to Cleveland, Ohio, in 1908. As a youth, he toyed with the name "Lester Hope" before opting for "Bob Hope" as his theatrical moniker. Years of dancing, singing, and joking in vaudeville paved his way to success on Broadway, in radio, and in motion pictures. Hope was one of America's top comedians.

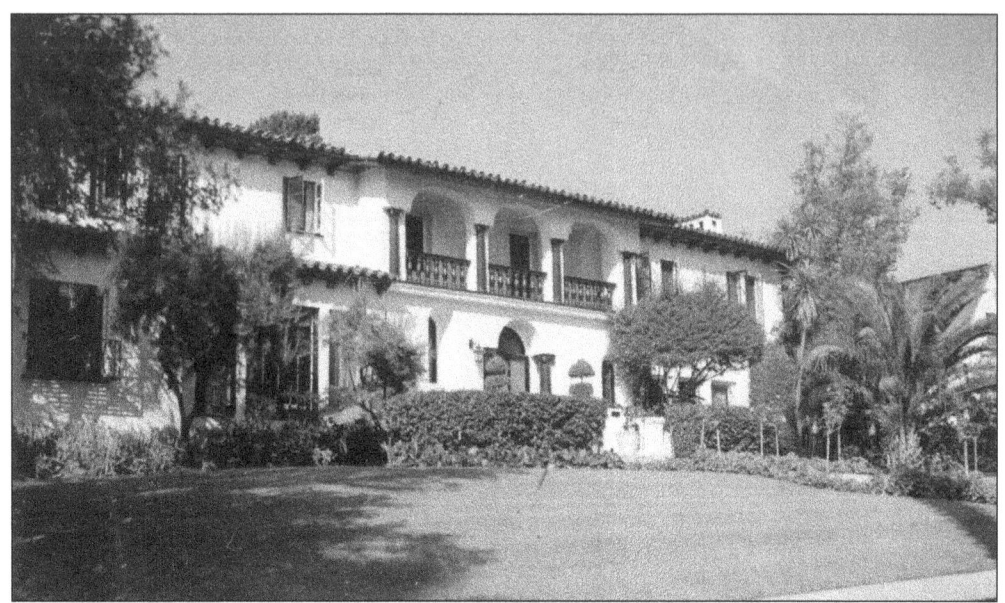

VAN JOHNSON. In the 1950s and 1960s, actor Van Johnson (1916–2008) lived in this mansion at 810 North Foothill Road, Beverly Hills. One of the top matinee idols of Hollywood in the 1940s and 1950s, Johnson's best-known films were made at Metro-Goldwyn-Mayer, and among them are *Thirty Seconds Over Tokyo*, *In the Good Old Summertime*, *Three Guys Named Mike*, *Grounds for Marriage*, *Too Young to Kiss*, *Invitation*, and *23 Paces to Baker Street*.

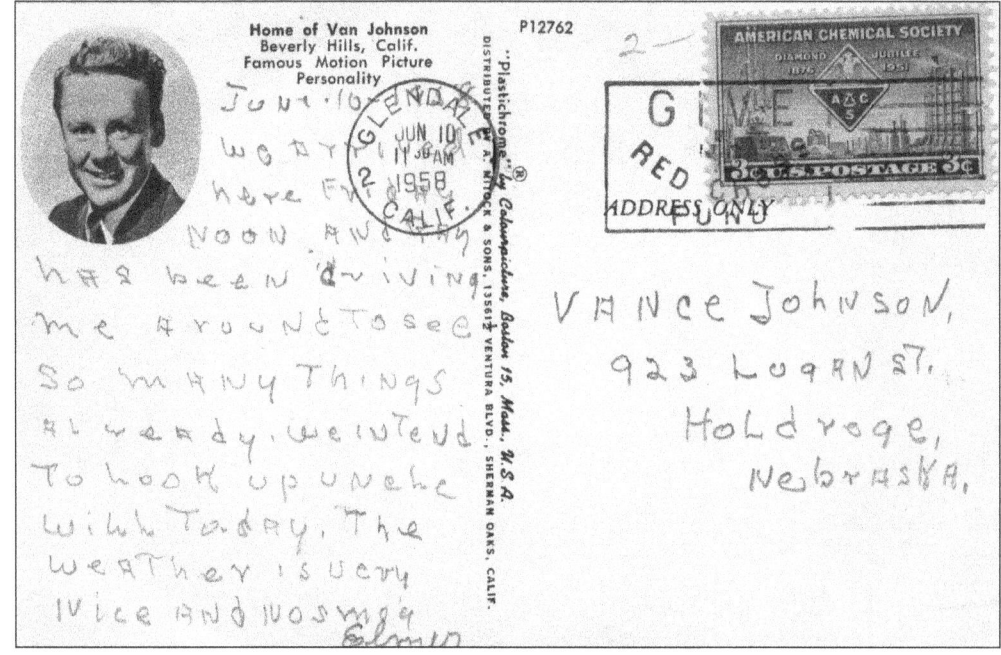

"THE WEATHER IS VERY NICE." This postcard showing Van Johnson's home was mailed to 923 Logan Street, Holdrege, Nebraska, on June 10, 1958. The message reads as follows: "We arrived here Friday noon and Ray has been driving me around to see so many things already. We intend to look up Uncle Will today. The weather is very nice . . . Elmer." The recipient was Vance Arthur Johnson (1903–1980), a lifelong Nebraskan.

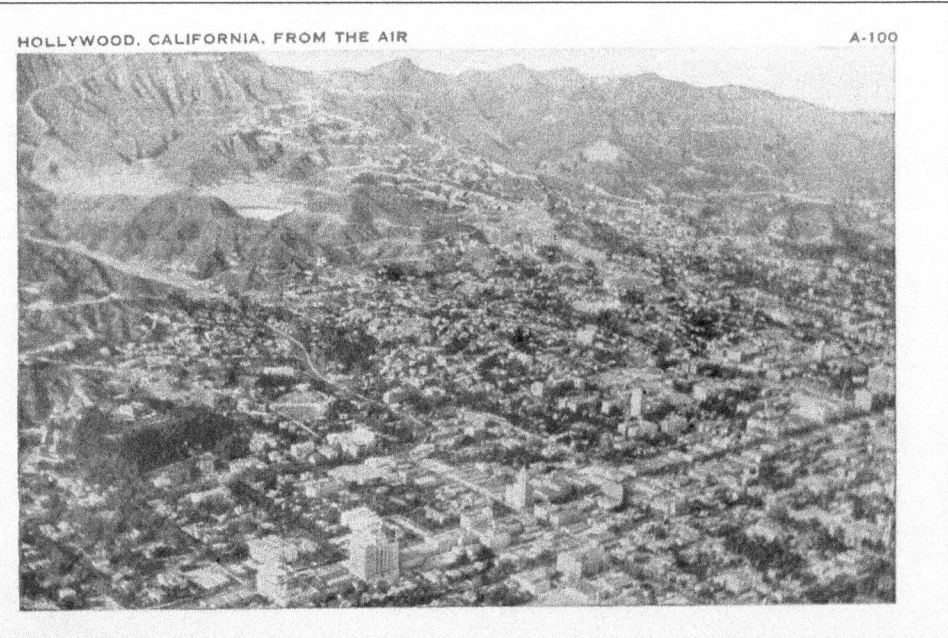

HOLLYWOOD, CALIFORNIA, FROM THE AIR   A-100

HOLLYWOOD FROM THE AIR.
Taken from a 1926 postcard, this
aerial shot of Hollywood shows a
sweeping view from the business
district in the foreground to the
Hollywood Hills in the background,
a section that housed the mansions
and hideaways of many of the
cinema's most admired actors and
movie makers.

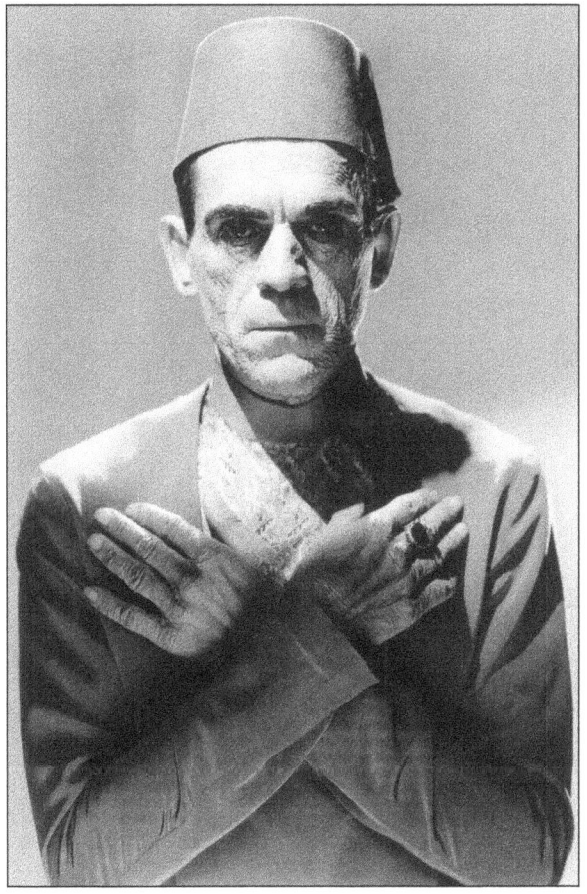

BORIS KARLOFF. The English actor
William Henry Pratt, better known
as Boris Karloff, is pictured in a
still from the British horror classic
The Mummy (1932). Karloff (1887–
1969), who retained his British
nationality despite his years in
Hollywood, lived in Beverly Hills at
2320 Bowmont Drive—the former
home of Katharine Hepburn—
until 1945, when he moved to 714
North Foothill Road. Karloff had
residences in England and New
York as well.

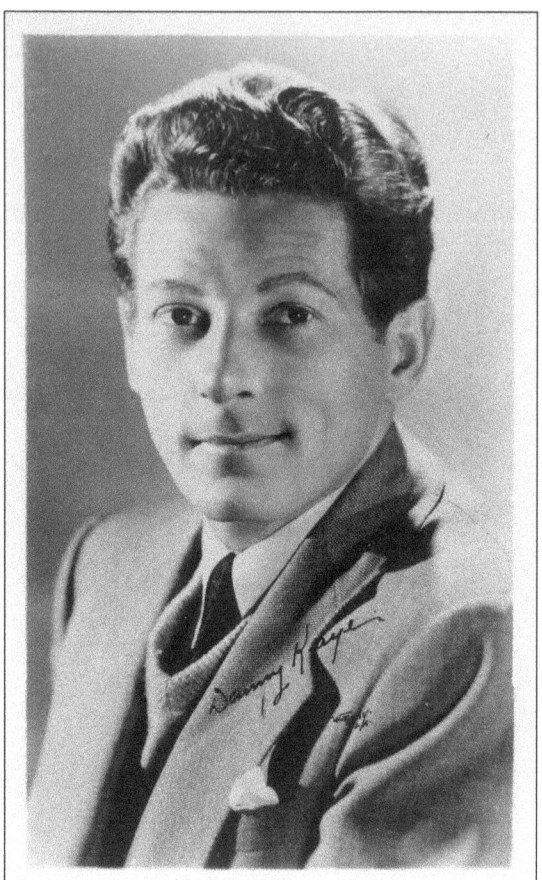

DANNY KAYE PICTURE POSTCARD. A unique talent, Danny Kaye (1911–1987) delighted audiences with his acting, singing, pantomime, and comedy. Born in Brooklyn, he made his mark in vaudeville and rose to stardom on Broadway in *Lady in the Dark* (1941). Among his best movies are *Wonder Man*, *The Kid from Brooklyn*, *The Secret Life of Walter Mitty*, *Hans Christian Andersen*, and *Knock on Wood*. Kaye lived at 1103 San Ysidro Drive, Beverly Hills.

BUSTER KEATON. At the height of his fame, comic genius Buster Keaton (1895–1966) and his wife, Natalie Talmadge-Keaton, lived in this exquisite Italian mansion at 1004 Hartford Way, Beverly Hills. The couple moved into the newly finished estate in 1926. Months after their divorce in August 1932, Natalie sold the showplace mansion. By 1949, English actor James Mason had bought it. Keaton's films include *Convict 13*, *One Run Elmer*, and *The Frozen North*.

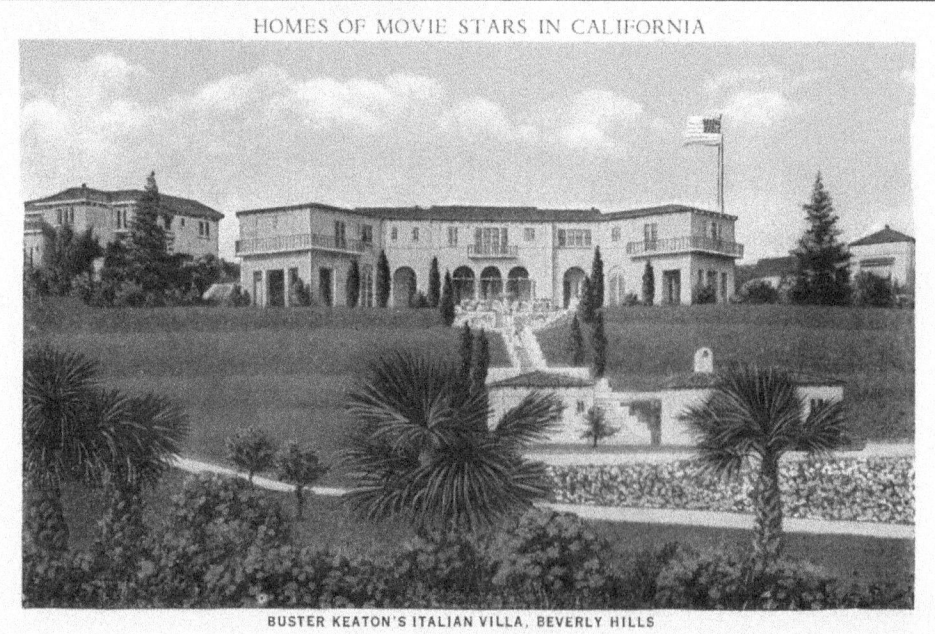

HOMES OF MOVIE STARS IN CALIFORNIA

BUSTER KEATON'S ITALIAN VILLA, BEVERLY HILLS

J. WARREN KERRIGAN IN 1915. In 1897,
Kentucky-born J. Warren Kerrigan rejected a
business career and went on the stage. In 1910,
he entered movies and became the decade's most
popular male star, second only to Francis X.
Bushman. In 1917, Kerrigan's refusal to serve in
the Army harmed his career. Nevertheless, one
of his last films, *The Covered Wagon* (1923), now a
Western classic, was a sensational hit and restored
his popularity.

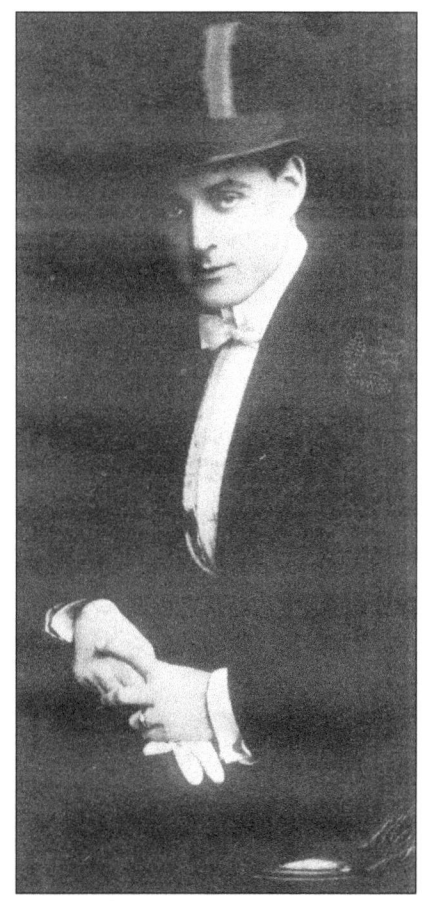

J. WARREN KERRIGAN. In the early 1920s, silent
film actor J. Warren Kerrigan (1879–1947) lived in
this house, located at 2307 Cahuenga Avenue, with
his mother, siblings, and private secretary, James
Vincent (1882–1957). One of the early matinee idols
of the screen, Kerrigan starred in *Come Again Smith*,
The Dream Cheater, *The House of Whispers*, *A Man's
Man*, *The Covered Wagon*, *The Girl of the Golden West*,
and *Captain Blood*.

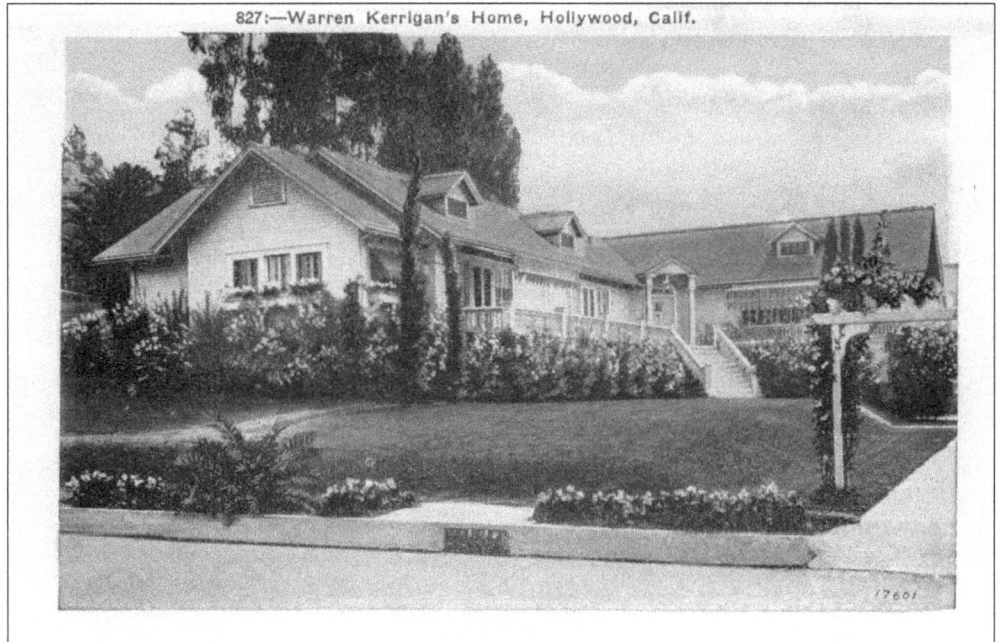

827:—Warren Kerrigan's Home, Hollywood, Calif.

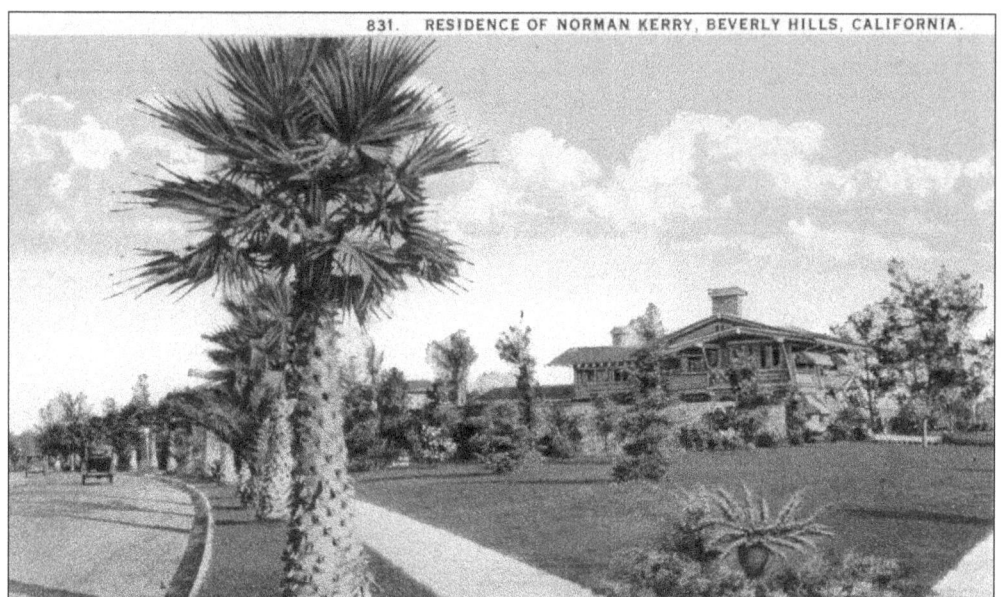

NORMAN KERRY. At the height of his popularity, Norman Kerry (1894–1956) lived at 910 North Bedford Drive, Beverly Hills. The house was originally in Los Angeles, but in 1923, Kerry bought and moved it to Beverly Hills. The style is high Craftsman. Kerry (né Arnold Kaiser) was a romantic favorite and starred in such blockbuster pictures as *The Hunchback of Notre Dame*, *The Phantom of the Opera*, and *The Unknown*.

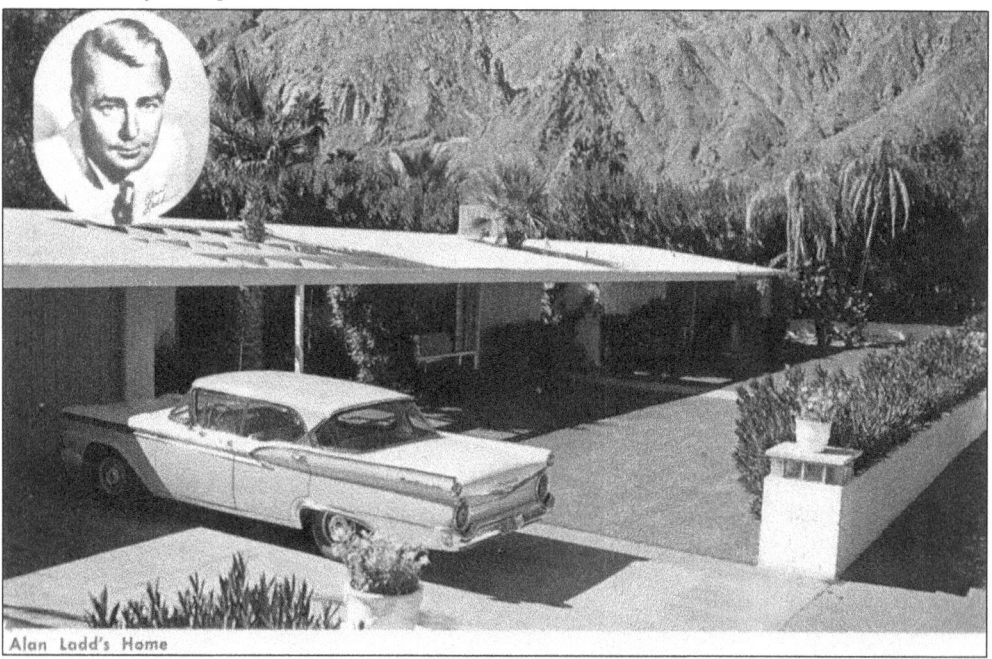

Alan Ladd's Home

ALAN LADD. Pictured here is Alan Ladd's hacienda-style home at 323 Camino Norte West, Palm Springs. Ladd and wife, Sue Carol (1906–1982), had the five-bedroom house built in 1955. Alan Ladd (1913–1964) died in his sleep there. An actor with a striking presence, he was in *This Gun for Hire*, *The Glass Key*, *And Now Tomorrow*, *The Blue Dahlia*, and *Shane*. His Holmby Hills mansion, constructed in 1949, was at 323 North Mapleton Drive.

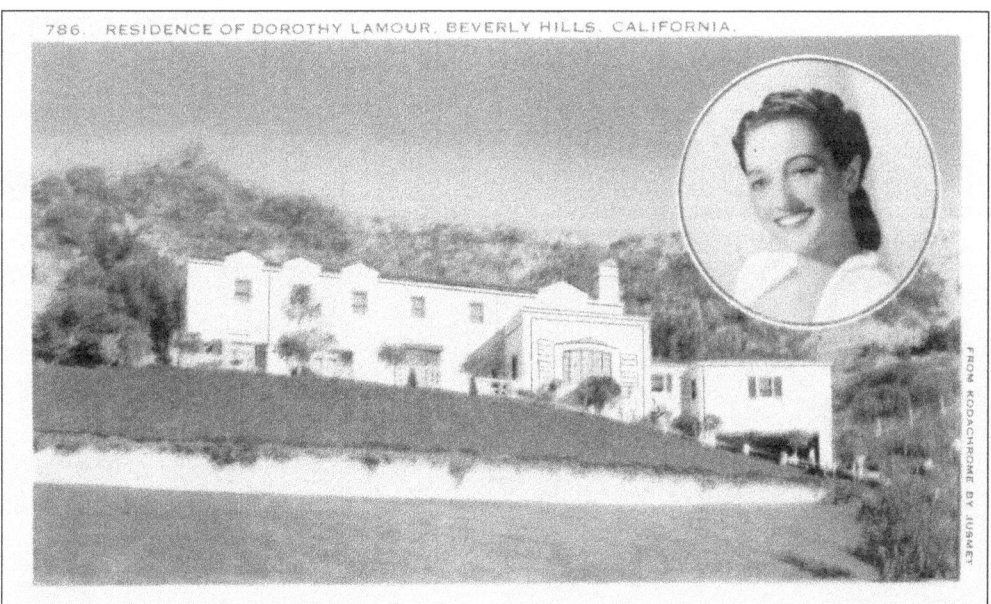

DOROTHY LAMOUR. Of French and English descent, Louisiana native Dorothy Lamour (1914–1996) struck it big in Hollywood and achieved fame as the leading lady in Bing Crosby and Bob Hope comedies, like *Road to Singapore*. She also starred in *The Jungle Princess*, *The Hurricane*, *Man About Town*, *Johnny Apollo*, *And the Angels Sing*, *My Favorite Brunette*, and *Slightly French*. Her address was 9131 Calle Juela Drive, Beverly Hills.

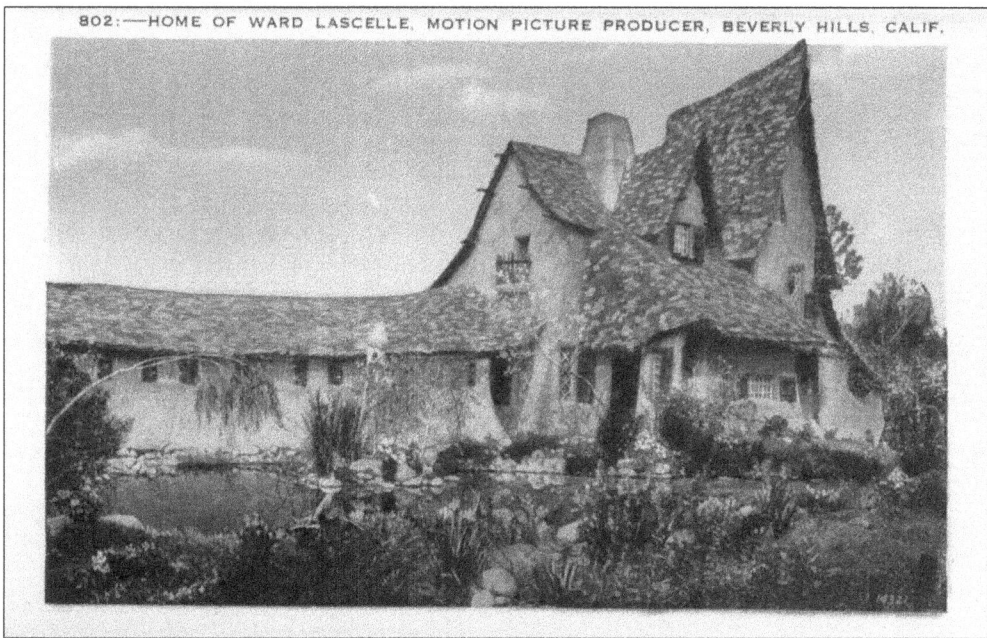

WARD LASCELLE. In 1921, Willat Studios of Culver City built this cottage for use in such silent films as *Hansel and Gretel*. In 1924, the Willat brothers sold their film studio, including the cottage, to director Ward Lascelle (1882–1941), who moved it to 516 North Walden Drive in Beverly Hills. His wife, Lilian (1887–1985), became the owner following their divorce. She subsequently married Louis E. Spadina (1883–1978).

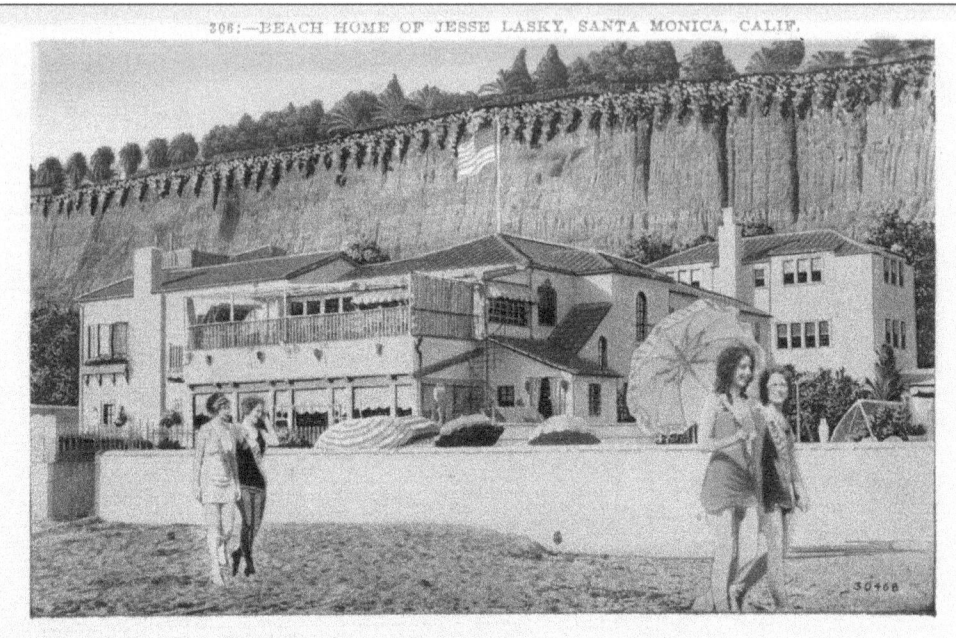

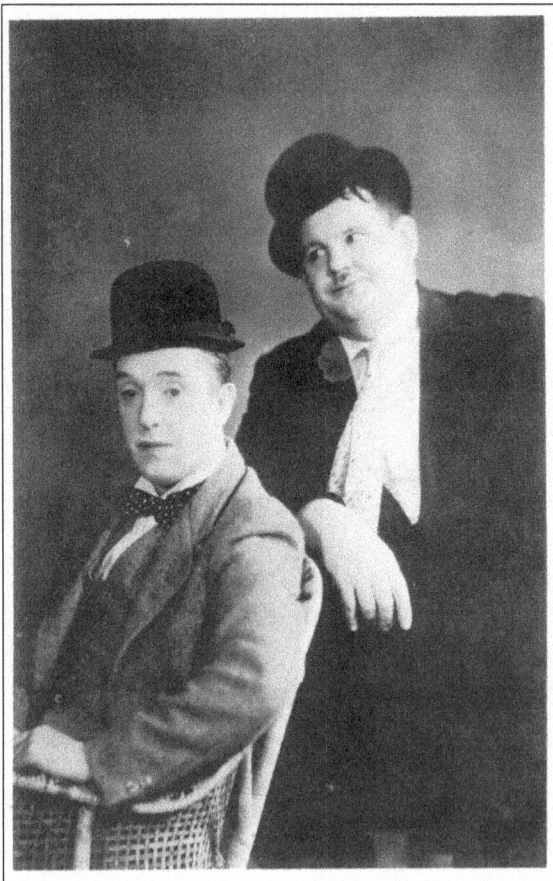

JESSE LASKY. Jesse Lasky (1880–1958), cofounder of Paramount Pictures with Adolph Zukor, owned this elegant beach house at 607 Palisades Beach Road, Santa Monica. In 1916, the pioneer producer merged with Zukor's Famous Players to create Famous Players-Lasky Corporation; its roster of stars included Fanny Ward, Pauline Frederick, Lou Tellegen, Wallace Reid, Owen Moore, Donald Brian, and Blanche Sweet. One of its greatest films is *The Covered Wagon* (1923).

LAUREL AND HARDY PICTURE POSTCARD. The renowned duo of Stan Laurel and Oliver Hardy is still unsurpassed in the world of comedy. Their films include *Another Fine Mess*, *Pack Up Your Troubles*, *Sons of the Desert*, *Babes in Toyland*, and *Way Out West*. Stan Laurel (1890–1965), who was an Englishman, lived at 718 North Bedford Drive, Beverly Hills, and Oliver Hardy (1892–1957), an American, lived at 621 Alta Drive, Beverly Hills.

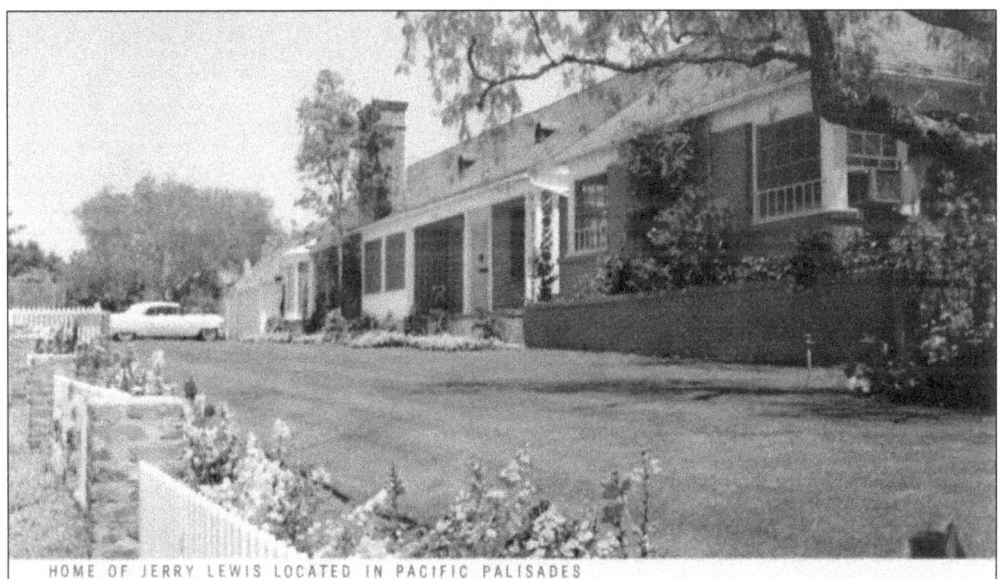

HOME OF JERRY LEWIS LOCATED IN PACIFIC PALISADES

JERRY LEWIS. In 1950, comedian Jerry Lewis and his family moved into this house at 1048 Amalfi Drive, Pacific Palisades. It was prestigious for Lewis, as a new face in Hollywood, to live in the same neighborhood as established stars, like Ronald Reagan and David Niven. Other than his delightful comedies with Dean Martin, Lewis pleased audiences with offerings like *The Bell Boy*, *The Errand Boy*, and *Who's Minding the Store?*

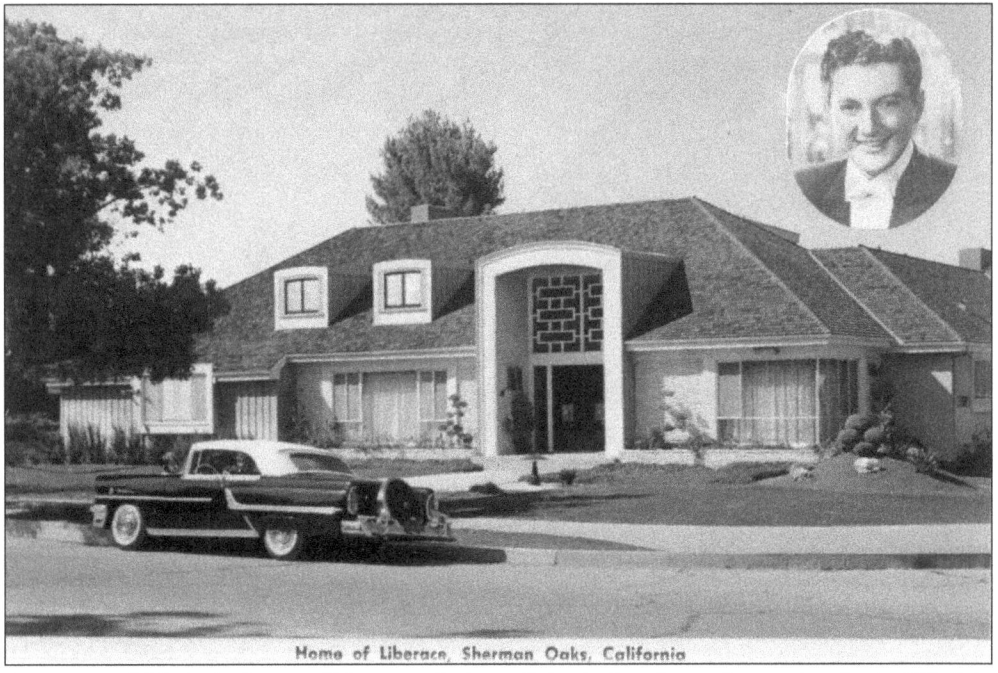

Home of Liberace, Sherman Oaks, California

LIBERACE. This is the home of that popularizer of classical and popular music, pianist Wladziu "Walter" Liberace (1919–1987). Liberace built this house, with its piano-shaped swimming pool, at 15405 Valley Vista Boulevard, Sherman Oaks, in 1954. After selling it, he later owned mansions in Hollywood Hills and Las Vegas. Liberace's syndicated television series, *The Liberace Show*, made him a star in the 1950s. His best-known film is *Sincerely Yours* (1955).

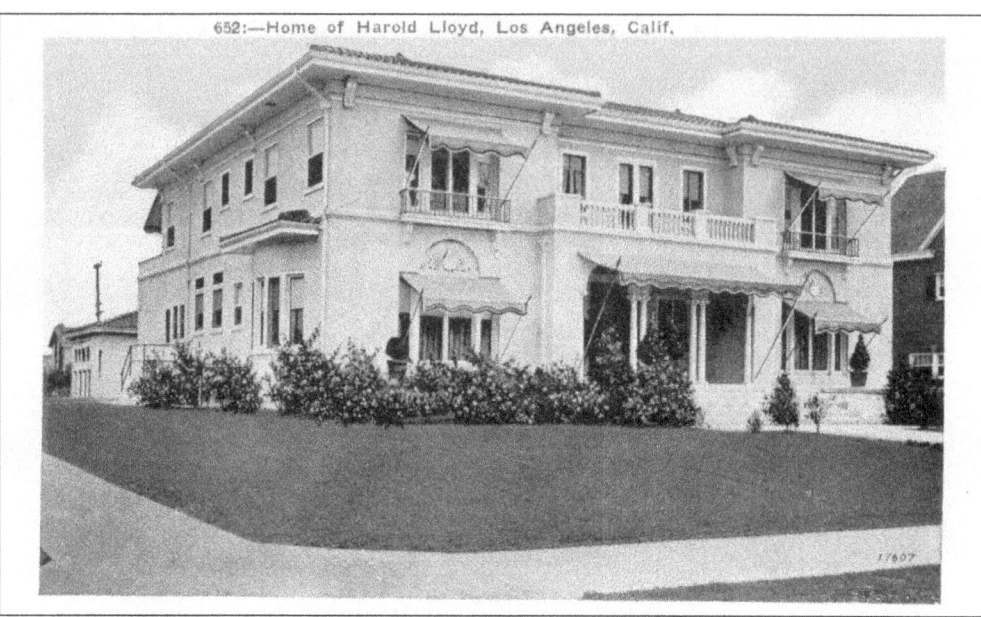

652:—Home of Harold Lloyd, Los Angeles, Calif.

HAROLD LLOYD. Comedian Harold Lloyd (1893–1971) had architect Sumner Spaulding design his mansion Greenacres in the Mediterranean Revival style. Located at 1740 Green Acres Drive, Beverly Hills, the 44-room house was completed in 1928. Among Lloyd's silent film classics are *Bashful*, *Grandma's Boy*, *Why Worry*, *Safety Last*, and *Girl Shy*. The most popular of his sound films include *Feet First*, *The Milky Way*, and *The Sin of Harold Diddlebock*.

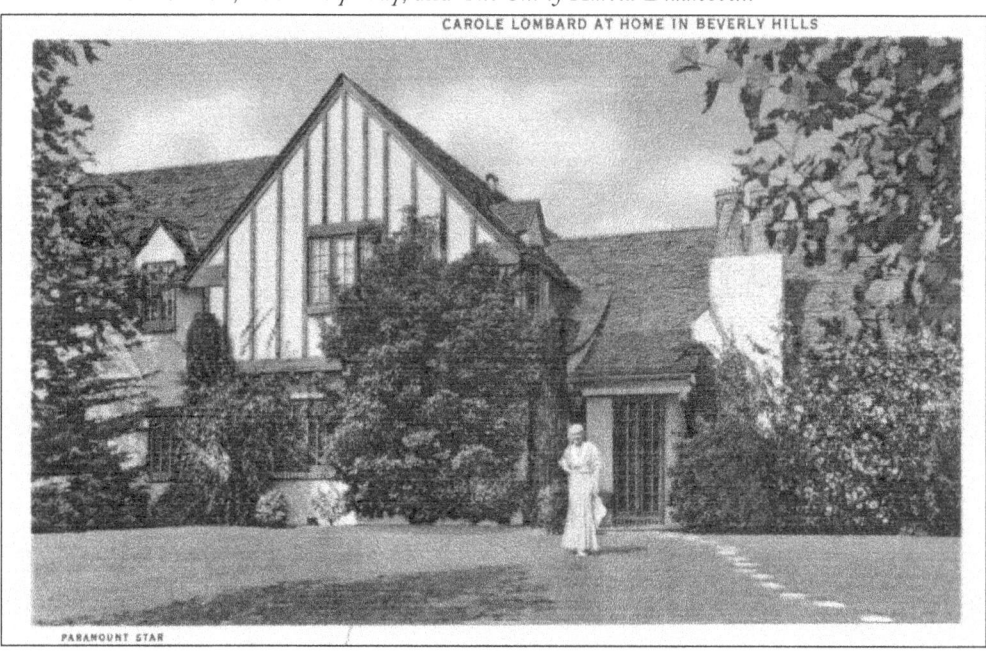

CAROLE LOMBARD AT HOME IN BEVERLY HILLS

CAROLE LOMBARD. This house at 533 North Beverly Drive, Beverly Hills, was Carole Lombard's home for a time in the 1930s. One of Hollywood's top stars, Indiana native Carole Lombard (1909–1942) blossomed into a virtuoso of screwball comedy acting. Among her best films are *Twentieth Century*, *Hands Across the Table*, *The Princess Comes Across*, *My Man Godfrey*, *Lady by Choice*, *Nothing Sacred*, *Mr. and Mrs. Smith*, and *To Be or Not to Be*.

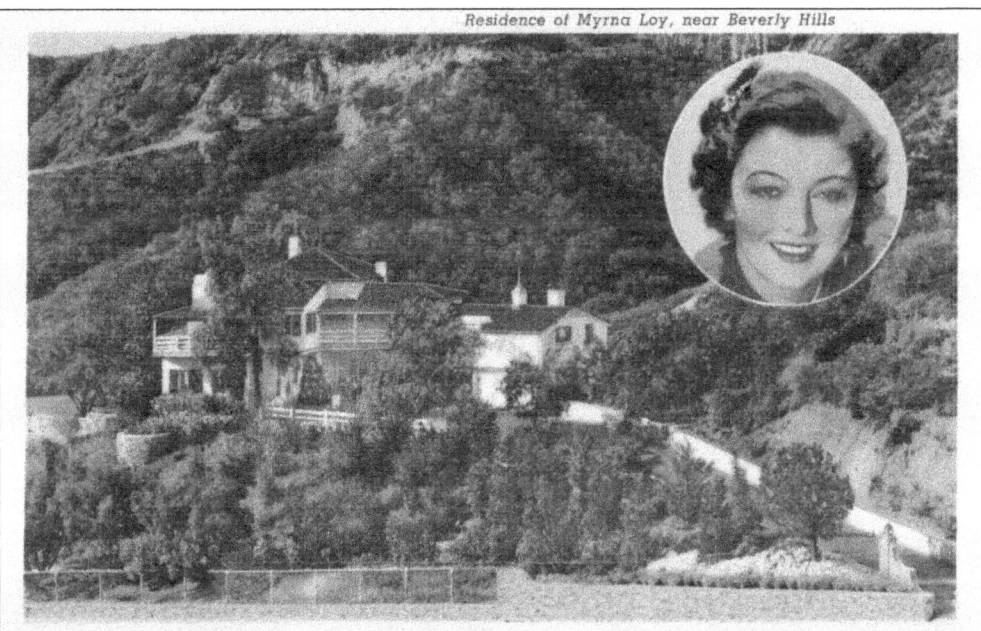

MYRNA LOY. Myrna Loy and her first husband, Arthur Hornblow Jr., who were married from 1936 to 1942, built this mansion at 9551 Hidden Valley Road, Hollywood Hills. She said: "A home . . . is a refuge." Myrna Loy (1905–1993), who won initial recognition playing vamps and femme fatales, finally won lasting acclaim for her elegant performances in films such as *The Thin Man* (and its sequels), *Wife vs. Secretary*, *Test Pilot*, *The Best Years of Our Lives*, and *The Bachelor and the Bobby-Soxer*.

JEANETTE MACDONALD. Sensational soprano Jeanette MacDonald (1903–1965) was one of filmdom's biggest stars in the 1930s. In 1937, she married actor Gene Raymond, and the couple moved into Raymond's wedding present to her, Twin Gables, at 783 Bel Air Road, Hollywood. Her films include *The Love Parade*, *The Vagabond King*, *One Hour with You*, *Love Me Tonight*, *The Merry Widow*, *Naughty Marietta*, *Rose Marie*, and *The Firefly*.

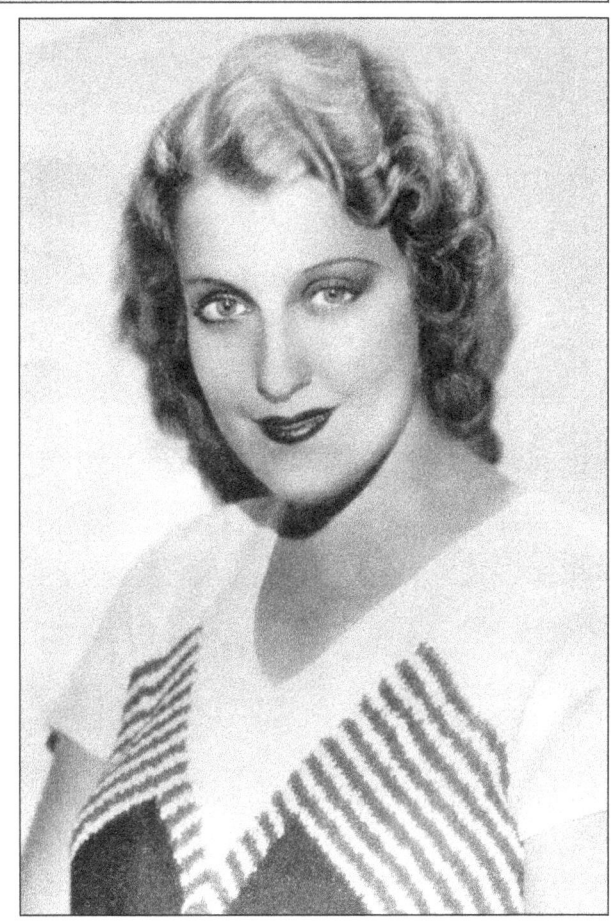

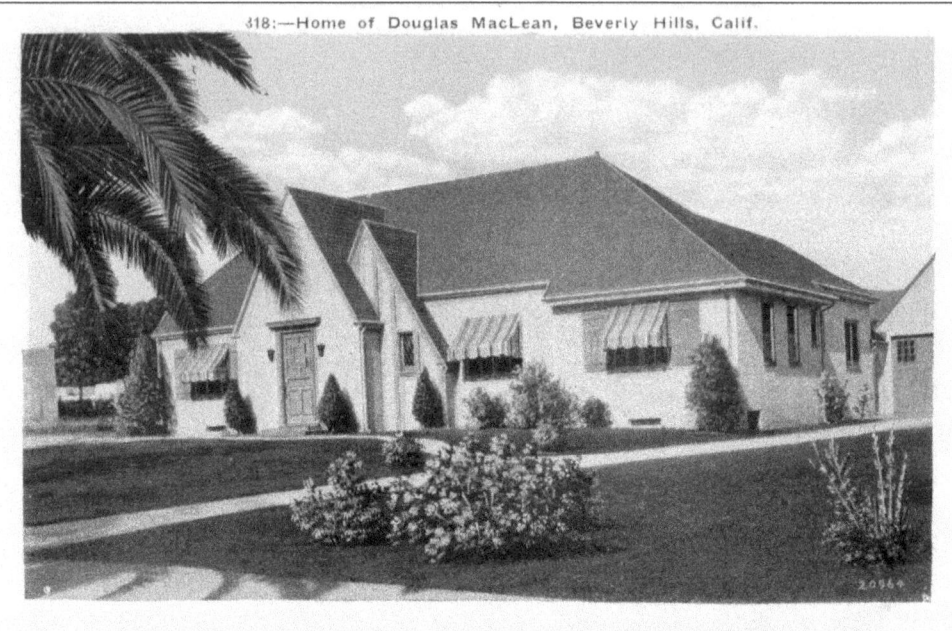

818:—Home of Douglas MacLean, Beverly Hills, Calif.

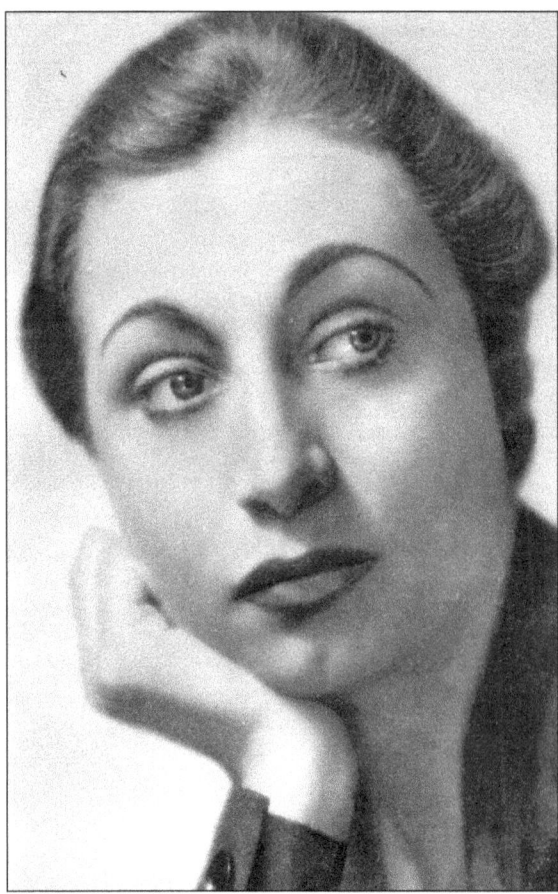

DOUGLAS MACLEAN. In 1922, silent film actor Douglas MacLean (1890–1967) built this "English-style" residence at 624 North Canon Drive, Beverly Hills. In September 1928, he sold it for $28,500; he and his wife, Faith MacLean, then moved to 711 North Palm Drive. MacLean starred in such comedies as *23 ½ Hours Leave*, *What's Your Husband Doing?*, *Chickens*, and *Hold That Lion*. In the 1930s and 1940s, he produced motion pictures.

ALINE MACMAHON. This talented actress enjoyed a long a career on stage and screen. She and her husband, Clarence Stein, lived at 117 North Roxbury Drive, Beverly Hills. The dramatic films of Aline MacMahon (1899–1991) include *The Mouthpiece*, with Warren William; *The World Changes*, with Paul Muni; and *Kind Lady*, with Basil Rathbone. With her frequent costar in comedy, Guy Kibbee, she starred in *Babbitt*, *Big-Hearted Herbert*, *Mary Jane's Pa*, and *While the Patient Slept*.

84

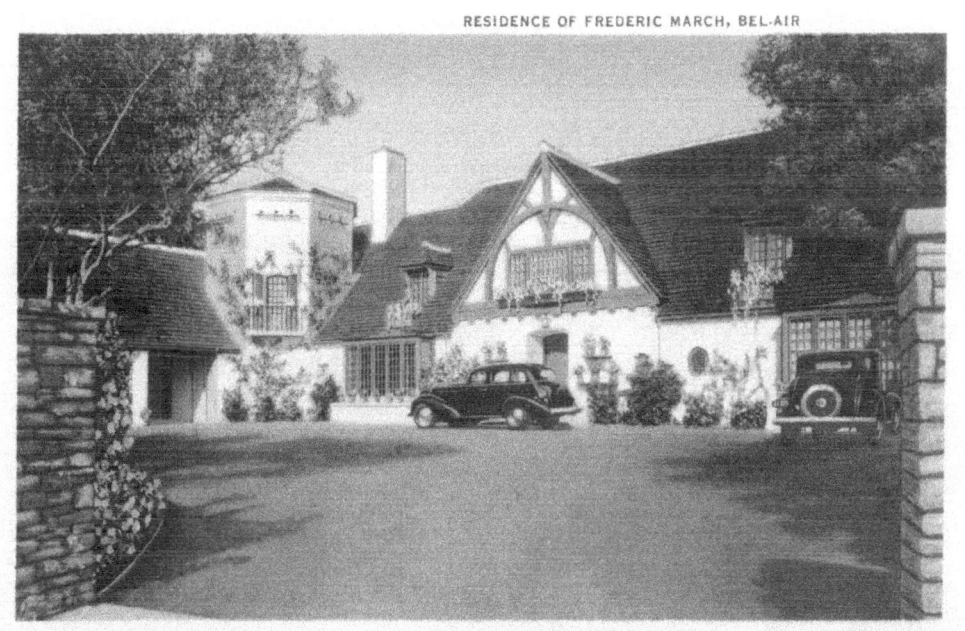

FREDRIC MARCH. Actor Fredric March (1897–1975) and his wife, actress Florence Eldridge, lived at 1065 Ridgedale Drive, Bel Air, in the 1930s. Designed for them by Wallace Neff, the three-story, Norman-style mansion had nine bedrooms. Fredric March won an Oscar for his incomparable performance in *Dr. Jekyll and Mr. Hyde* (1931). His other films include *Anna Karenina, A Star Is Born, Death of a Salesman, Executive Suite,* and *Seven Days in May.*

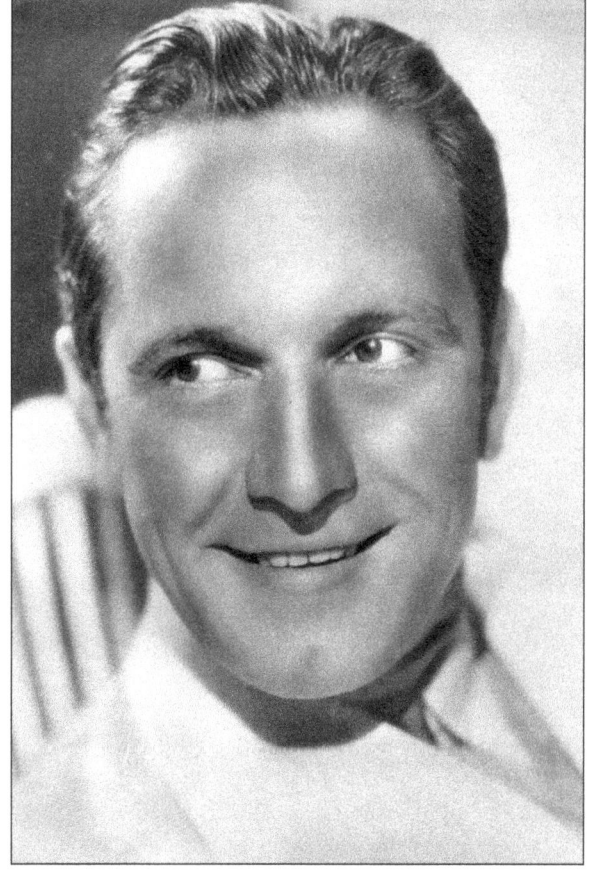

FREDRIC MARCH PORTRAIT. Even as a stage actor in the 1920s, Fredric March was hailed for his versatility. His reputation brought him to Hollywood, where he soon won his first Academy Award. The future actor was born Ernest Frederick McIntyre Bickel in Wisconsin, the third son of John and Cora Bickel. March's wife, Florence Eldridge, appeared in such films as *Mary of Scotland* and *An Act of Murder* with her husband.

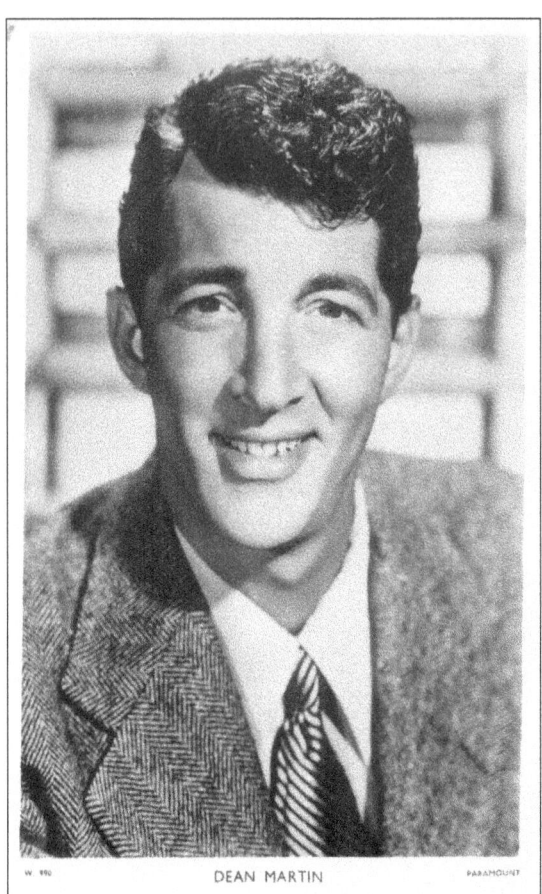

DEAN MARTIN

DEAN MARTIN. Actor and singer Dean Martin (1917–1995) was one of Hollywood's most popular personalities. His NBC television variety-comedy series, *The Dean Martin Show* (1965–1974), was a major hit. Martin had several homes, including 601 Mountain Drive, Beverly Hills, where he lived from 1955 to 1972. Martin's films include his comedies with Jerry Lewis, from *My Friend Irma* to *Hollywood or Bust*, as well as his solo films, like *The Young Lions*, *Rio Bravo*, and *Oceans 11*.

TONY MARTIN AND CYD CHARISSE. In 1958, Tony Martin (1913–2012) and Cyd Charisse (1922–2008) moved into their new home at 679 West Camino Sur, Palm Springs. Martin was a popular recording artist and actor. After marrying Alice Faye, his first wife, he starred in films, such as *Winner Take All*, *Music in My Heart*, and *Sally, Irene and Mary*. His second wife, dancer Cyd Charisse, starred in *Sombrero*, *Silk Stockings*, and *Party Girl*.

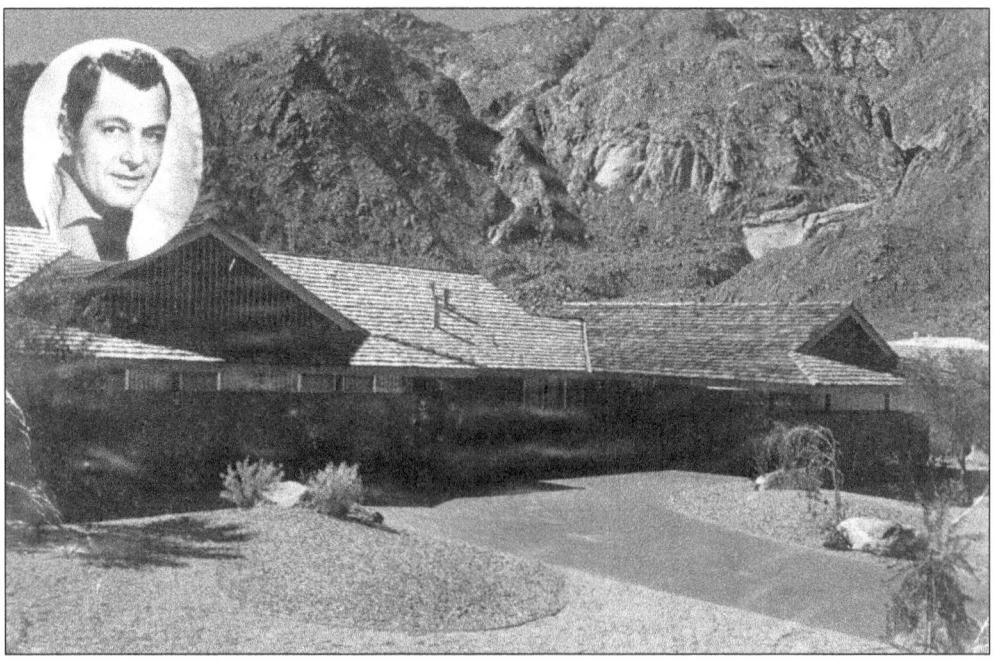

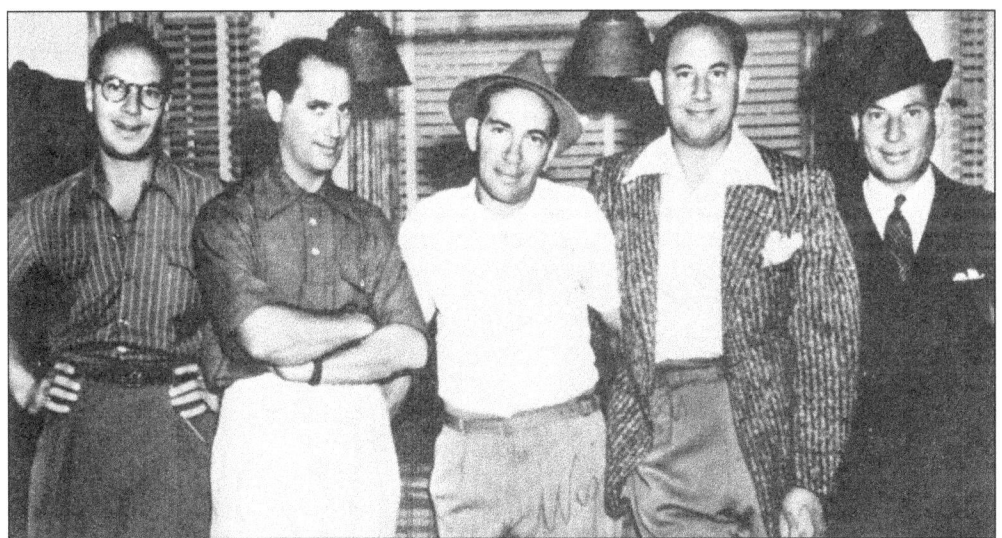

THE MARX BROTHERS IN MUFTI. Pictured here are the legendary Marx Brothers—Zeppo, Groucho, Chico, Gummo, and Harpo—without their makeup and costumes on. The brothers' real names were Herbert "Zeppo" (1901–1979), Julius "Groucho" (1890–1977), Leonard "Chico" (1887–1961), Milton "Gummo" (1893–1977), and Arthur "Harpo" (1888–1964). Among their classic films are *The Cocoanuts*, *Horse Feathers*, *Animal Crackers*, *Monkey Business*, *Duck Soup*, *A Night at the Opera*, *A Day at the Races*, and *Room Service*.

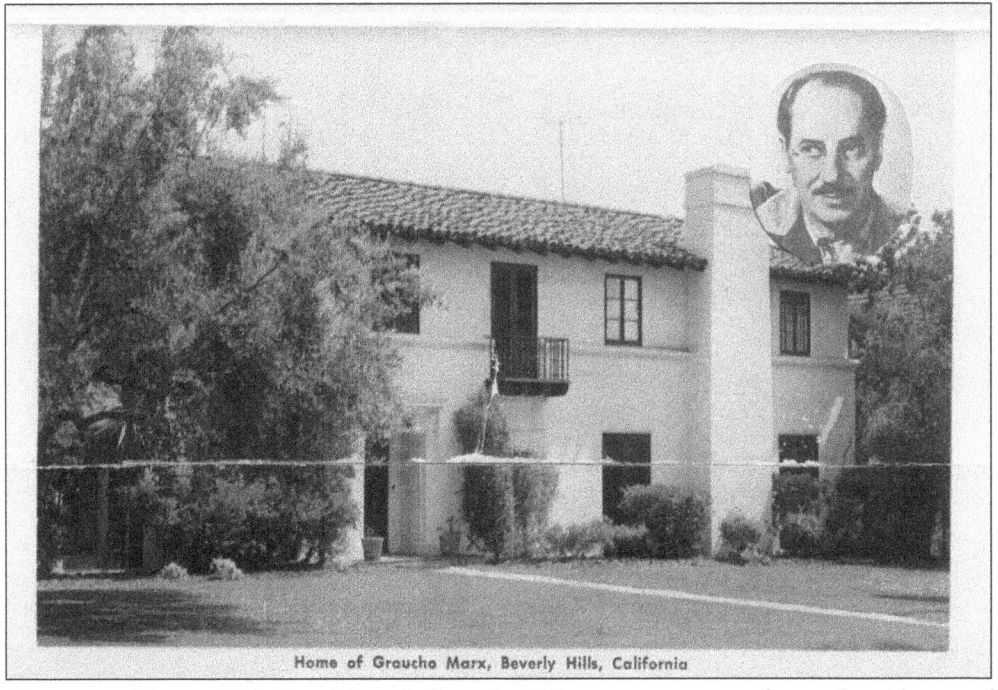

Home of Groucho Marx, Beverly Hills, California

GROUCHO MARX. This Spanish-style Beverly Hills estate was one of several residences of Groucho Marx; it had eight bedrooms. Marx began his career with his brothers Chico, Gummo, Harpo, and Zeppo in vaudeville. By the 1920s, they were major stars in vaudeville, and this led to Broadway and motion picture stardom. From 1929 to 1949, Groucho, Chico, and Harpo starred in 14 classic comedies. Their last film together was *The Story of Mankind* (1957).

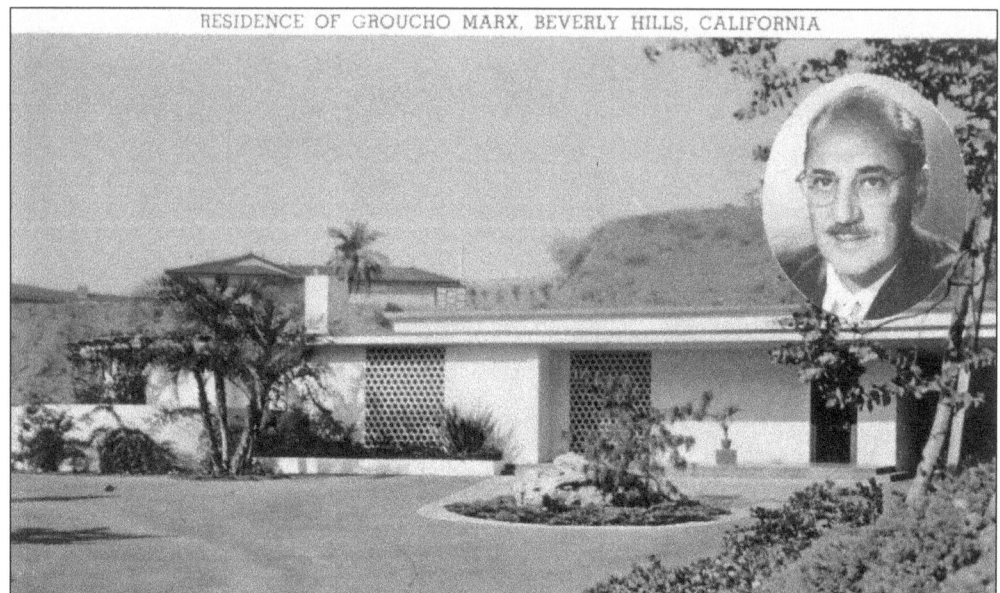

GROUCHO MARX'S LAST HOME. In 1956, Wallace Neff designed this house at 1083 Hillcrest Road for the legendary comedian Groucho Marx. The one-story Beverly Hills residence has five bedrooms, six bathrooms, a swimming pool, and sauna. Groucho lived there until his death. Aside from the classic comedies he starred in with his brothers, he also made *Copacabana* and *Double Dynamite* as well as his television game show *You Bet Your Life* (1950–1961).

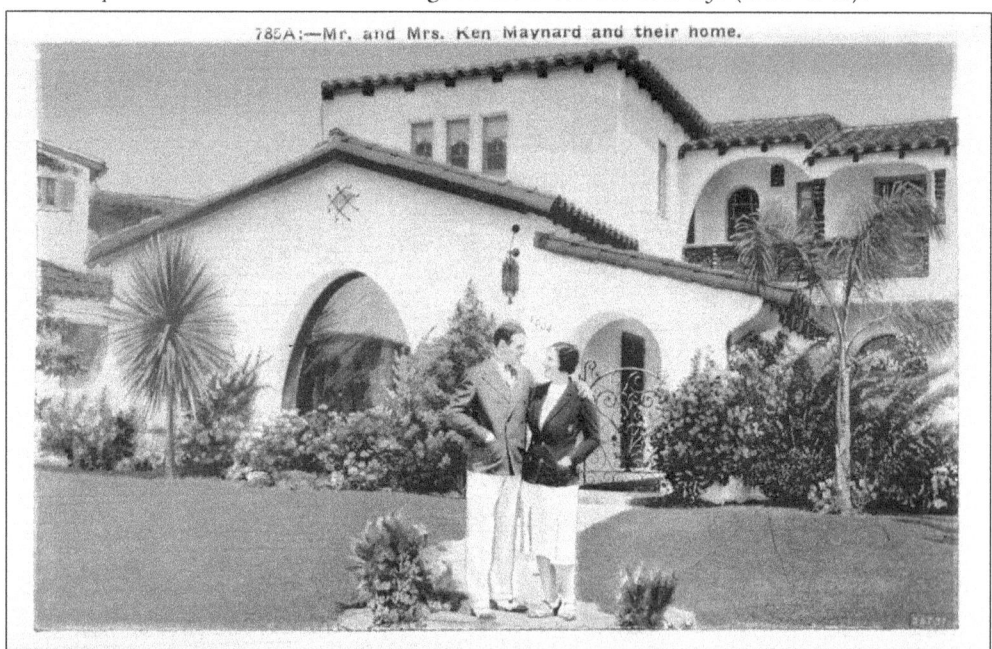

785A:—Mr. and Mrs. Ken Maynard and their home.

KEN MAYNARD. Cowboy star Ken Maynard (1895–1973) began as a stuntman and character actor in silent pictures. He benefitted from the emergence of sound films and became a star. In the 1930s, Maynard lived in this Mediterranean-style house at 315 South Las Palmas Avenue, Beverly Hills. Among his films are *Sons of the Saddle, Mountain Justice, Smoking Guns, Western Courage, Heroes of the Range, Six Shootin' Sheriff*, and *Death Valley Rangers*.

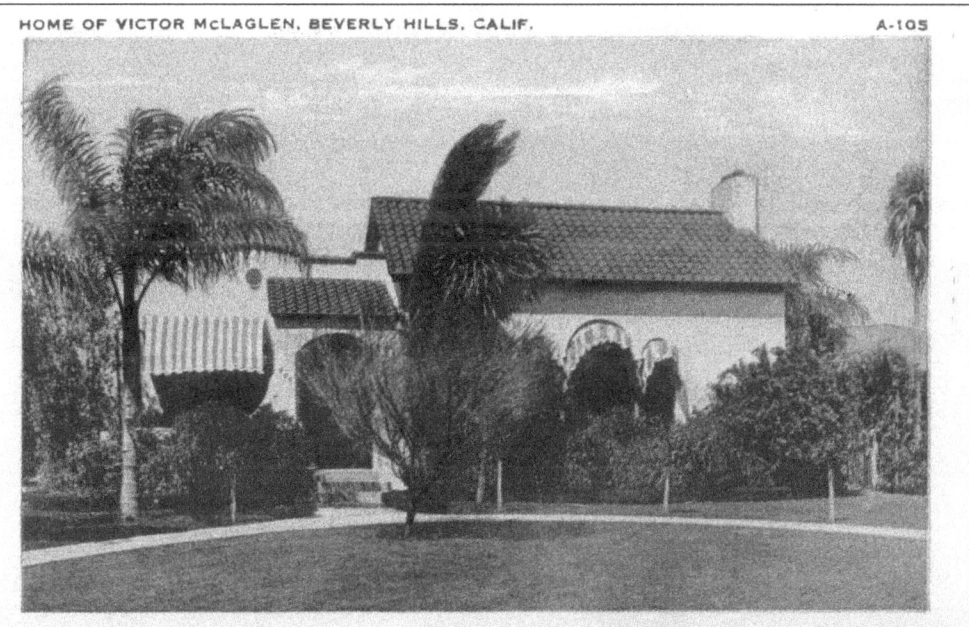

VICTOR McLAGLEN. After years as an athlete, England's Victor McLaglen (1886–1959) tried his luck in Hollywood in the 1920s. With a rough, feisty Anglo-Irish image, he rose to stardom in silent pictures, such as *What Price Glory* and *The Unholy Three*. In talkies, he remained popular and won an Oscar for *The Informer* (1935). His other films include *The Lost Patrol*, *Gunga Din*, and *The Quiet Man*. In 1930, he and his wife, Enid, lived at 226 North Rexford Drive, Beverly Hills.

RAY MILLAND. Published in London, this postcard in Kinematograph's "Picture Series of Cinema Stars" depicts screen star Ray Milland. Welsh-born Milland (1907–1986) costarred in *The Flying Scotsman* (1929), with Moore Marriott, in England. His Hollywood pictures include *French Without Tears*, *Beau Geste*, *Arise My Love*, *The Lost Weekend* (Oscar, 1945), *The Big Clock*, and *Dial M for Murder.* He lived at 726 North Elm Drive, Beverly Hills.

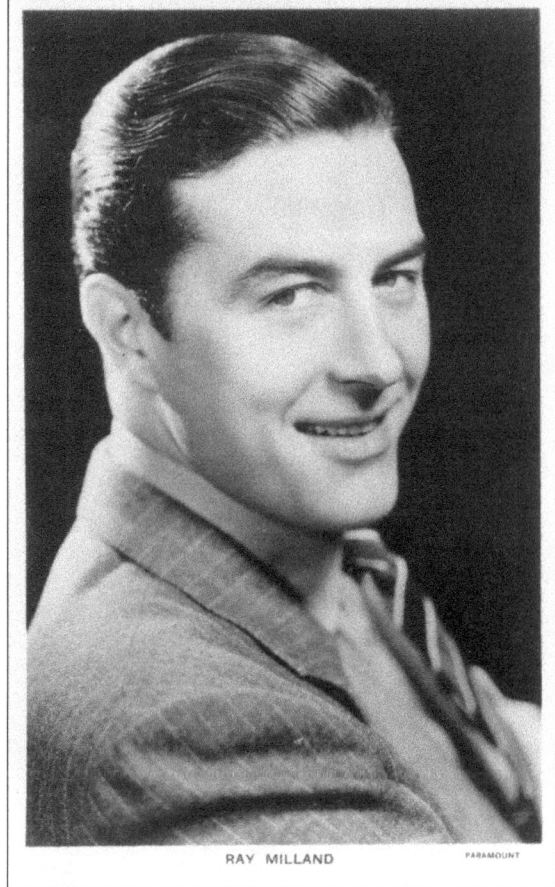

RAY MILLAND   PARAMOUNT

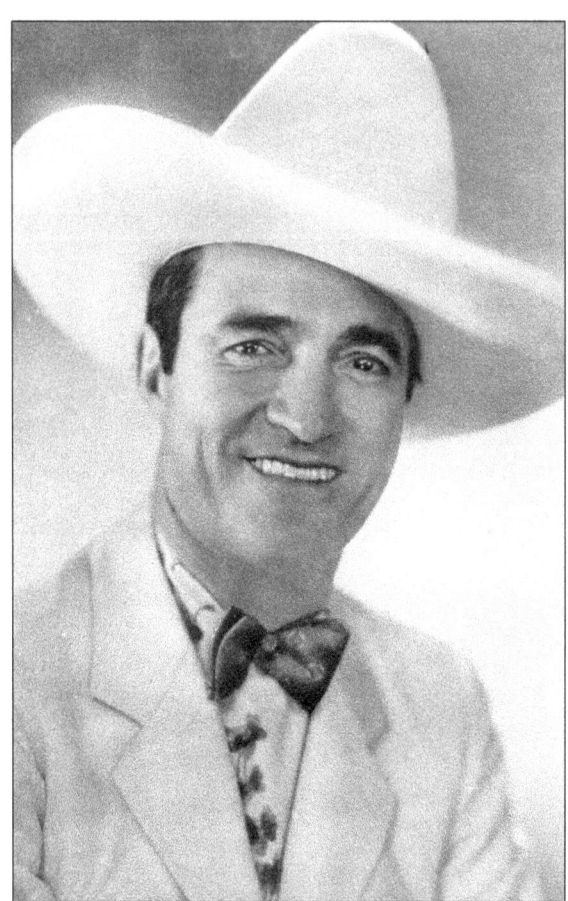

TOM MIX PORTRAIT. The future Western star was born Thomas Hezekiah Mix (1880–1940) in Pennsylvania. Yet as an actor, he preferred to claim Texas as his birthplace. The often-wedded Mix married his fifth and last wife, Mabel (1902–1991), in 1932. In 1940, Mix was killed when his 1937 yellow Cord Phaeton motorcar swung into a gully in Arizona, overturned, and crashed. Actor Monte Blue read the ritual, and Rudy Vallée sang "Empty Saddles" at his Masonic funeral.

TOM MIX. From 1922 to 1929, cowboy superstar Tom Mix (1880–1940) and his fourth wife, Victoria, lived in this mansion at 1018 Summit Drive, Beverly Hills; the six-acre estate required a retinue of servants. Tom and Victoria also had a smaller house at 5841 Carlton Way, Los Angeles. Their neighbors included Douglas Fairbanks, Corinne Griffith, and Charlie Chaplin. Among Mix's films are *Western Blood*, *The Wilderness Trail*, *Riders of the Purple Sage*, and *The Texan*.

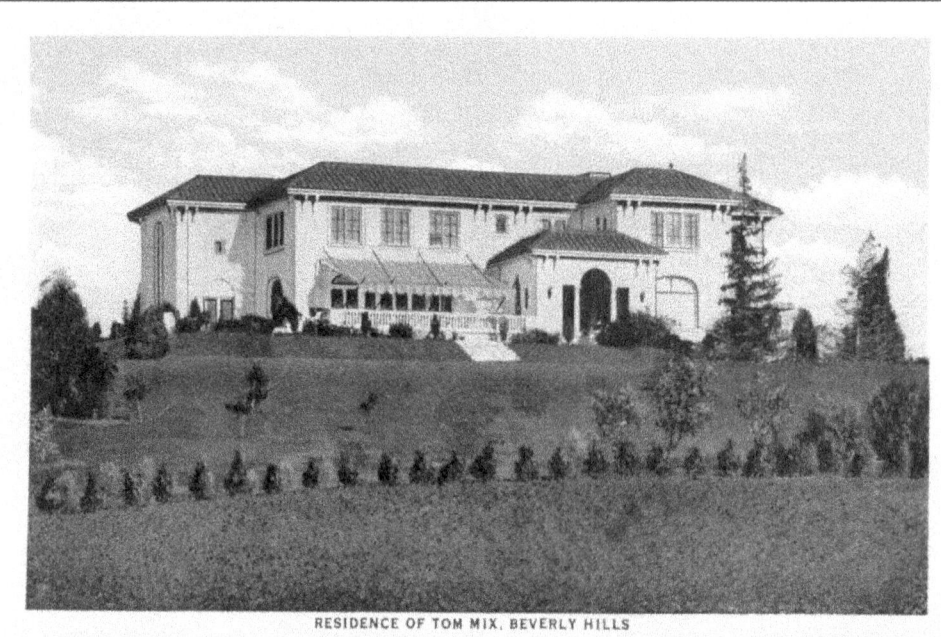

RESIDENCE OF TOM MIX, BEVERLY HILLS

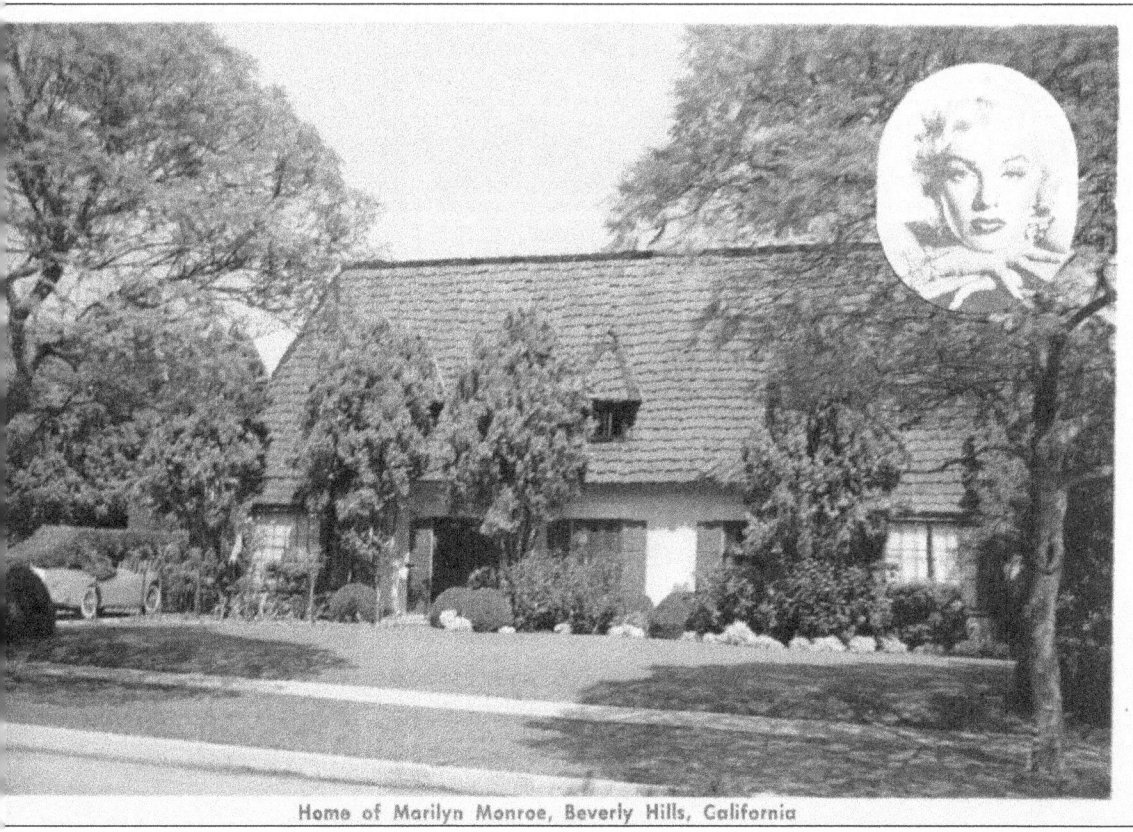

Home of Marilyn Monroe, Beverly Hills, California

MARILYN MONROE. Screen star Marilyn Monroe (1926–1962) had many residences, including this home in Beverly Hills. The screen icon was born Norma Jeane Mortenson at General Hospital in Los Angeles. Transforming herself into an actress with the name "Marilyn Monroe," she starred in such memorable films as *Niagara*, *Gentlemen Prefer Blondes*, *The Seven Year Itch*, *Bus Stop*, and *Some Like It Hot*. The only house she ever owned is the house she died in, 12305 Fifth Helena Drive, Brentwood.

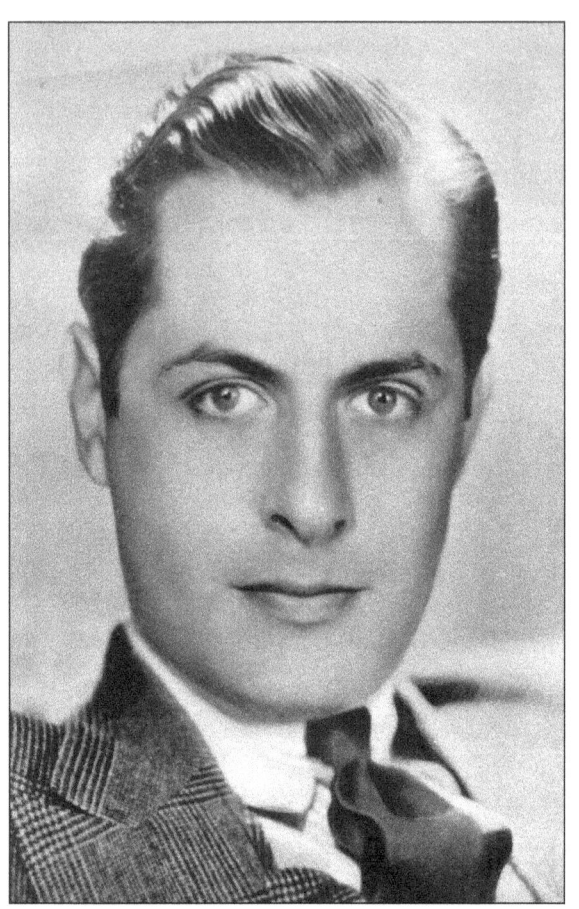

ROBERT MONTGOMERY PORTRAIT. During the 1930s and 1940s, Robert Montgomery was one of Hollywood's most popular actors. MGM principally cast him in light-hearted romantic comedies, a genre in which he excelled. However, it was the 1937 drama *Night Must Fall* that garnered him critical acclaim. His other dramas include *The Big House*, *Rage in Heaven*, *The Earl of Chicago*, and the film noir classic, *Lady in the Lake*.

ROBERT MONTGOMERY. From about 1938 to 1942, Robert Montgomery (1904–1981) lived in this hillside New England–style mansion at 144 Monovale Drive, Beverly Hills; he later moved to 10430 Bellagio Road. One of the screen's versatile stars, Montgomery's films include *Shipmates*, *The Man in Possession*, *But the Flesh Is Weak*, *Busman's Honeymoon* (as Lord Peter Wimsey), *Here Comes Mr. Jordan*, *The Saxon Charm*, and *June Bride*.

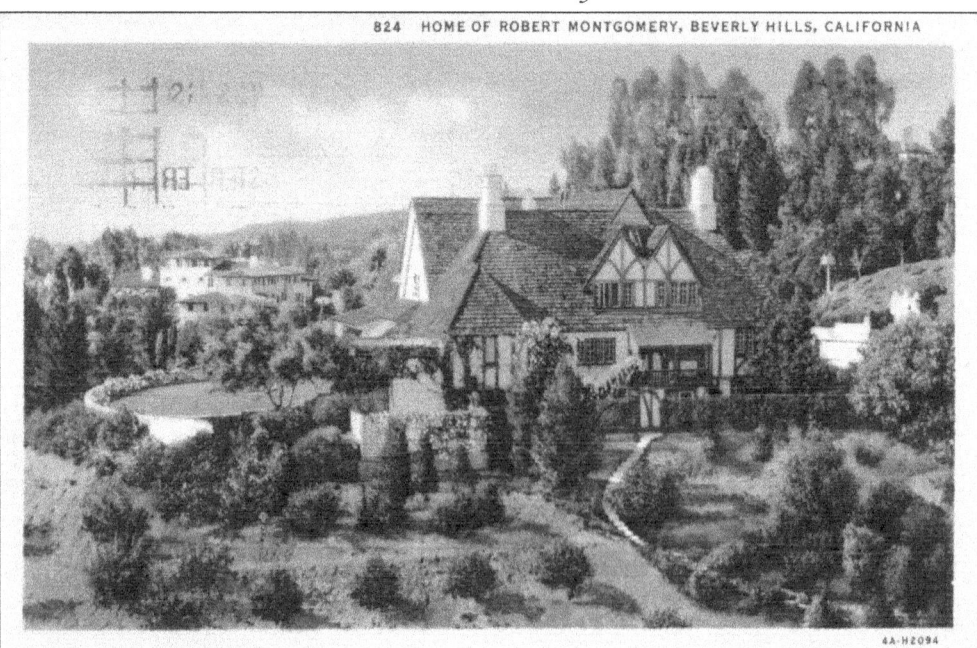

824 HOME OF ROBERT MONTGOMERY, BEVERLY HILLS, CALIFORNIA

4A-H2094

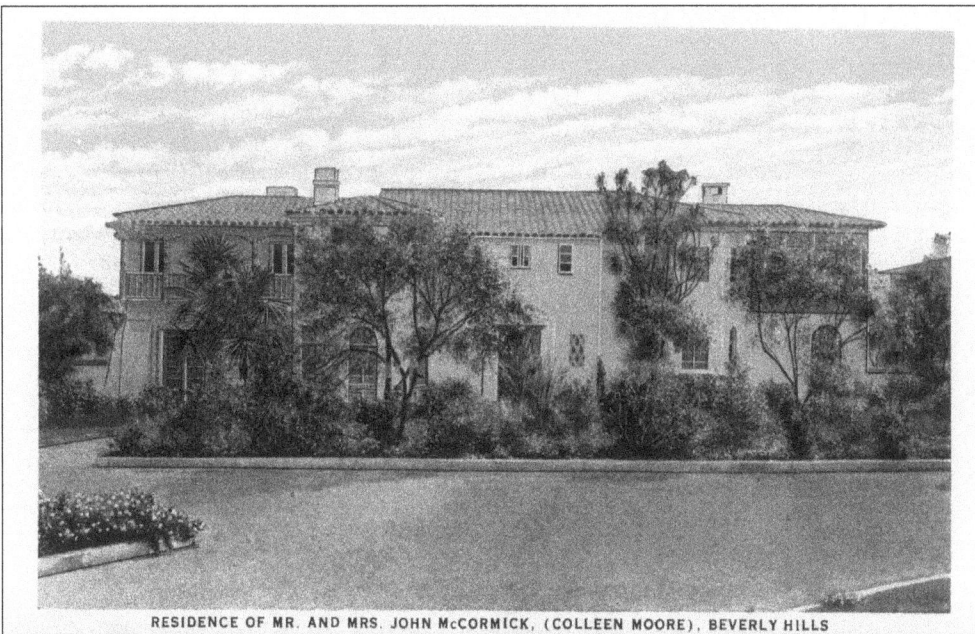

RESIDENCE OF MR. AND MRS. JOHN McCORMICK, (COLLEEN MOORE), BEVERLY HILLS

COLLEEN MOORE. The screen beauty known for her trademark bobbed hair and bangs, Colleen Moore (1899–1988) lived in this house at 345 St. Pierre Road, Bel Air, with her first husband, movie producer John McCormick (1893–1961). This highly paid star graced silent films, such as *Forsaking All Others*, *April Showers*, *Flaming Youth*, *The Perfect Flapper*, *So Big*, *Ella Cinders*, and *Lilac Time*. *Social Register* (1934) is one of her sound films.

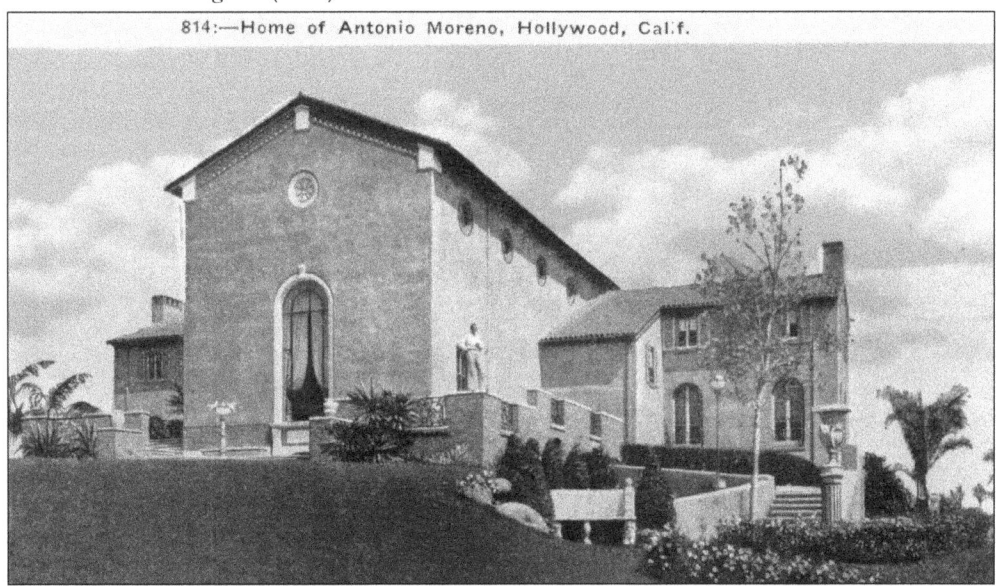

814:—Home of Antonio Moreno, Hollywood, Calif.

ANTONIO MORENO. The romantic Spaniard of the silent screen, Antonio Moreno (1887–1967) lived in Crestmount, a Mediterranean-style mansion at 1923 Micheltorena Street, Silver Lake, with his wife, oil heiress Daisy Canfield Moreno, and stepchildren. Crestmount was the scene of countless Hollywood parties. Among Moreno's silent films are *Mare Nostrum*, *The Flaming Forest*, *It*, and *Venus of Venice*. His sound films include *The Midnight Taxi* and *Creature from the Black Lagoon*.

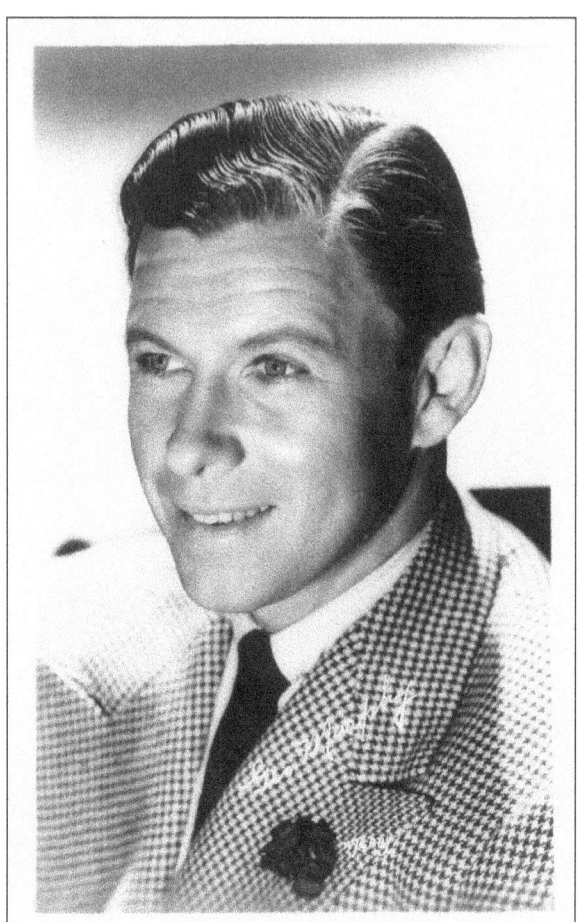

GEORGE MURPHY PICTURE POSTCARD. Nightclub dancer George Murphy (1902–1992) broke into movies in 1934. He danced in *The Broadway Melody of 1938* and *For Me and My Gal*. His other credits include *The Public Menace*, *Broadway Rhythm*, *Step Lively*, *Border Incident*, *Walk East on Beacon*, and *Tom, Dick and Harry*. Murphy later served as a US senator (1964–1970). He lived at 807 North Rodeo Drive, Beverly Hills.

CONRAD NAGEL. Stage and screen star Conrad Nagel (1897–1970) lived in this house at 715 North Palm Drive, Beverly Hills. Nagel was the leading man in silent films, like *Lights of Old Broadway*, *Quality Street*, and *London After Midnight*. In the talking era, his credits include *Dynamite*, *East Lynne*, *The Reckless Hour*, *Dangerous Corner*, and *One New York Night*. He hosted television shows *Celebrity Time* (1948–1952) and *Hollywood Preview* (1955–1956).

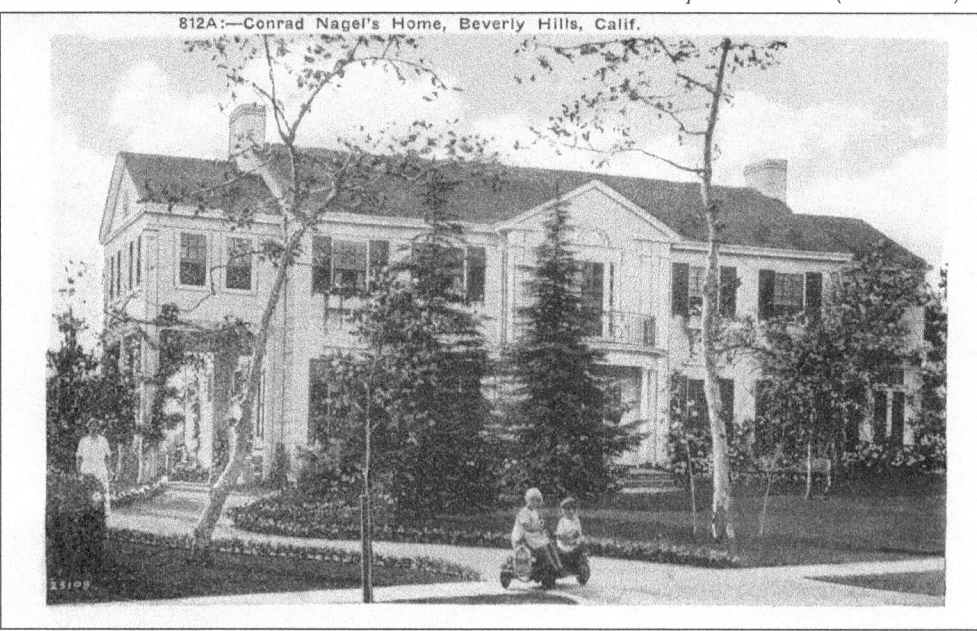

812A:—Conrad Nagel's Home, Beverly Hills, Calif.

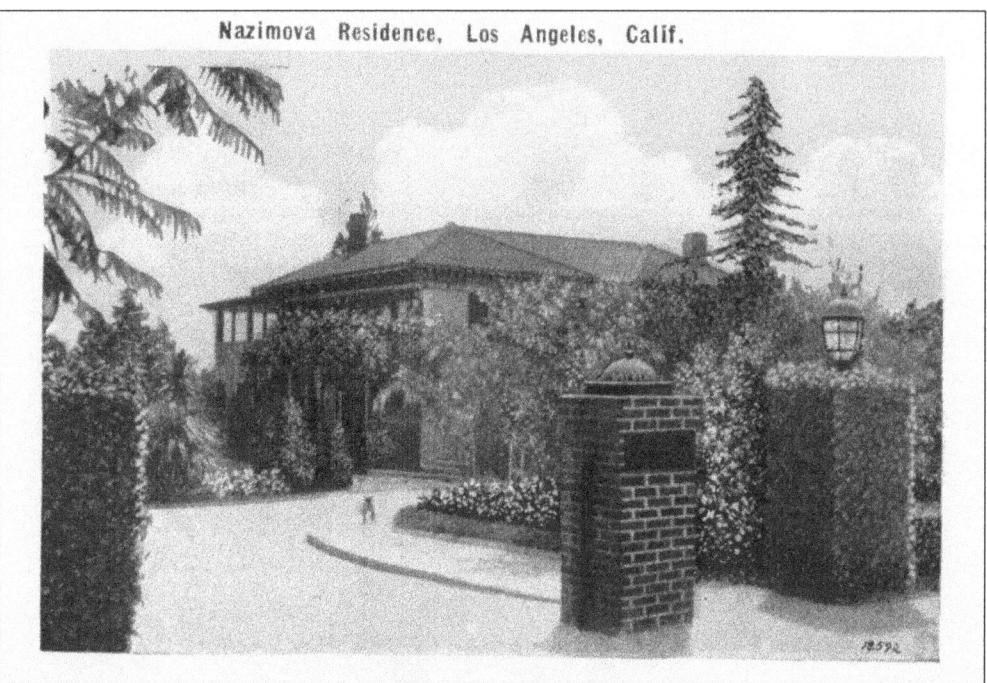

Nazimova Residence, Los Angeles, Calif.

ALLA NAZIMOVA. From 1919 to 1926, Russian actress Alla Nazimova (1879–1945) lived at 8152 Sunset Boulevard, Hollywood. After her screen career faded, she changed it into a residential estate of 25 villas and christened it the Garden of Alla. Nazimova was a great star with such films as *Revelation, Out of the Fog, The Red Lantern, A Doll's House*, and *Salomé*. Her first sound film, *Escape* (1940), was another triumph for her.

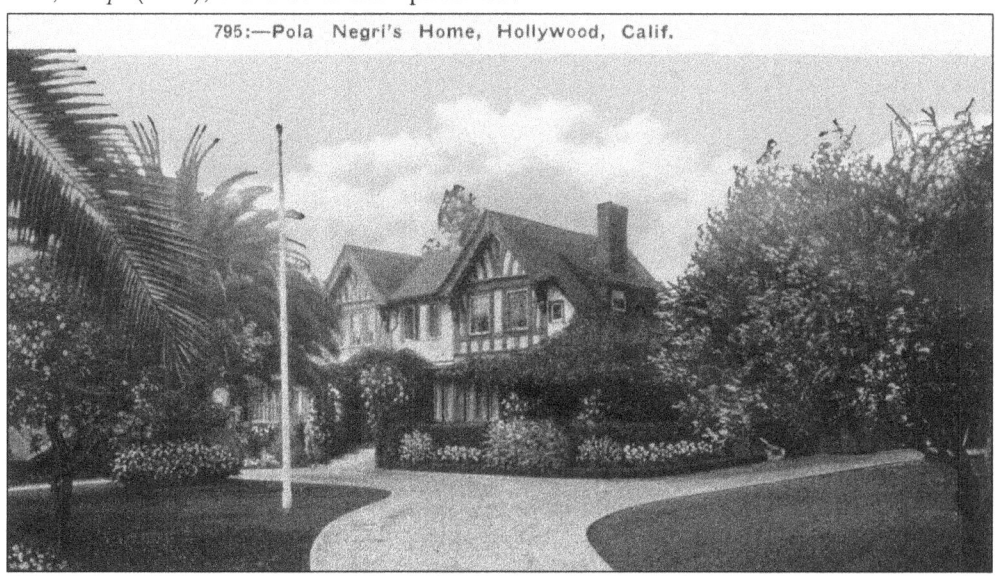

795:—Pola Negri's Home, Hollywood, Calif.

POLA NEGRI. In September 1922, the Polish actress Pola Negri (1897–1987) sailed to America to seek a film career in Hollywood. One of her temporary residences in Hollywood appears on this 1923 postcard. She was in top form for the silent screen and won acclaim for such films as *Bella Donna, Forbidden Paradise, Shadows of Paris, East of Suez*, and *Hotel Imperial*. The advent of sound films drove her back to Europe.

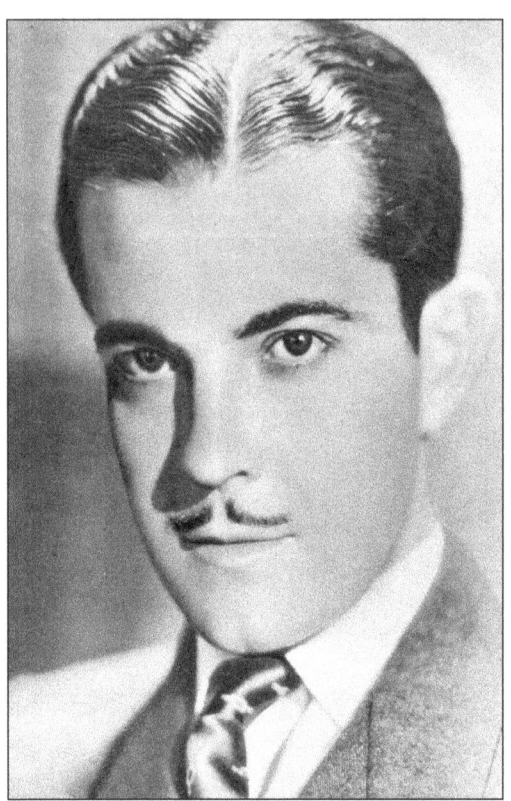

RAMÓN NOVARRO PORTRAIT. Here, legendary actor Ramón Novarro (1899–1968) is depicted in a scene from *Where the Pavement Ends* (1923), with Alice Terry. Novarro was born José Ramón Samaniego to a prominent family in Durango, Mexico. The Mexican Revolution sent him fleeing to California. In Hollywood, Novarro was compared favorably with Rudolph Valentino. In 1942, he returned to Mexico and starred in the religious classic *La Virgen que Forjó una Patria* (1942). His cousin was actress Dolores del Río.

RAMÓN NOVARRO. One of the silent screen's great romantic stars, Ramón Novarro lived in this mansion at 6609 Valley Oak Drive in the 1930s; he later lived at 3110 Laurel Canyon Drive. Novarro, a Mexican, settled in Los Angeles in 1913. His classic films include *The Prisoner of Zenda*, *The Midshipman*, *Ben-Hur*, *The Pagan* (in which he sang his enchanting "Pagan Love Song"), *Devil-May-Care*, *Mata Hari*, and *The Night Is Young*.

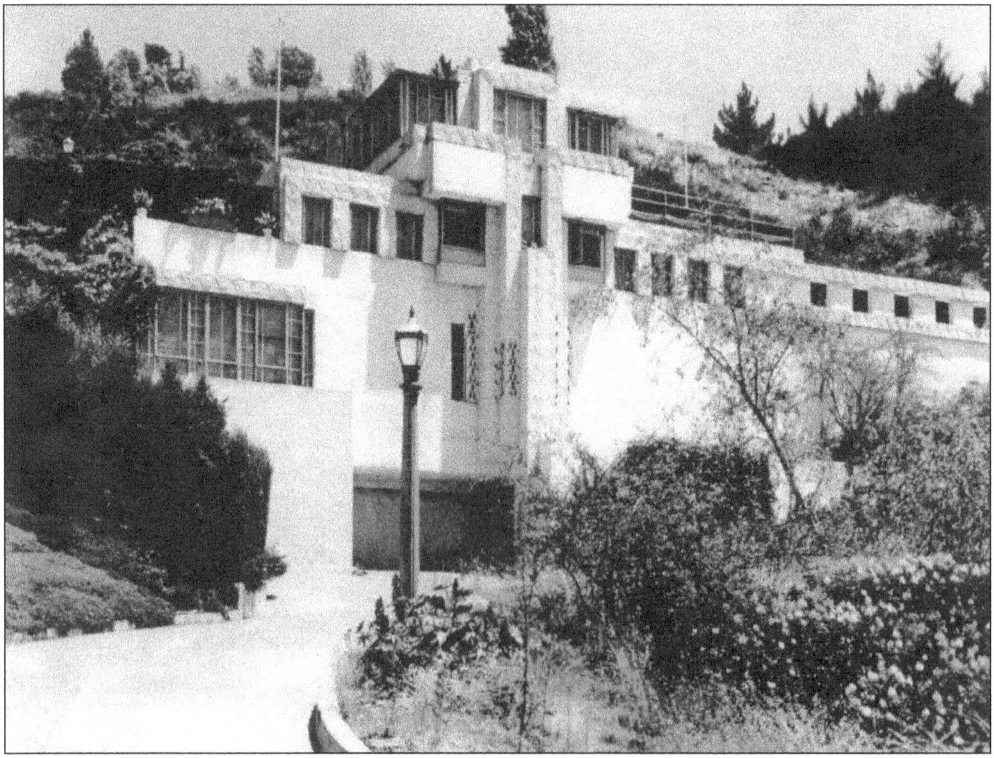

Four

JACK PALANCE TO LORETTA YOUNG

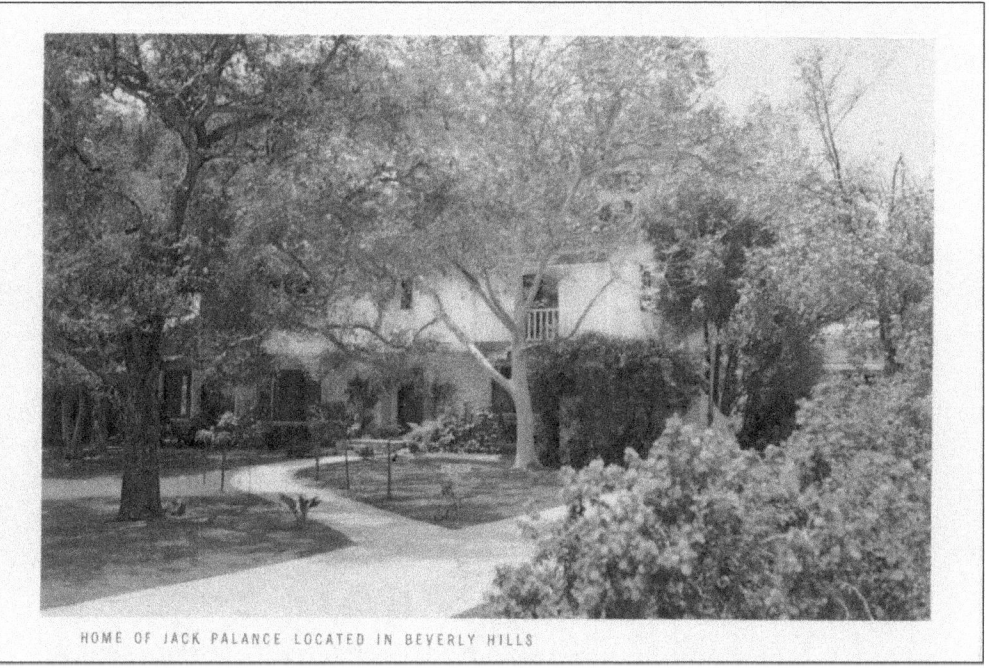

HOME OF JACK PALANCE LOCATED IN BEVERLY HILLS

JACK PALANCE. Built in 1949, actor Jack Palance's estate at 1006 Hartford Drive, Beverly Hills, was richly appointed. A unique presence, Jack Palance (1919–2006) gave outstanding performances in the 1950s in *Halls of Montezuma, Sudden Fear, Shane, Arrowhead, The Big Knife, Attack, I Died a Thousand Times,* and *Man in the Attic.* Years later, he won an Oscar for *City Slickers* (1992).

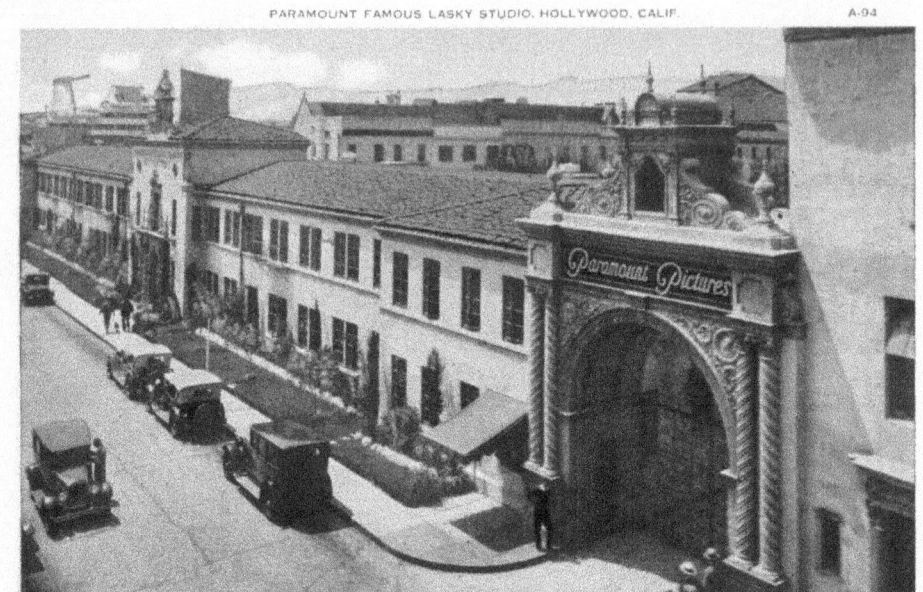

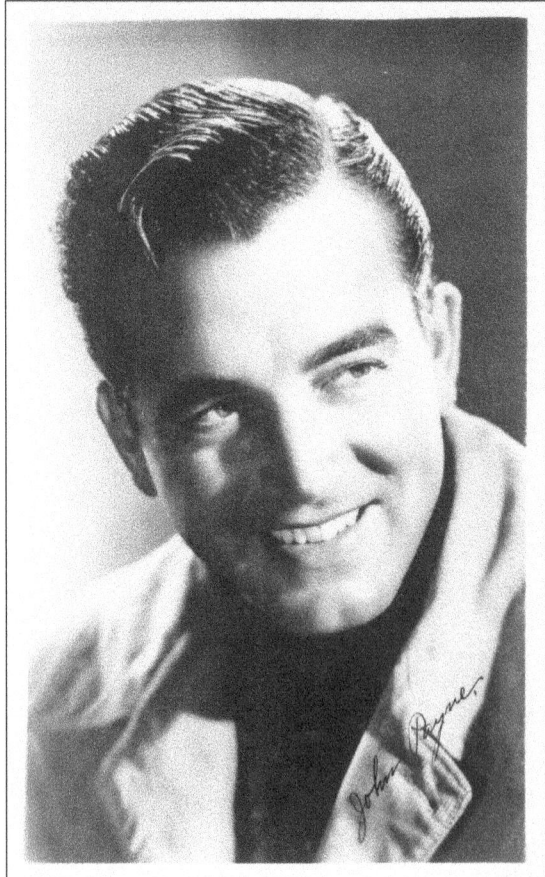

PARAMOUNT PICTURES. Originating as Famous Players Film Company in 1912, Paramount Pictures developed into one of Hollywood's foremost studios. This 1926 postcard shows its legendary entrance gate on Bronson Avenue. The studio's thousands of stars include Gloria Swanson, Wallace Reid, Florence Vidor, Rudolph Valentino, Thomas Meighan, Bebe Daniels, Richard Dix, Clara Bow, Maurice Chevalier, Claudette Colbert, W.C. Fields, Marlene Dietrich, Bing Crosby, Mae West, Cary Grant, Bob Hope, and William Holden.

JOHN PAYNE PICTURE POSTCARD. Noted as a star of film noirs and dramas as well as for his role in *Miracle on 34th Street*, John Payne (1912–1989) was born in Virginia. A stage actor, he broke into movies in 1936. Among them are *Tin Pan Alley*, *Weekend in Havana*, *Sentimental Journey*, and *Slightly Scarlet*. In 1940, he and his wife, actress Anne Shirley (1918–1993), lived at 8800 Evanview Drive, Hollywood.

MARY PICKFORD PICTURE POSTCARD. Born Gladys Smith in Toronto, Canada, Mary Pickford (1892–1979) became one of the greatest stars of the silent screen. She seemed to reign over Hollywood. From poverty, she and her family struggled as traveling stage actors, until Mary made her mark as the first world-famous movie star. Her credits include *A Good Little Devil*, *Hearts Adrift*, *Tess of the Storm Country*, and *Poor Little Rich Girl*.

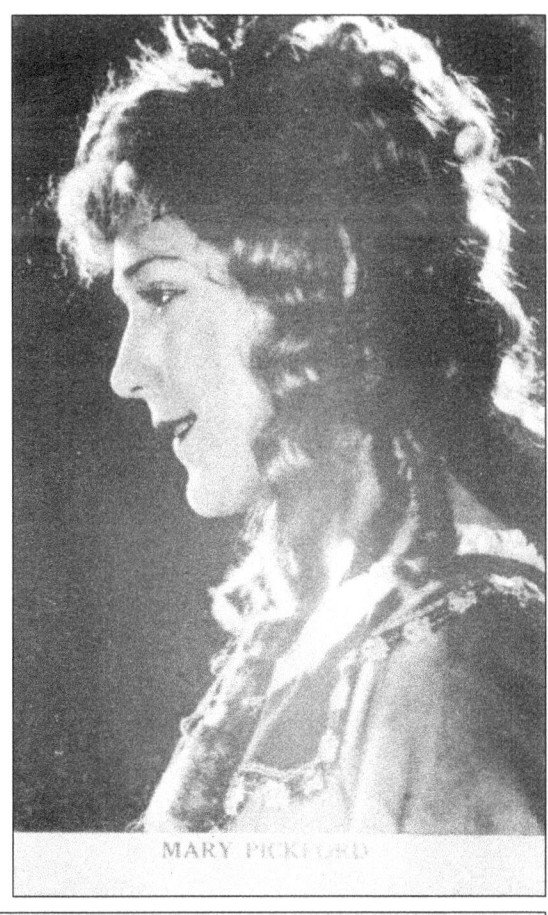

MARY PICKFORD

MARY PICKFORD. In her 1935–1936 divorce settlement with Douglas Fairbanks, Mary Pickford kept Pickfair, their lavish 18-acre Beverly Hills estate. The next year, she married bandleader and actor Charles "Buddy" Rogers. The couple lived there for decades until her death at the age of 87. One of the richest stars of the silent screen, she left most of her vast fortune, including Pickfair, to her own private charity, the Mary Pickford Foundation.

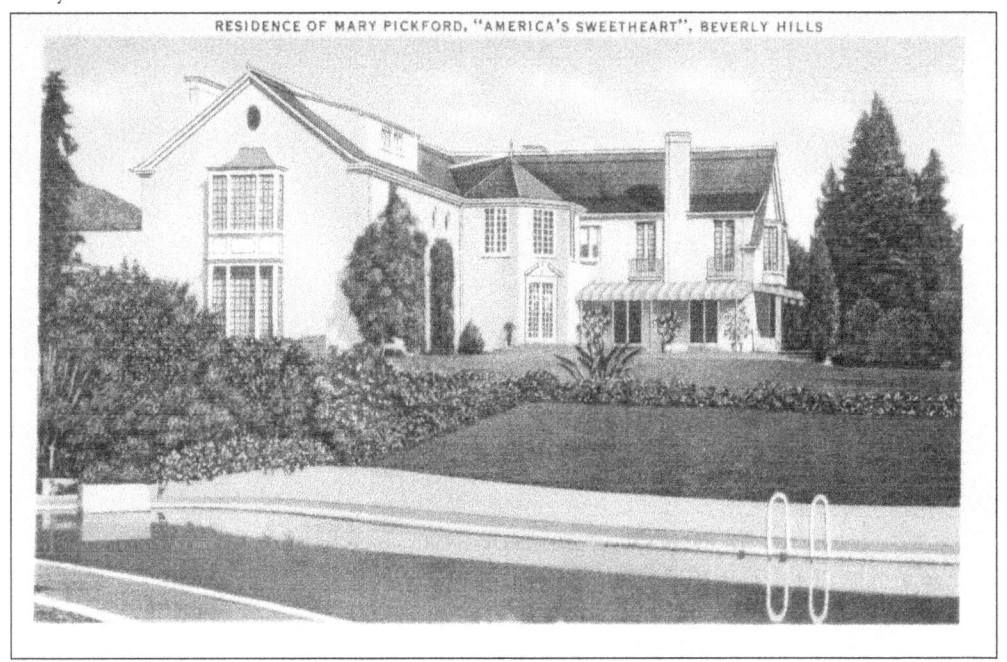

RESIDENCE OF MARY PICKFORD, "AMERICA'S SWEETHEART", BEVERLY HILLS

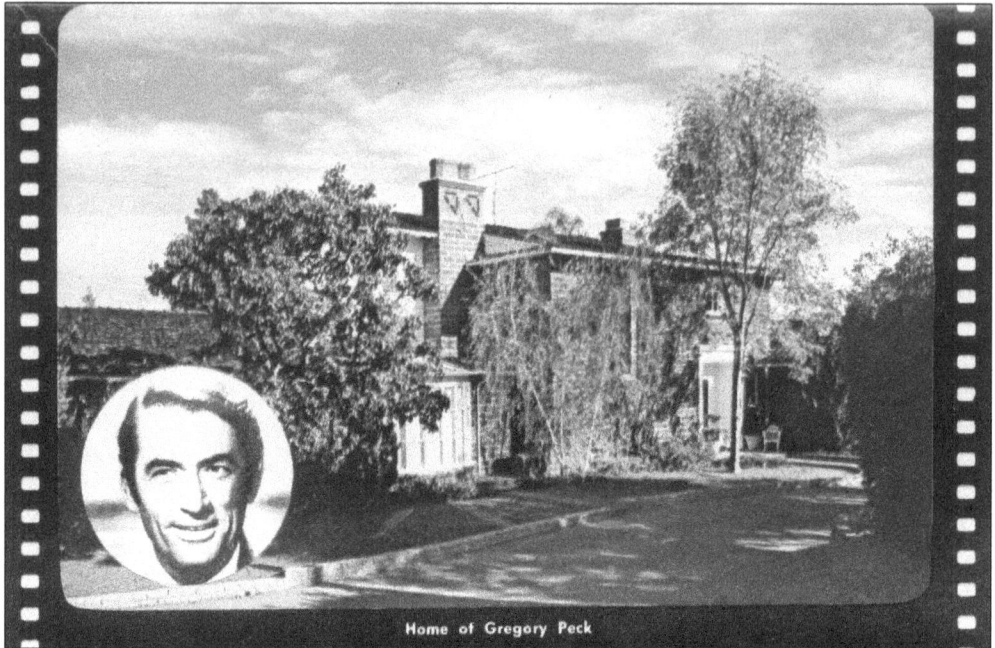

Home of Gregory Peck

GREGORY PECK. For years, Gregory Peck lived in this estate at 266 South Cliffwood Avenue, Brentwood. The grounds included a pavilion, tennis courts, a guesthouse, and a vast meadow. Beginning as a stage actor, Gregory Peck (1916–2003) emerged into a major screen star in 1944. His films include *Keys of the Kingdom*, *The Yearling*, *Duel in the Sun*, *Gentlemen's Agreement*, *Spellbound*, *Roman Holiday*, and *To Kill a Mockingbird* (Oscar, 1962).

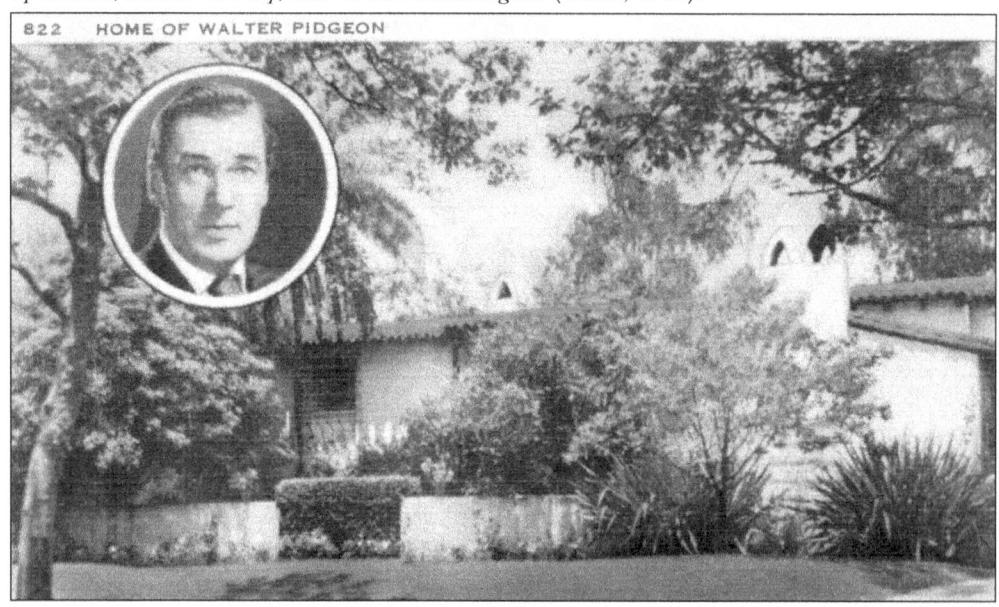

822   HOME OF WALTER PIDGEON

WALTER PIDGEON. In the 1930s and 1940s, Walter Pidgeon (1897–1984) and his family lived in this house at 710 North Walden Drive, Beverly Hills. He became a successful actor and singer in Hollywood thanks to the advent of sound films. Pidgeon's films include *Melody of Love* (1928), *Society Lawyer* (1939), *How Green Was My Valley* (1941), *Mrs. Miniver* (1942), *Calling Bulldog Drummond* (1951), *Advise and Consent* (1962), and *Funny Girl* (1968).

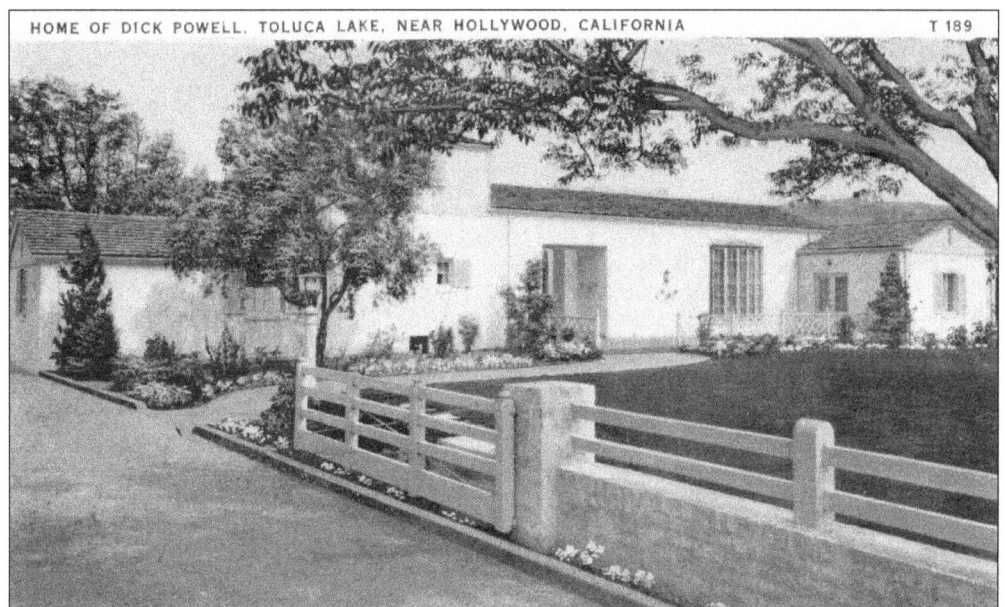

DICK POWELL. One of Warner Bros.'s popular movie stars was the romantic crooner Dick Powell. He starred opposite dancer Ruby Keeler in musicals, like *42nd Street*, *Gold Diggers of 1933*, *Footlight Parade*, and *Dames*. As a crooner, he introduced "We're in the Money," "I Only Have Eyes for You," and "Lullaby of Broadway." Beginning in 1932, Powell (1904–1963) lived in this Spanish-style house in Toluca Lake.

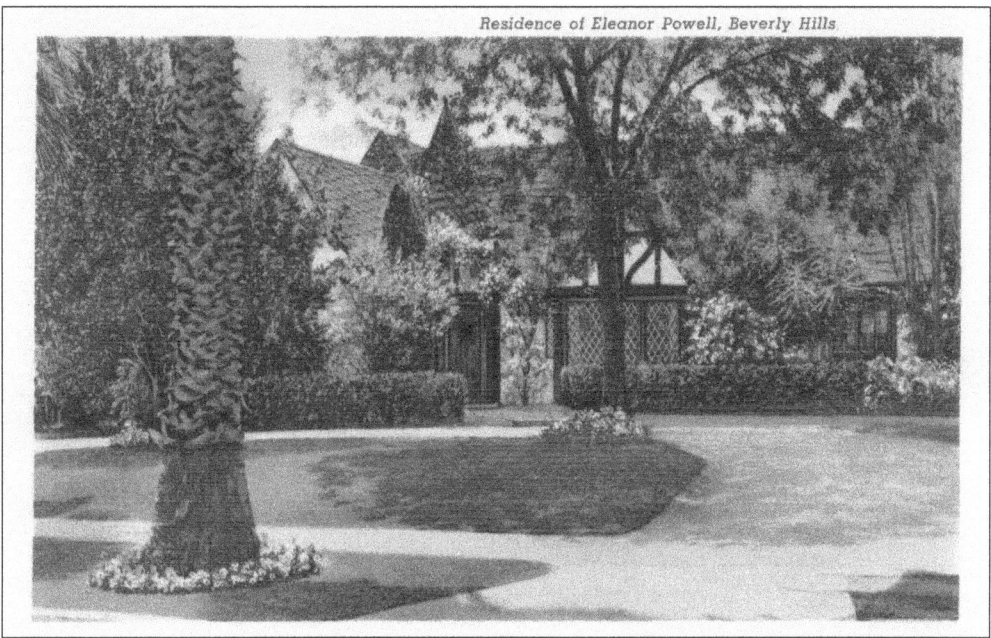

ELEANOR POWELL. In the 1930s and 1940s, actress-dancer Eleanor Powell (1912–1982) rented this house at 727 North Bedford Drive from Marion Davies and lived there with her mother. In 1943, she married actor Glenn Ford, and the couple eventually purchased a mansion. Celebrated for her tap dancing, Eleanor Powell starred in *Broadway Melody of 1936*, *Born to Dance*, *Rosalie*, *Honolulu*, *Lady Be Good*, *Ship Ahoy*, and *I Dood It*.

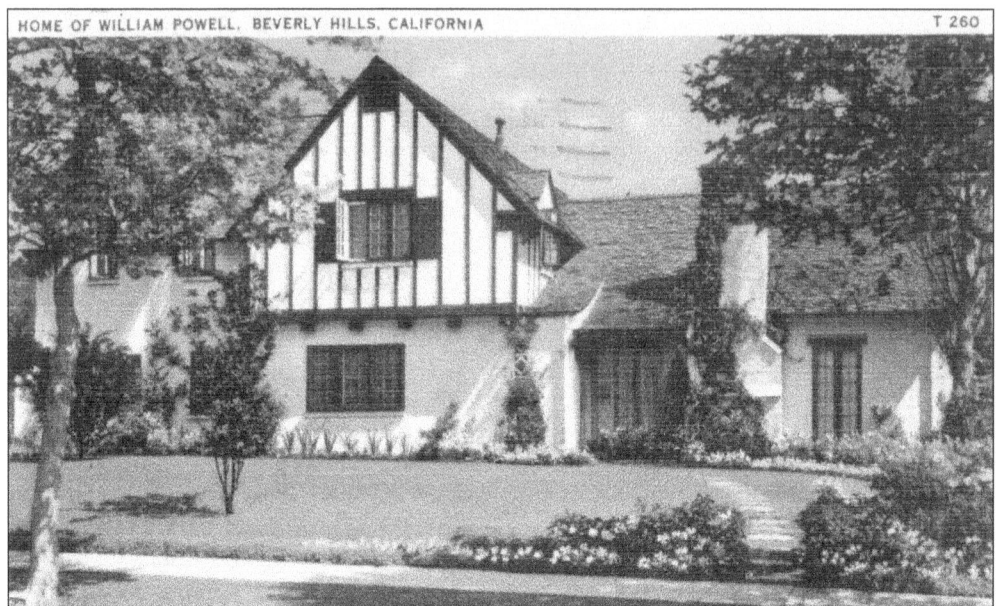

WILLIAM POWELL. Shown here is a former home of actor William Powell. By about 1935, he had moved to 1113 Tower Road, Beverly Hills. A respected stage actor, William Powell only entered silent films to augment his income in 1922. But when talkies came in, his mastery of dialogue made him a major star. His credits include *Manhattan Melodrama, The Thin Man, The Great Ziegfeld, My Man Godfrey,* and *Life with Father.*

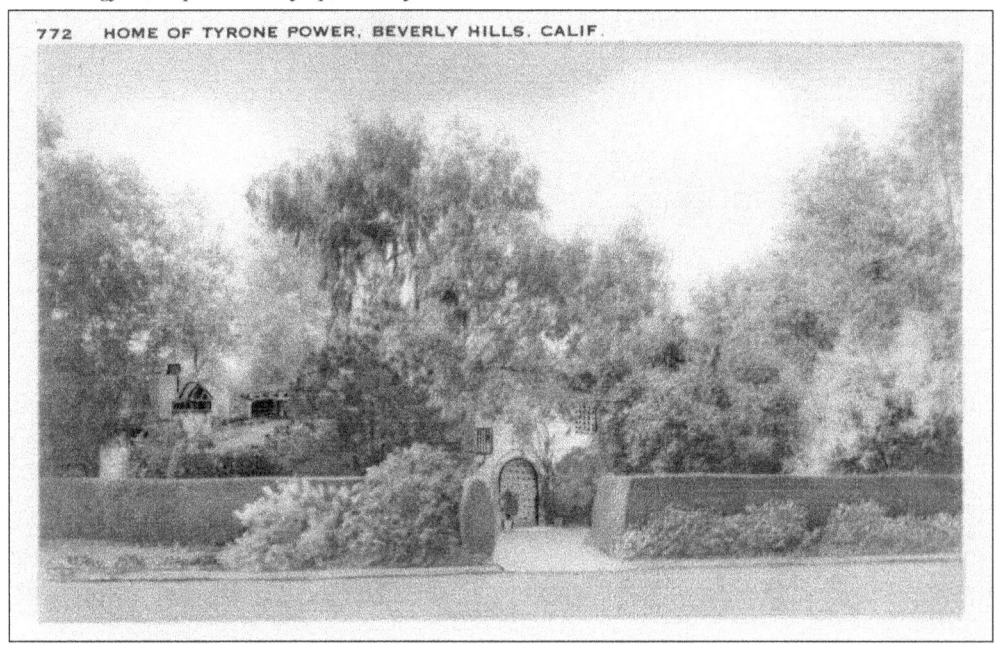

TYRONE POWER. In 1938, screen great Tyrone Power lived in this house at 635 Perugia Way, Bel Air. After Power (1913–1958) and wife, Annabella, moved out in 1939, later residents included Lana Turner, Jennifer Jones, Robert Walker, and, in the 1960s, Elvis Presley. Among Tyrone Power's most admired films are *The Mark of Zorro, Blood and Sand, The Razor's Edge, Captain from Castile,* and *Witness for the Prosecution.*

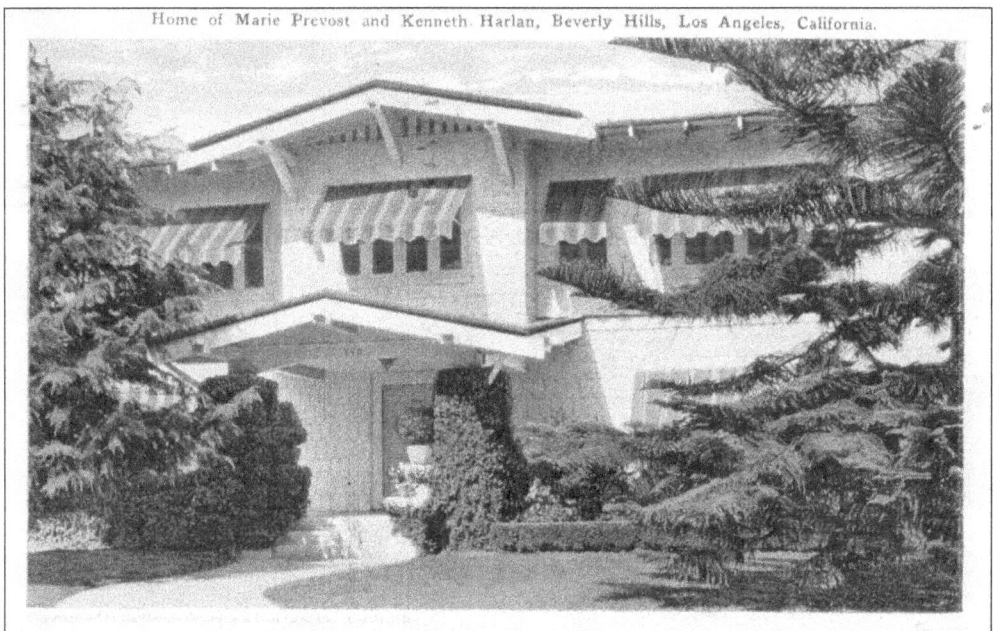

Home of Marie Prevost and Kenneth Harlan, Beverly Hills, Los Angeles, California.

MARIE PREVOST AND KENNETH HARLAN. Married from 1924 to 1927, these two movie favorites lived here at 810 North Camden Drive, Beverly Hills. Marie Prevost (1896–1937) and Kenneth Harlan (1895–1967) costarred in *The Beautiful and the Damned* and *Bobbed Hair*. Prevost also starred in *The Marriage Circle*, *Three Women*, *Kiss Me Again*, and *Seven Sinners*, while Harlan's credits include *Toll of the Sea*, *Poisoned Paradise*, *The Virginian*, and *The Crowded Hour*.

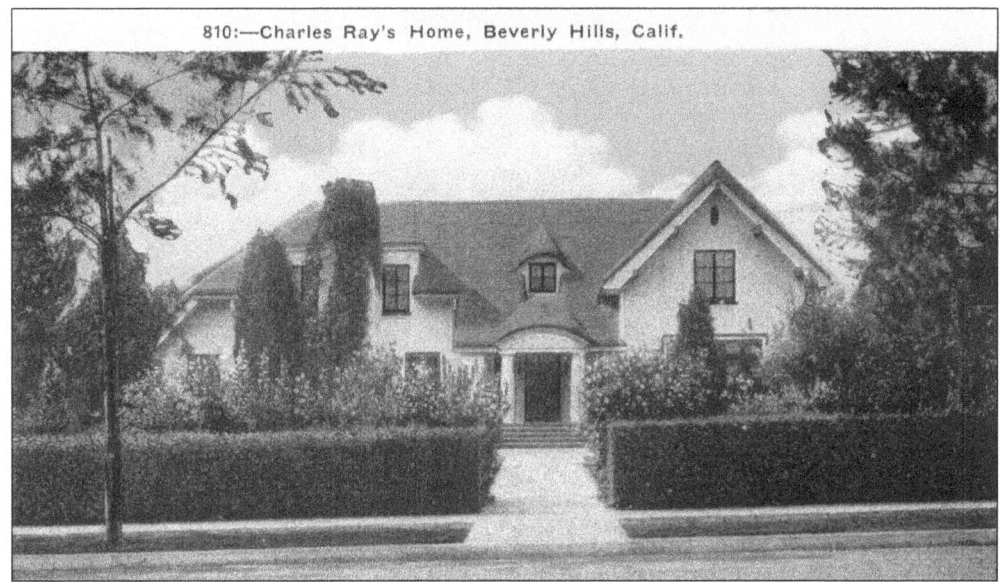

810:—Charles Ray's Home, Beverly Hills, Calif.

CHARLES RAY. Admired for his wholesome country bumpkin characterizations, Charles Ray (1891–1943) and his wife, Clara, lived at 901 Camden Drive, Beverly Hills (1920). A spendthrift, he eventually went bankrupt (1925). After 1930, he only had bit parts in talkies. By 1942, he and his new wife, Yvonne, lived modestly on Berendo Street, Los Angeles. Ray's films include *The Clodhopper*, *His Mother's Boy*, *Alarm Clock Andy*, *The Old Swimmin' Hole*, and *Bright Lights*.

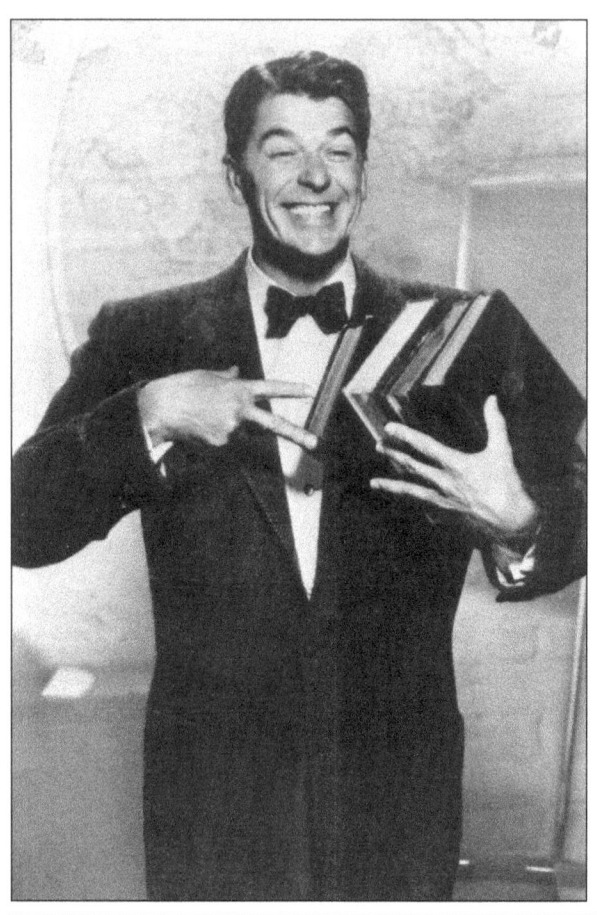

RONALD REAGAN. Movie star Ronald Reagan (1911–2004) is shown in a publicity still for the 1952 comedy *She's Working Her Way Through College*, in which he starred opposite screen beauty Virginia Mayo. Reagan, a popular leading man, starred in such films as *King's Row*, *Desperate Journey*, *Stallion Road*, *The Voice of the Turtle*, and *Storm Warning*. Reagan lived in Pacific Palisades for years. His last home was at 668 St. Cloud Road, Bel Air.

WALLACE REID. In 1920, movie star Wallace Reid (1891–1923) and his wife, actress Dorothy Davenport (1895–1977), purchased this Italianate mansion at 8327 De Longpre Avenue, Hollywood. Known as "the screen's most perfect lover," Reid was in *Valley of the Giants*, *The Roaring Road*, *Double Speed*, *Excuse My Dust*, and *The Affairs of Anatole*, among others. Following Reid's untimely death from his morphine addiction, his wife produced a film about addiction called *Human Wreckage*.

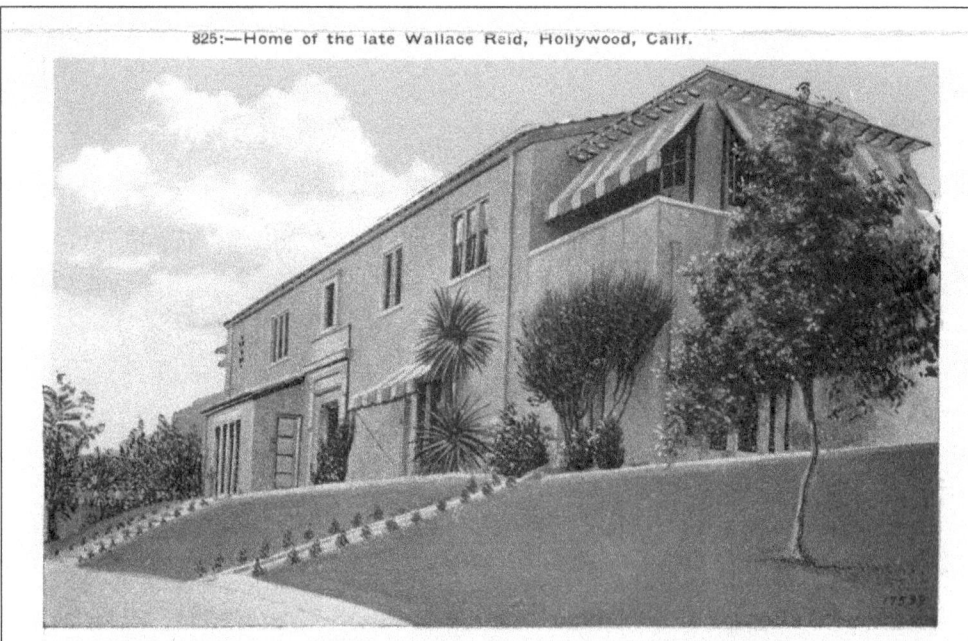

825:—Home of the late Wallace Reid, Hollywood, Calif.

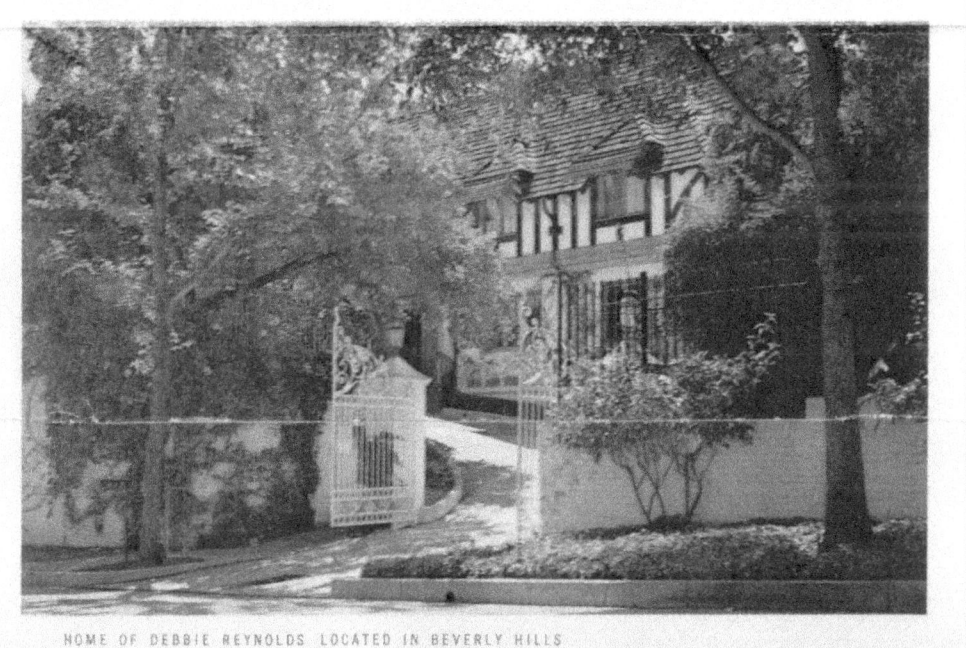

HOME OF DEBBIE REYNOLDS LOCATED IN BEVERLY HILLS

DEBBIE REYNOLDS. During the early years of her career, Debbie Reynolds (1932–2016) lived in this Tudor-style mansion in Beverly Hills. A dynamic entertainer, Reynolds enjoyed many years in show business from the Golden Age of Hollywood to television (*The Debbie Reynolds Show*, NBC-TV), cabaret, and even Broadway (*Irene*). Her films include *Singin' in the Rain*, *Susan Slept Here*, *The Catered Affair*, *Tammy and the Bachelor*, and *The Unsinkable Molly Brown*.

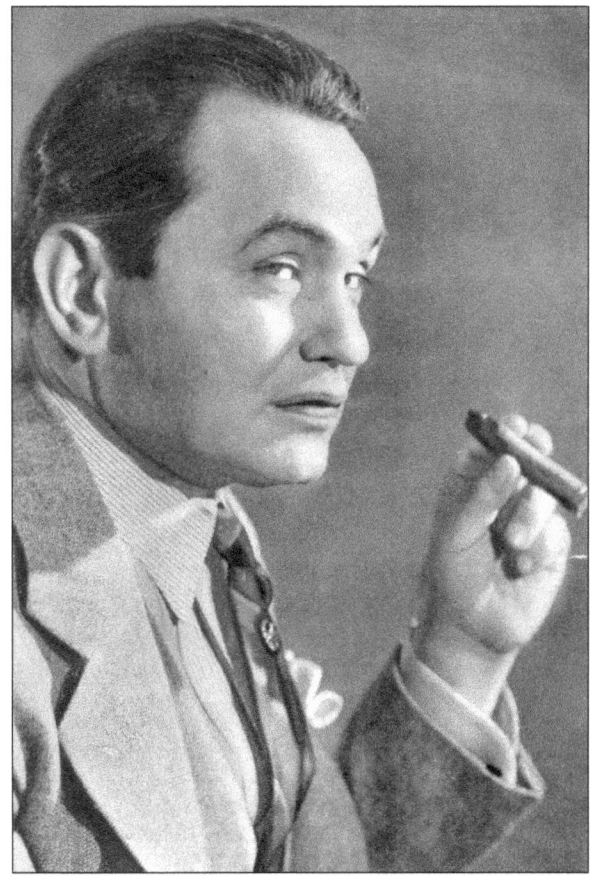

EDWARD G. ROBINSON. Born in Romania, Edward G. Robinson (1893–1973) emigrated to America in 1904. Later, as a New York actor, he gained success on Broadway. This led to his rise to screen stardom in such films as *Little Caesar*, *Smart Money*, *The Little Giant*, *Bullets or Ballots*, *The Woman in the Window*, *Scarlet Street*, and *Key Largo*. An avid art collector, he lived at 910 North Rexford Drive, Beverly Hills, for 42 years.

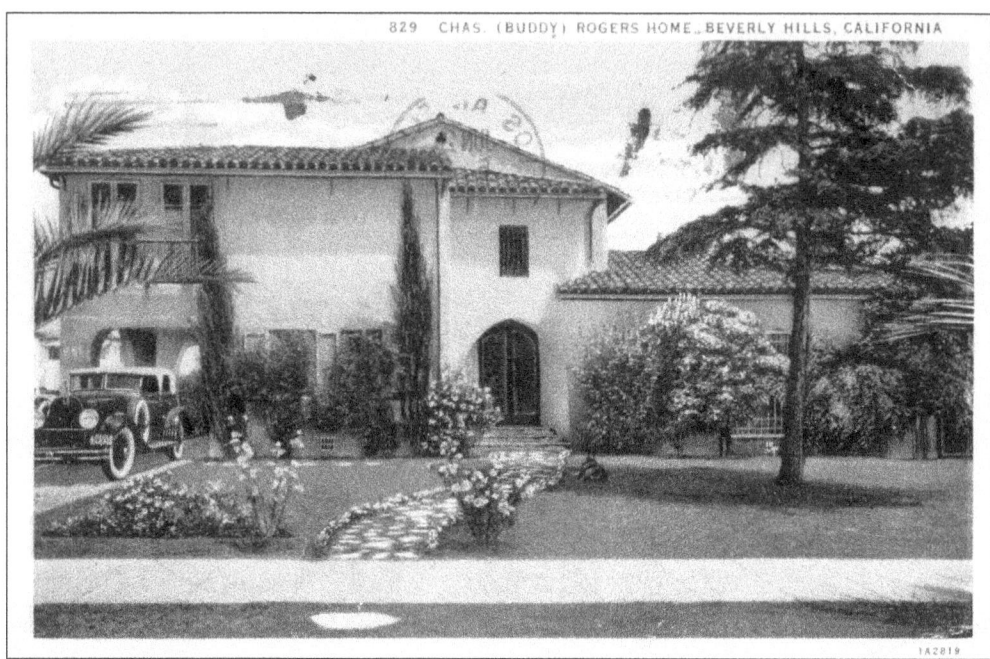

CHARLES "BUDDY" ROGERS. In 1932, the young actor and bandleader lived in this house, possibly at 606 North Bedford Drive, Beverly Hills. In 1937, Rogers (1904–1999) built a new house and married Mary Pickford, his leading lady in *My Best Girl* (1927). Rogers's other credits include *Fascinating Youth, Wings, Halfway to Heaven, The Lawyer's Secret, This Reckless Age, Dance Band, This Way Please*, and *The Mexican Spitfire's Baby*.

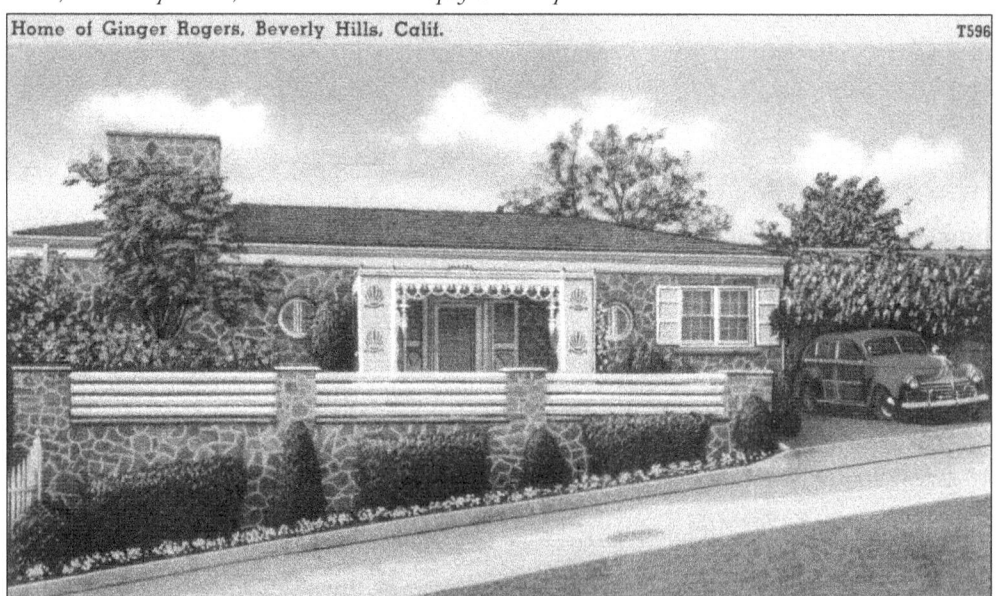

GINGER ROGERS. In 1936, Ginger Rogers had this ranch house built at 1605 North Gilcrest Drive, Beverly Hills. Designed by Carroll Clark of RKO Radio Pictures, the single-story stone-and-frame house, standing on a crest, boasted a solarium and library. Talented and very popular with theater audiences, Ginger Rogers was in *Star of Midnight, Top Hat, Shall We Dance, Bachelor Mother, Kitty Foyle* (Oscar, 1940), *I'll Be Seeing You, Storm Warning*, and *Dreamboat*.

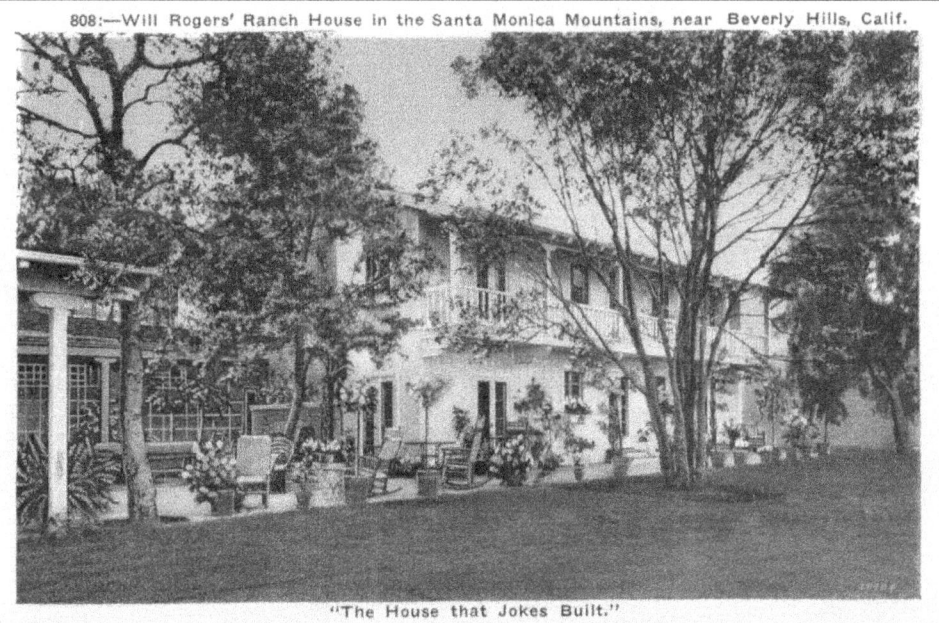

808:—Will Rogers' Ranch House in the Santa Monica Mountains, near Beverly Hills, Calif.

"The House that Jokes Built."

WILL ROGERS. Describing his new Beverly Hills house in 1920, Will Rogers (1879–1935) told *Photoplay* magazine the following: "I call this 'The House That Jokes Built,' cause I done it with money." Topping a crest, the mansion was flanked by trees and shrubbery. The beloved folksy comedian starred in *The Headless Horseman, Lightnin', Too Busy to Work, State Fair, David Harum, The County Chairman, Judge Priest,* and *Doubting Thomas.*

CESAR ROMERO. From the 1930s to the 1940s, Cesar Romero (1907–1994) lived at 1325 Hayward Avenue and, from the 1940s through the 1960s, at 3631 Saltair Avenue, Brentwood. The legendary actor of Spanish Italian descent starred in many films, including *The Devil Is a Woman* (1935), *15 Maiden Lane* (1936), and six Cisco Kid Westerns (1939–1941). Romero scored hits on television with *Passport to Danger* (1954–1958) and as the Joker on *Batman* (1966–1968).

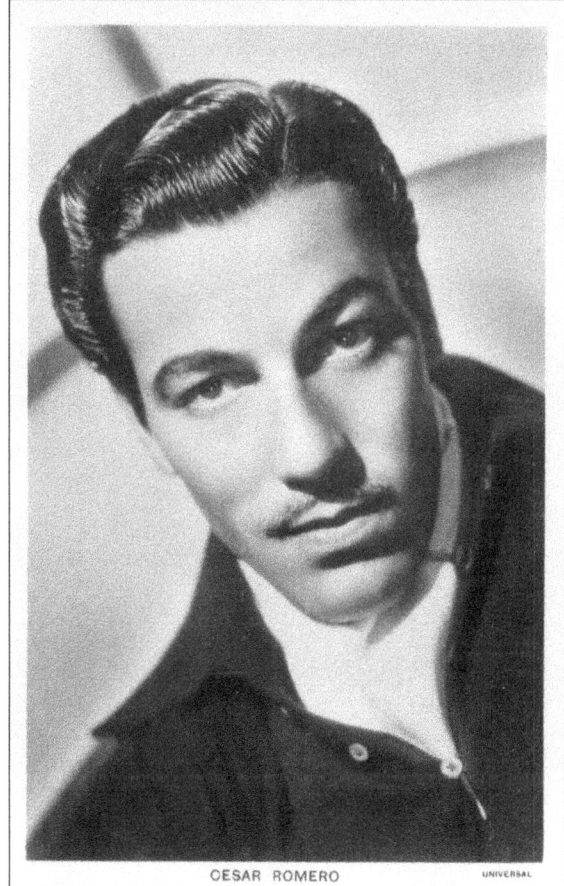

CESAR ROMERO   UNIVERSAL

107

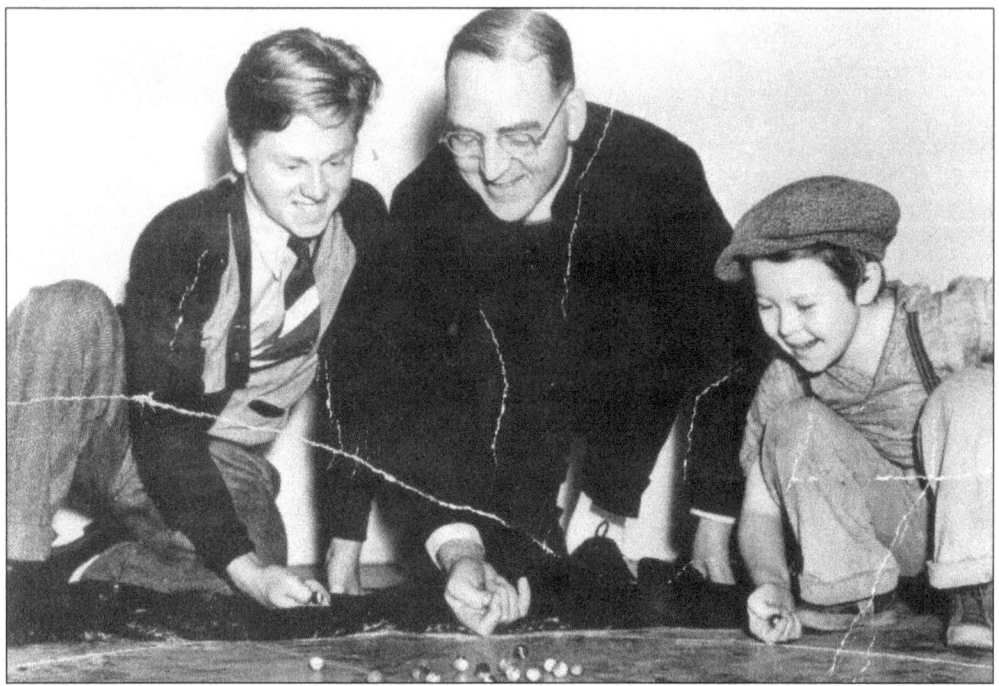

MICKEY ROONEY PICTURE POSTCARD. In 1938, actor Mickey Rooney (left) is seen playing marbles with Fr. Edward Flanagan and child actor Bobs Watson in a relaxing moment between filming scenes of *Boys Town*, which was partly shot at Father Flanagan's Boys Town in Nebraska. The Metro-Goldwyn-Mayer biographical drama, highlighting juvenile delinquency and underprivileged children and the challenges of correction and reform, starred Spencer Tracy and Mickey Rooney.

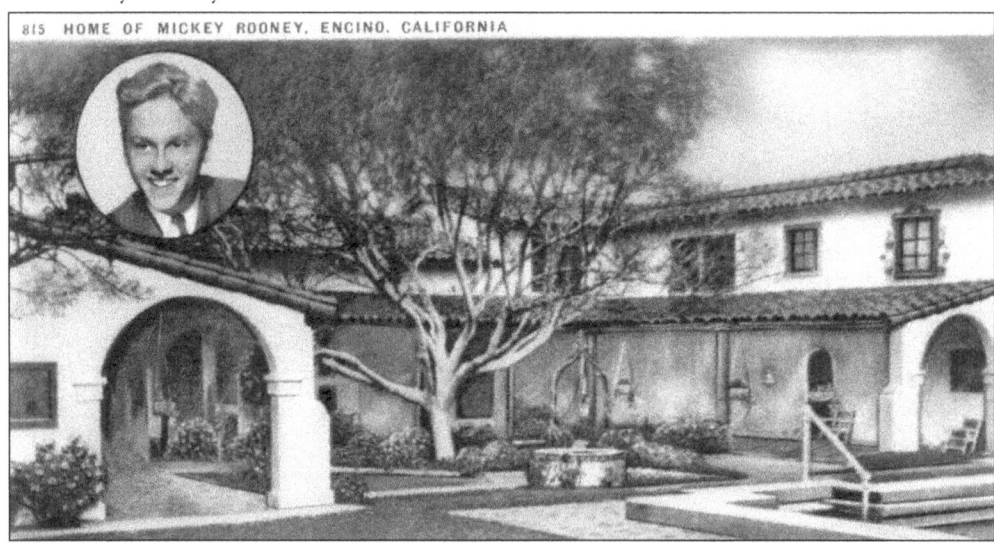

MICKEY ROONEY. In the 1940s, actor Mickey Rooney (1920–2014) lived in this house at 16780 Oak View Drive, Encino. Rooney, born Joseph Yule Jr., had a career that lasted 88 years. Aside from the 16 films he was featured in as Andy Hardy (1937–1958), his other films include *A Midsummer Night's Dream*, *Boys Town*, *Stablemates*, *Young Tom Edison*, *The Human Comedy*, *Girl Crazy*, *National Velvet*, *Words and Music*, and *Quicksand*.

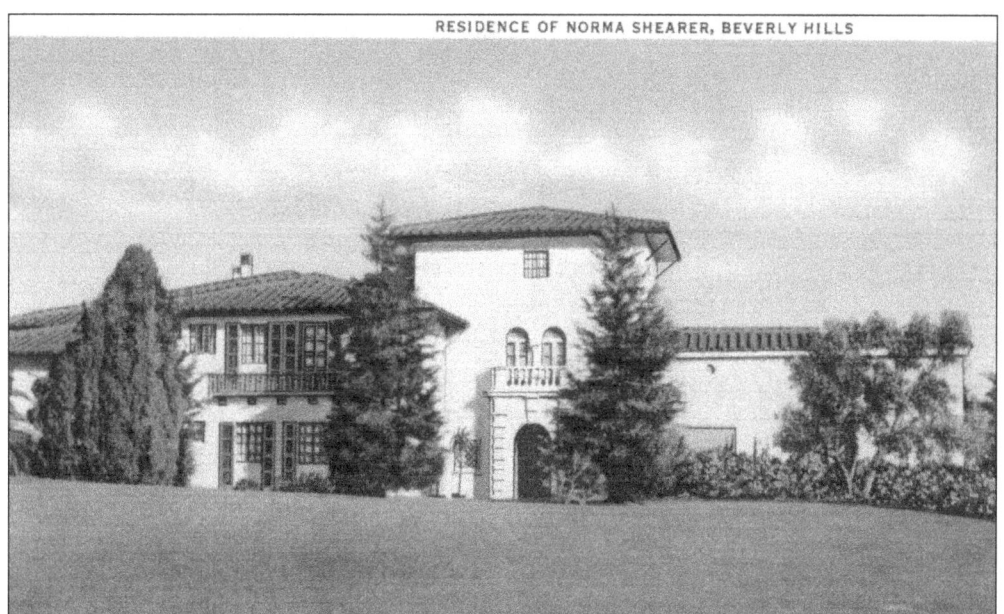

NORMA SHEARER. Accomplished actress and film star Norma Shearer (1902–1983) and her husband, MGM producer Irving Thalberg, lived at 724 North Linden Drive, Beverly Hills. Norma Shearer rose to stardom in silent films, such as *He Who Gets Slapped*, *Lady of the Night*, and *The Demi-Bride*. She continued as a major star in sound films, which include *A Free Soul*, *Strange Interlude*, *Riptide*, *Marie Antoinette*, and *Idiot's Delight*.

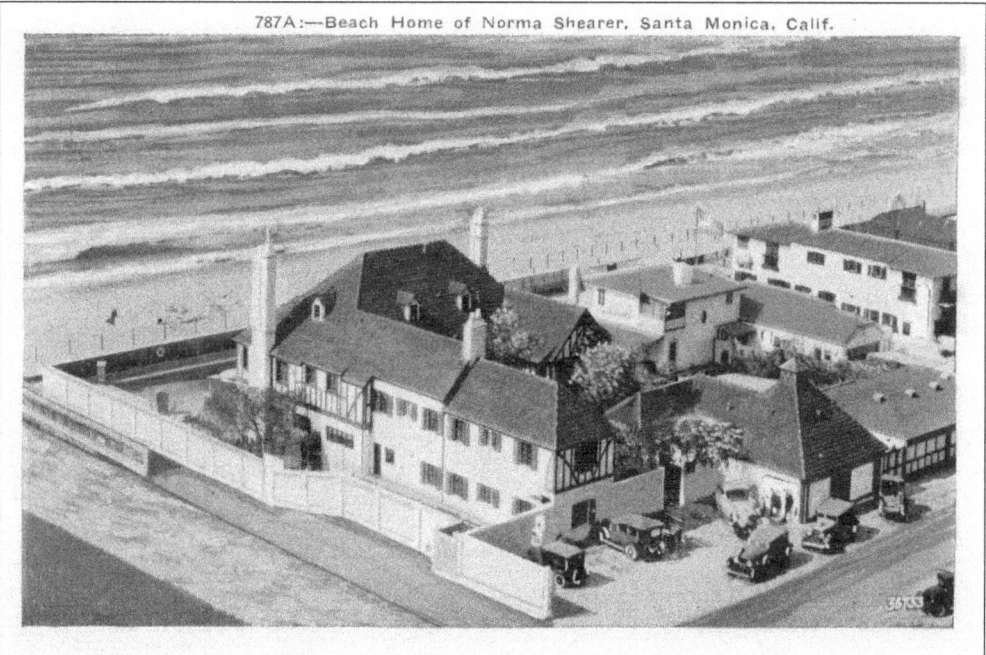

787A:—Beach Home of Norma Shearer, Santa Monica, Calif.

NORMA SHEARER'S BEACHFRONT ESTATE. This was the Santa Monica beachfront estate of Norma Shearer and husband, Irving Thalberg (1899–1936), a motion picture producer. The French Provincial–style residence was designed by John Byers (1875–1966) and built on Ocean Front Avenue in 1931. Among its luxuries was a screening room for the projection of motion pictures.

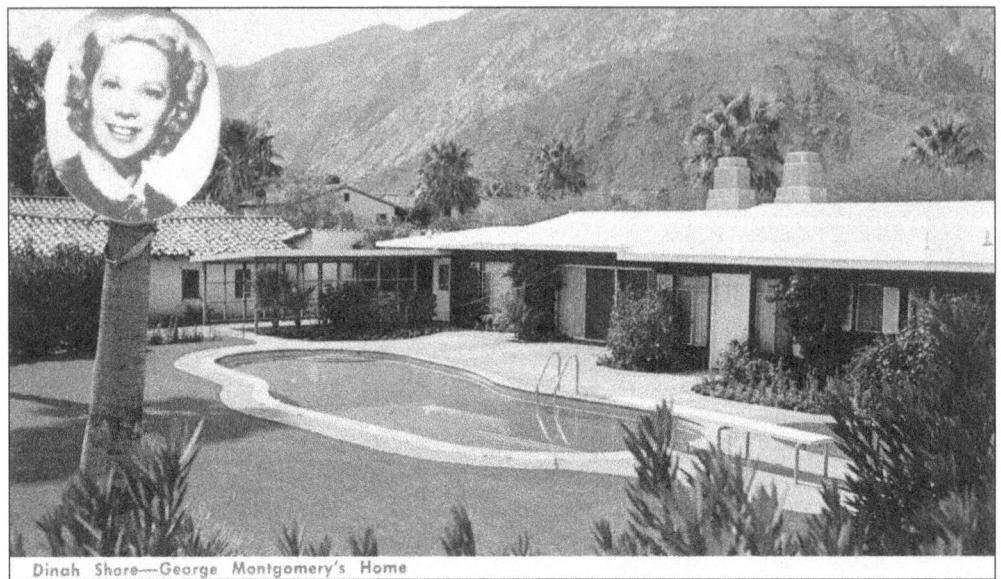

Dinah Shore—George Montgomery's Home

DINAH SHORE AND GEORGE MONTGOMERY. Here is the home of Dinah Shore and George Montgomery, one of Hollywood's popular couples, who were married from 1943 to 1963, at 317 Camino Norte West, Palm Springs. Dinah Shore (1916–1994), a popular band singer and recording artist, later became a perennial television personality with shows like *The Dinah Shore Chevy Show* and *Dinah's Place*. Montana-born George Montgomery (1916–2000) was a romantic leading man and then a star of Westerns, including television's *Cimarron City*.

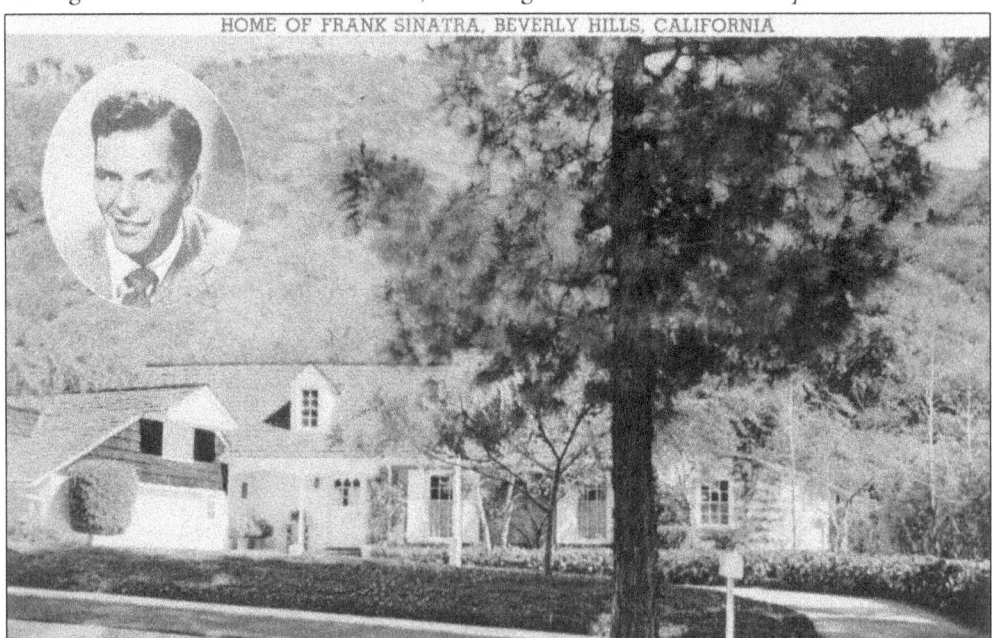

HOME OF FRANK SINATRA, BEVERLY HILLS, CALIFORNIA

FRANK SINATRA. Singer–actor Frank Sinatra (1915–1998) lived in this house in Beverly Hills in the 1950s. Although his later homes were more lavish, this postcard highlights Sinatra's lifestyle when he was younger. In the early 1950s, Sinatra, after a career slump, reasserted himself as a top recording artist and became a popular actor. His films included *From Here to Eternity*, *Guys and Dolls*, *Young at Heart*, *High Society*, and *Pal Joey*.

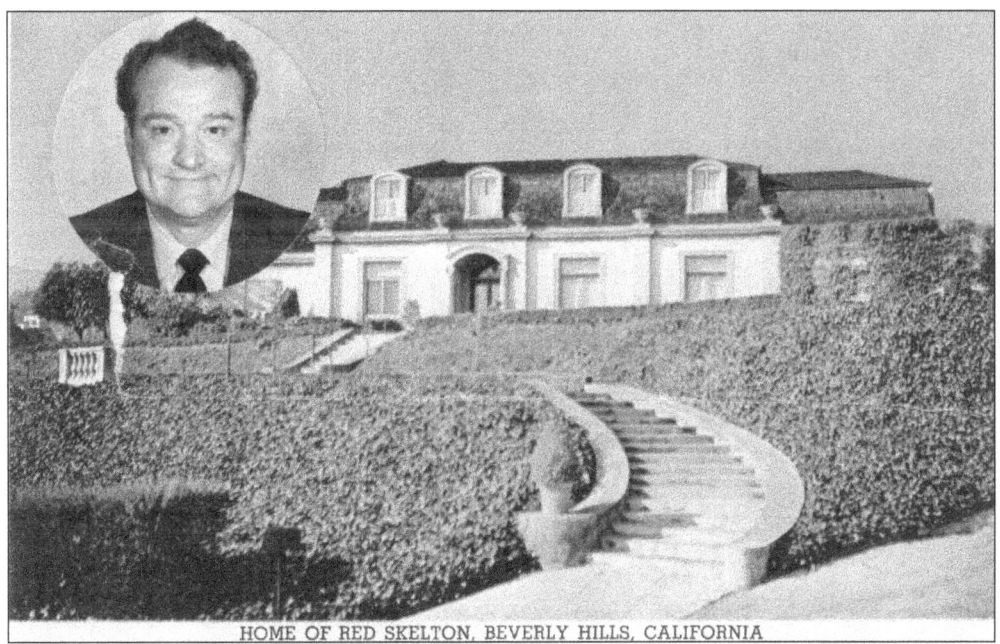

HOME OF RED SKELTON, BEVERLY HILLS, CALIFORNIA

RED SKELTON. Pictured here is Red Skelton's 13-bedroom mansion at 801 North Sarbonne Road, Bel Air. In 1957, Skelton suffered a nearly fatal asthma attack there. Skelton, one of the most original and beloved comedians of his time, starred in such films as *Whistling in the Dark*, *A Southern Yankee*, *The Fuller Brush Man*, and *The Clown* as well as on his hit television program *The Red Skelton Show* (1951–1971).

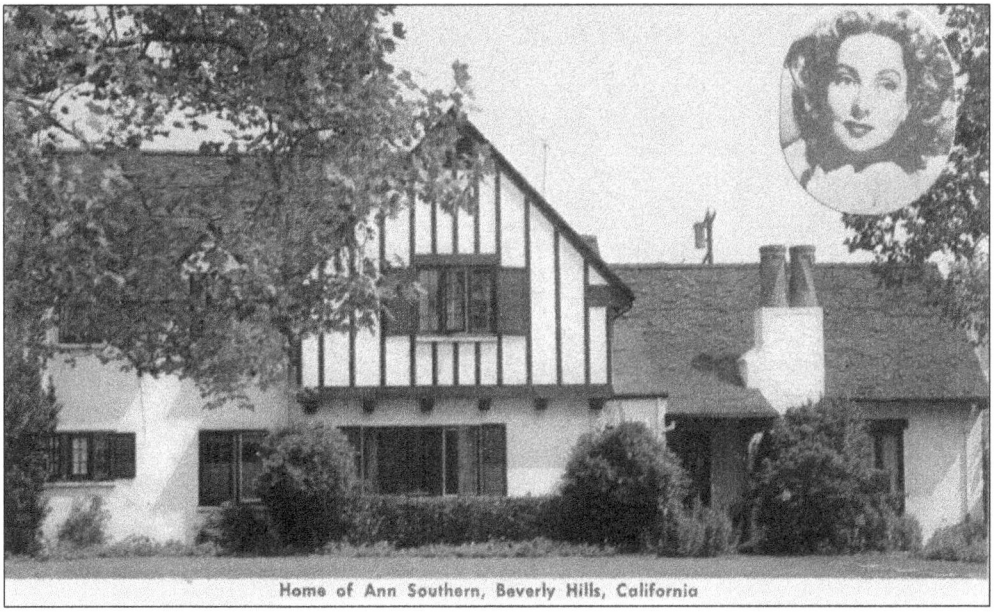

Home of Ann Southern, Beverly Hills, California

ANN SOTHERN. This 1960s postcard depicts the Beverly Hills home of Ann Sothern (1909–2001); the house was once labeled as "one of the beautiful homes of the stars." At the time of the postcard, Sothern was a television favorite; however, her career was a long one. Her screen credits go back to the 1930s with *The Smartest Girl in Town*, *Danger—Love at Work*, *Walking on Air*, *Panama Hattie*, and a series of 10 MGM comedies as showgirl Maisie Ravier (1939–1947).

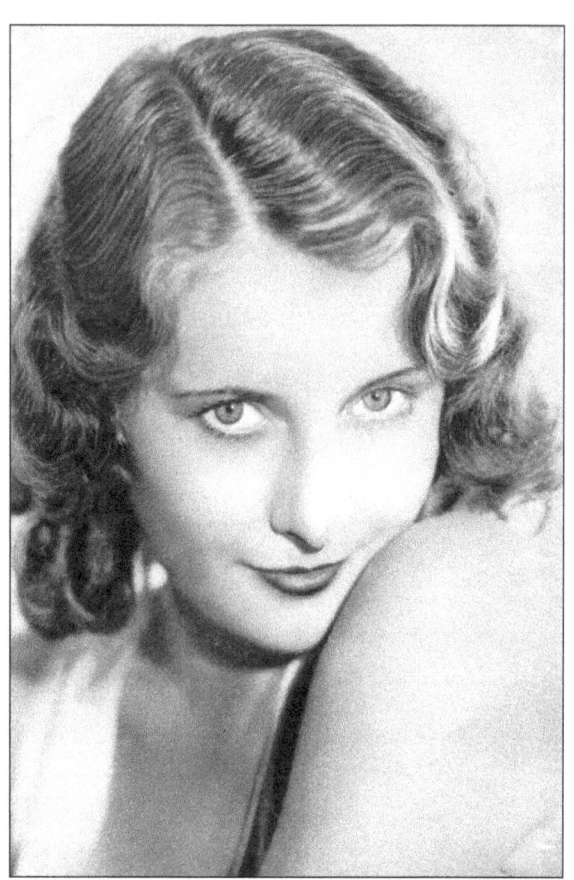

BARBARA STANWYCK PORTRAIT.
Pictured here is Barbara Stanwyck
when she captivated audiences in
the beginning of her career. Her
first starring films were *The Locked
Door* and *Mexicali Rose* (both 1929)
and *Ladies of Leisure* (1930). From
1928 to 1935, she was the wife of
vaudeville's master comedian of wit
and barbs, Frank Fay, who later made
a spectacular comeback on Broadway
as Elwood P. Dowd in *Harvey* (1944).

BARBARA STANWYCK. Barbara
Stanwyck lived in this house in
Beverly Hills in the 1950s and 1960s.
One of the screen's enduring favorites,
Stanwyck (1907–1990) starred in *So
Big*, *Baby Face*, *The Ladies They Talk
About*, and *The Lady Eve* and received
Oscar nominations for *Stella Dallas*,
Ball of Fire, *Double Indemnity*, and
Sorry, Wrong Number. She was married
twice, first to funnyman Frank
Fay and then to movie heartthrob
Robert Taylor.

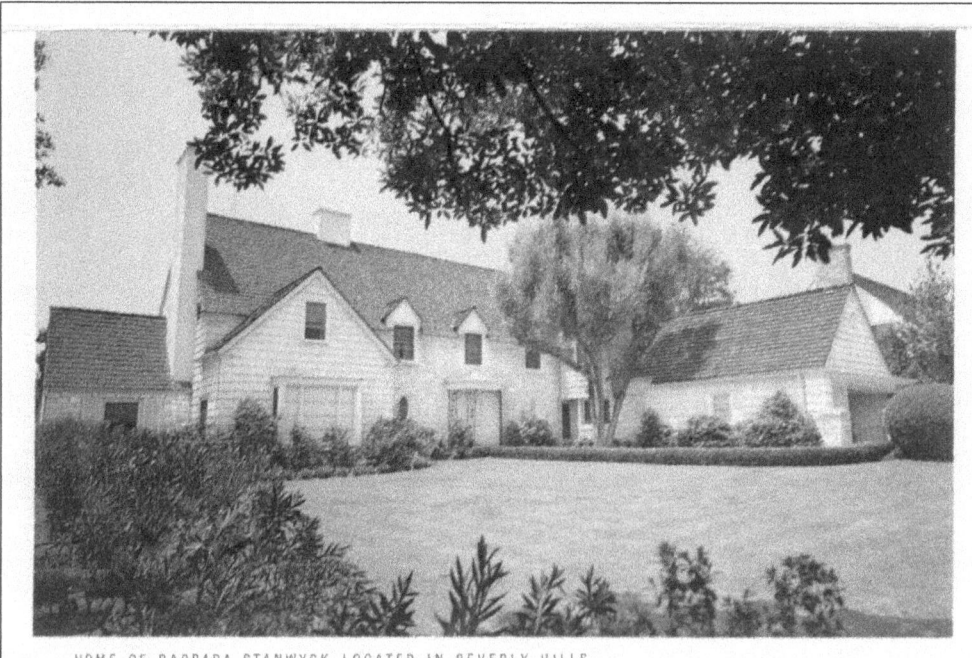

HOME OF BARBARA STANWYCK LOCATED IN BEVERLY HILLS

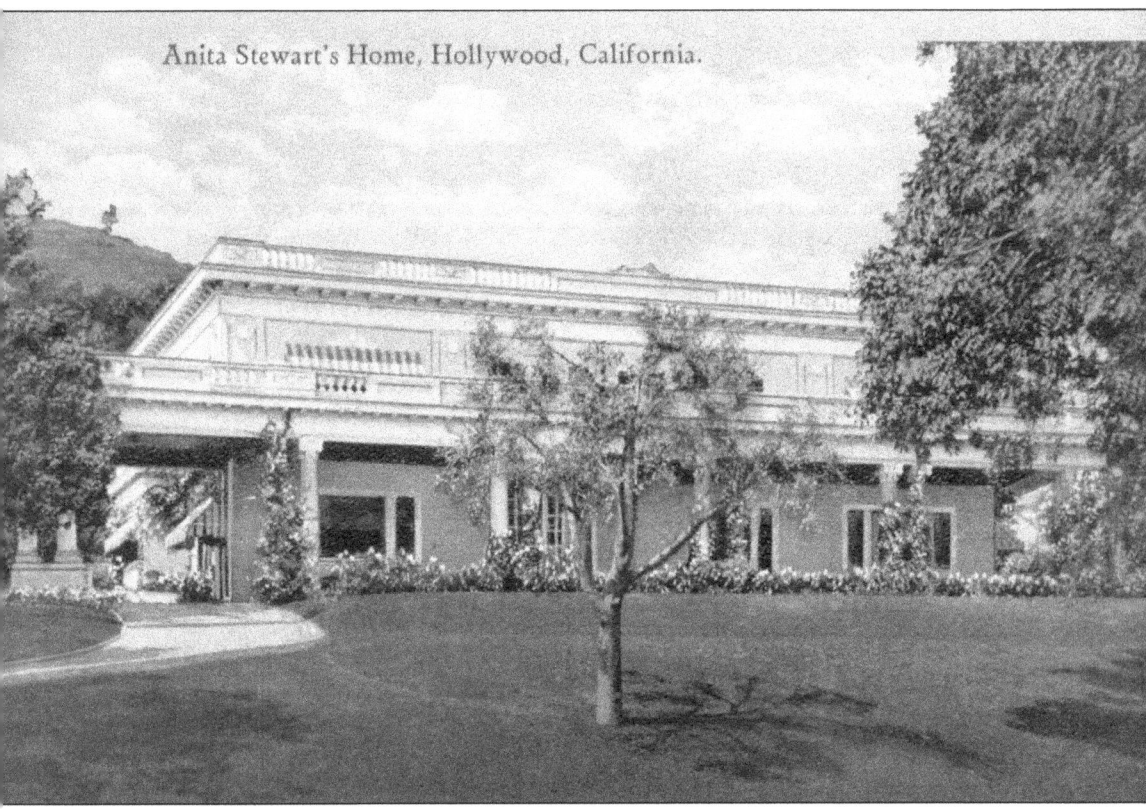

Anita Stewart's Home, Hollywood, California.

ANITA STEWART. In 1925, silent film idol Anita Stewart (1895–1961) bought this palatial mansion at 7425 Franklin Avenue, Hollywood. It was gorgeous, inside and out. Stewart's popularity once even rivaled Mary Pickford's. Stewart's films include *The Glory of Yolanda*, *Shadows of the Past*, *The Painted World*, *Human Desire*, *My Lady's Slippers*, and *Rose of the Sea*. In 1935, she penned *The Devil's Toy*, a mystery novel. On the back of this Anita Stewart postcard is the following message: "They all have such beautiful homes that I think I'll try and get into the movies. Ha, ha. I wish you folks lived here." The Western Publishing & Novelty Company, headed by immigrant entrepreneur Theodore Sohmer (1880–1938), published the card.

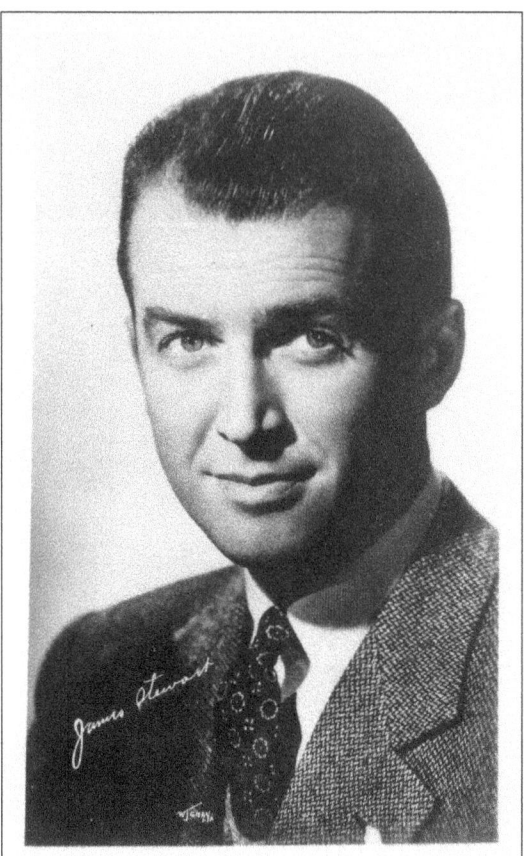

JAMES STEWART PICTURE POSTCARD. A native son of Indiana, Pennsylvania, the future actor was born James Maitland Stewart. His father, Alexander Stewart, was a hardware merchant, and his mother, Elizabeth, was a housewife. There were also two sisters, Mary and Virginia. Stewart began acting while at his alma mater, Princeton University (1928–1932). His professional career on the stage began after graduation. He made his screen debut as Shorty in *The Murder Man* (1935).

JAMES STEWART. James Stewart (1908–1997) enjoyed a long career as a major star. His home was at 918 North Roxbury Drive, Beverly Hills. With a down-to-earth manner and superb acting skills, he took on diverse roles in such films as *The Shop Around the Corner, Mr. Smith Goes to Washington, The Philadelphia Story* (Oscar, 1940), *You Can't Take It with You, It's a Wonderful Life, Harvey, The Spirit of St. Louis,* and *Vertigo.*

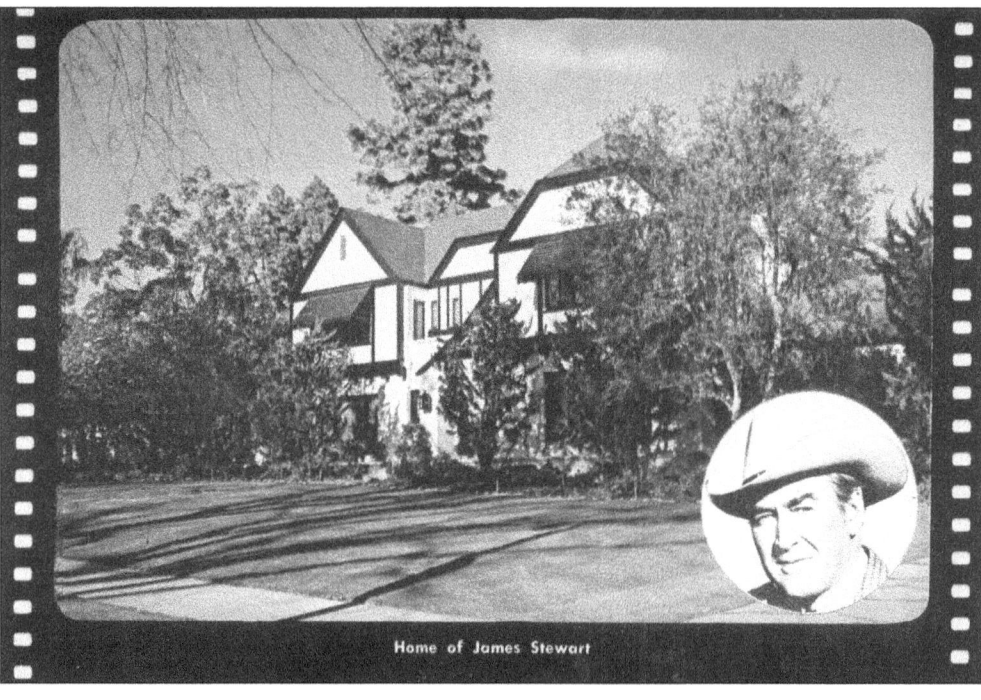

Home of James Stewart

Gloria Swanson Picture Postcard. Published in Paris in the noted cinema stars series "Les Vedettes de Cinéma," this postcard features Gloria Swanson holding a copy of *The Shulamite* in a scene promoting her new film, *Under the Lash*, a 1921 dramatization of the stage play and Edwardian novel pictured. Swanson was marvelous, but the film did not fare well at the box office.

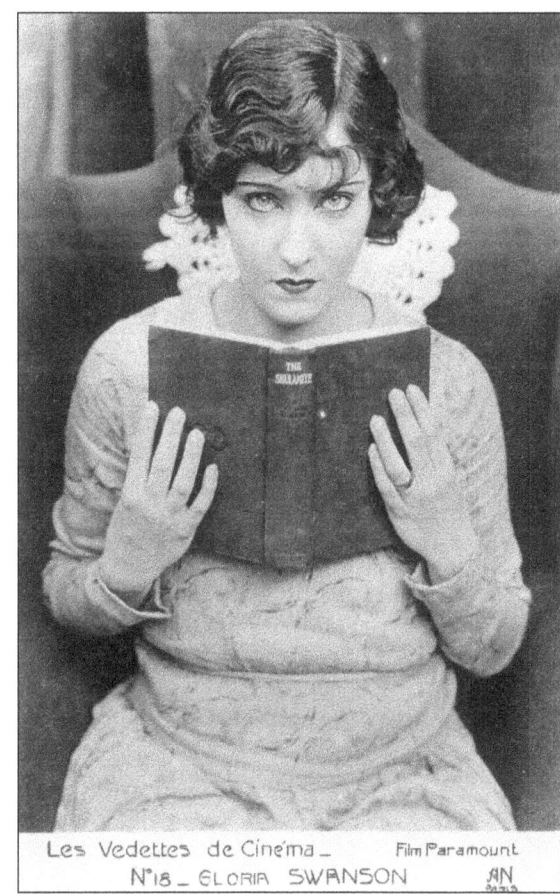

Les Vedettes de Cinéma _   Film Paramount
N°18 _ GLORIA SWANSON

Gloria Swanson. In 1922, superstar Gloria Swanson (1899–1983) paid safety razor blade inventor King Gillette $200,000 for this 22-room Italian Renaissance mansion at 904 North Crescent Drive, Beverly Hills. By 1938, her film career was in decline, so she gave up the mansion and moved to New York. Swanson's films include *Her Gilded Cage*, *Manhandled*, *The Coast of Folly*, and *Sadie Thompson*. In 1950, she made a dazzling comeback in the unforgettable drama *Sunset Boulevard*.

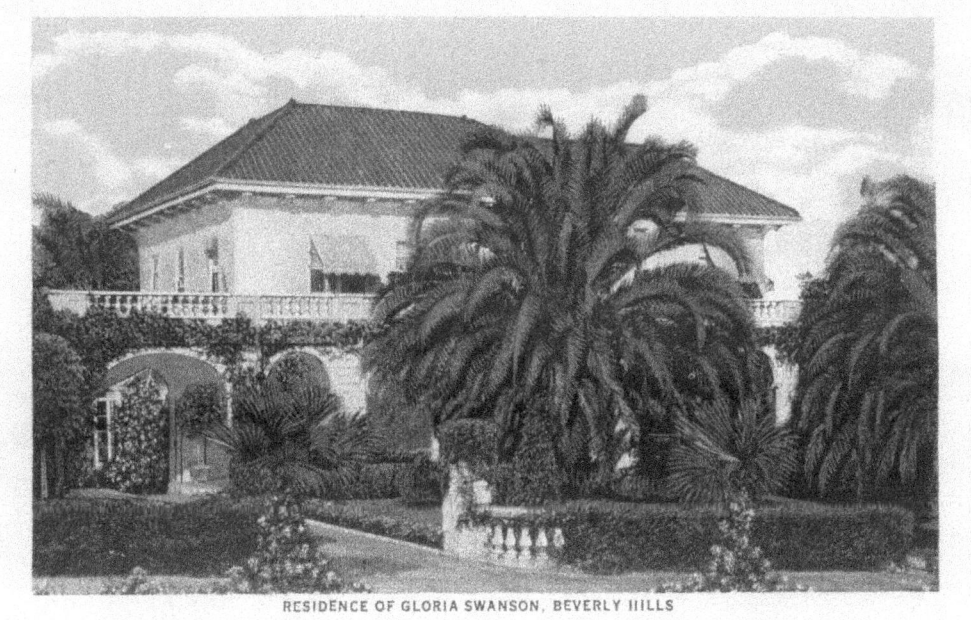

RESIDENCE OF GLORIA SWANSON, BEVERLY HILLS

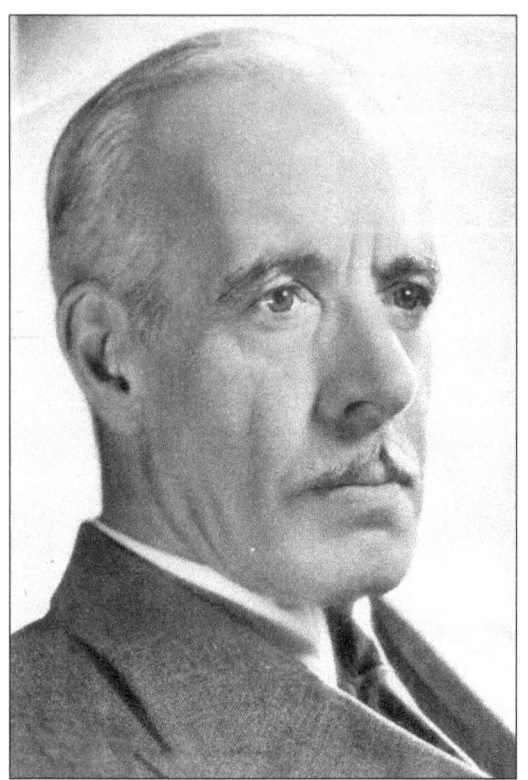

LEWIS STONE PORTRAIT. Actor Lewis Stone had a long career on stage and on screen. He starred in silent films, including *The Prisoner of Zenda* (1922). Later, he had a flourishing career in the sound era and is especially remembered as Judge Hardy in the 14 Andy Hardy movies. From 1930 until his death, Stone lived at his Spanish ranch La Casa Sueno at 5700 Rhodes Avenue, North Hollywood.

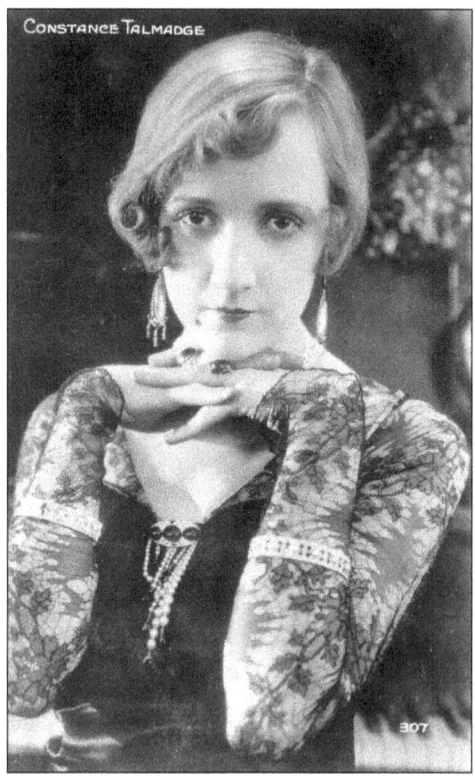

CONSTANCE TALMADGE. Vivacious Constance Talmadge (1898–1973) was deft at romantic comedy as is evident in sparkling comedies like *A Pair of Silk Stockings*, *The Love Expert*, and *Her Sister from Paris* (1925), in which she portrays a neglected wife who has her glamorous twin sister brazenly flirt with her husband, portrayed by Ronald Colman, to test his devotion. Talmadge and her second husband, Townsend Netcher, lived at 1020 Palisades Beach, Santa Monica.

NORMA TALMADGE PORTRAIT.
Constance Talmadge's older and more famous sister Norma Talmadge is seen here in a still from *Secrets* (First National). Directed by Frank Borzage in 1924, *Secrets* was a highly successful drama that delighted her fans. Her leading man was Eugene O'Brien. The film was remade as a sound film in 1933 with Norma Talmadge's friend Mary Pickford in the leading role.

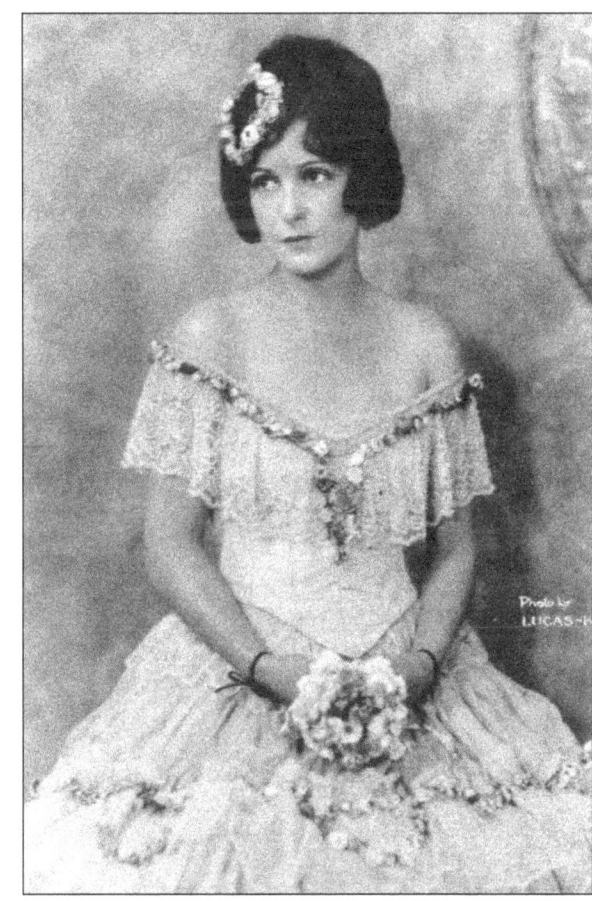

NORMA TALMADGE. Norma Talmadge (1894–1957) was one of the greatest stars of the 1920s with a string of smash hits, including *Smilin' Through*, *Secrets*, *Song of Love*, *Kiki*, and *Camille*. Later, like others terrified by talkies, she took speaking lessons. But she only took a chance on two talkies, *New York Nights* and *Du Barry, Woman of Passion*. She and her husband, producer Joseph Schenck, lived at 7269 Hollywood Boulevard.

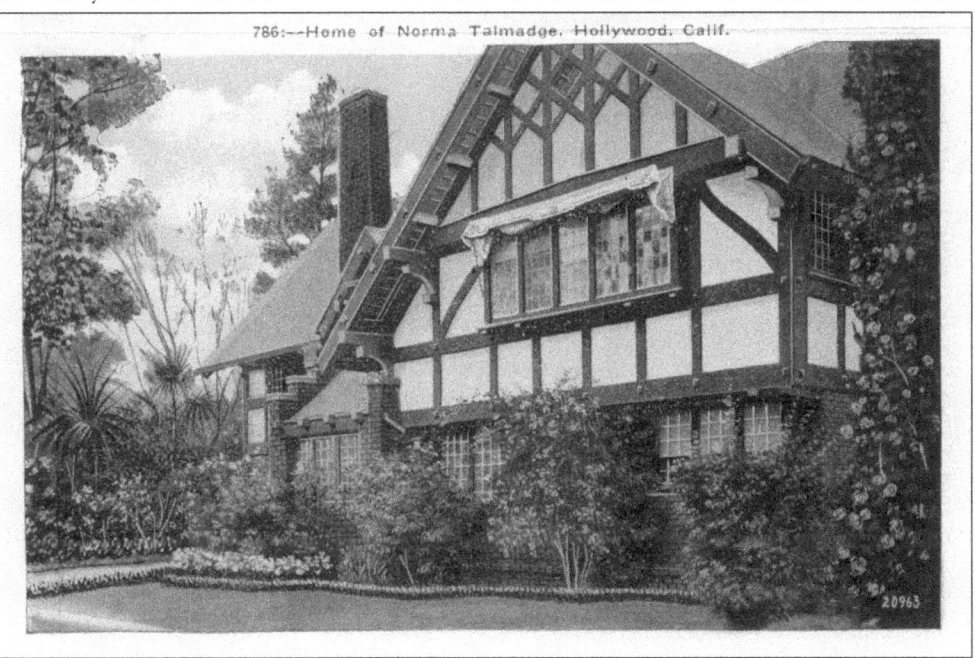

786:--Home of Norma Talmadge. Hollywood, Calif.

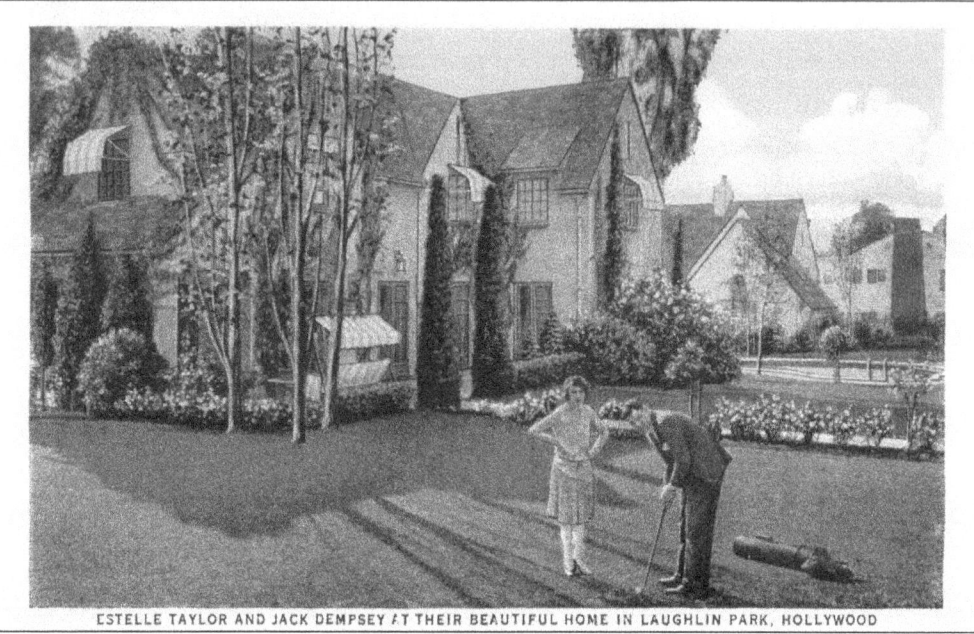

ESTELLE TAYLOR AND JACK DEMPSEY AT THEIR BEAUTIFUL HOME IN LAUGHLIN PARK, HOLLYWOOD

ESTELLE TAYLOR. In 1925, actress Estelle Taylor (1894–1958) lived at 5254 Los Feliz Boulevard, Hollywood, with her second husband, heavyweight champion boxer Jack Dempsey (1895–1983). Their matrimonial venture ended in a Reno, Nevada, divorce court in 1931. The popular screen star's silent films include *Tiger Love*, *Passion's Pathway*, *Playthings of Desire*, and *Where East Is East*. Her sound films include *Lilliom*, *Cimarron*, *Street Scene*, and *The Southerner* (1945), with Zachary Scott.

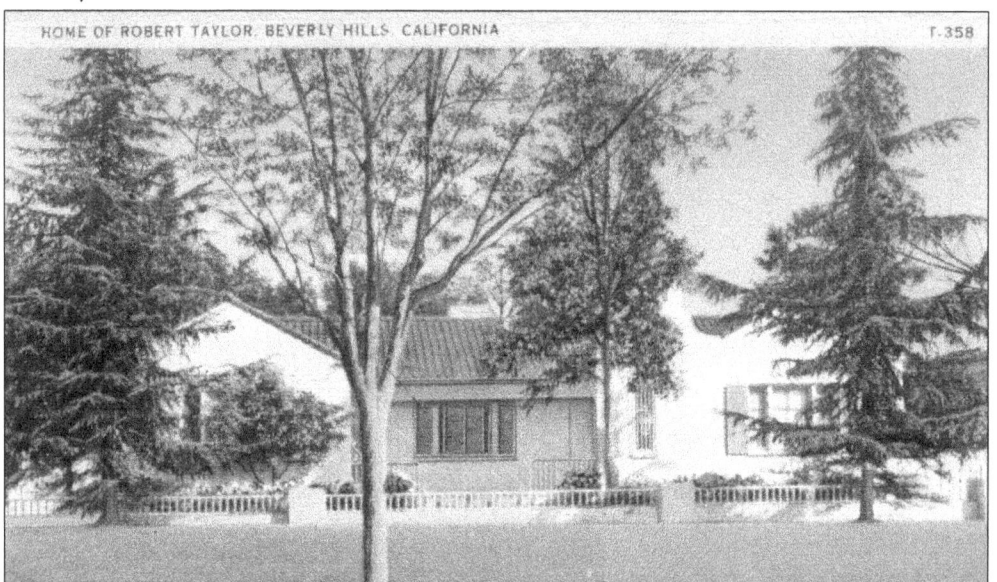

HOME OF ROBERT TAYLOR, BEVERLY HILLS, CALIFORNIA T-358

ROBERT TAYLOR. After achieving success in the 1930s, actor Robert Taylor (1911–1969) lived in this house at 510 North Roxbury Drive, Beverly Hills. In 1939, he married actress Barbara Stanwyck and moved away. A major star, Taylor was in *Magnificent Obsession*, *Camille*, *A Yank at Oxford*, *Billy the Kid*, *Her Cardboard Lover*, *Bataan*, *Ivanhoe*, and *Rogue Cop*. In 1966, he succeeded Ronald Reagan as host of television's *Death Valley Days*.

SHIRLEY TEMPLE PORTRAIT.
Shirley Temple had a career in
motion pictures that spanned 17
years and 44 films. As she grew
up, she essayed adult roles despite
the consternation of her fans.
In this period, her top leading
men included Guy Madison
(*Kiss and Tell*), Cary Grant (*The
Bachelor and the Bobby-Soxer*), and
Ronald Reagan (*That Hagen Girl*).
From 1958 to 1961, she starred
on NBC television in *Shirley
Temple's Storybook.*

SHIRLEY TEMPLE. The screen's
greatest child star was Shirley
Temple, who lived with her
parents, George and Gertrude
Temple, and her brothers,
Jack and George Jr., at 227
North Rockingham Avenue,
Brentwood. Phenomenally
talented, Shirley Temple (1928–
2014) topped the bill in such
films as *Little Miss Marker, Bright
Eyes, The Little Colonel, Curly
Top, Stowaway, Poor Little Rich
Girl, Heidi, The Little Princess,* and
Rebecca of Sunnybrook Farm.

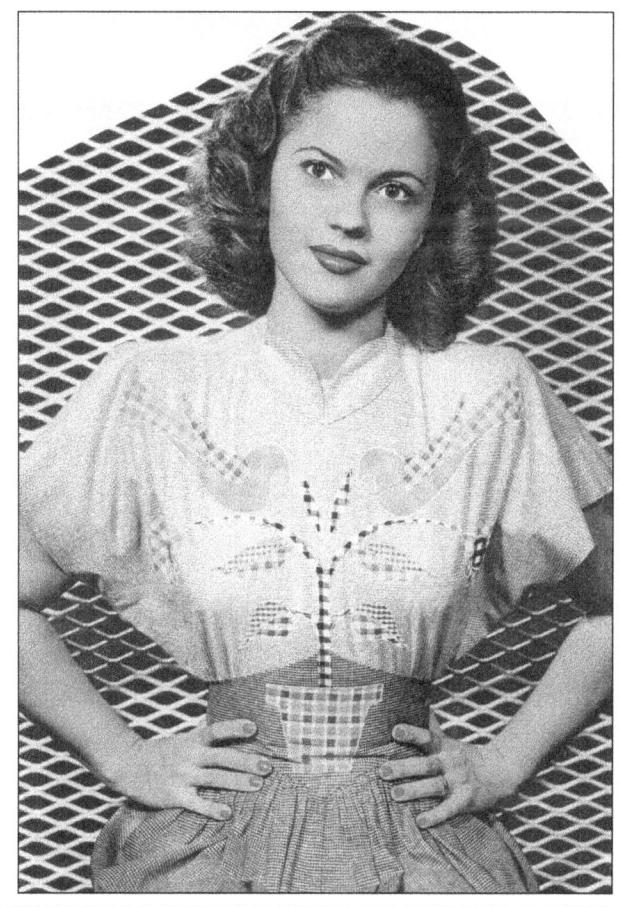

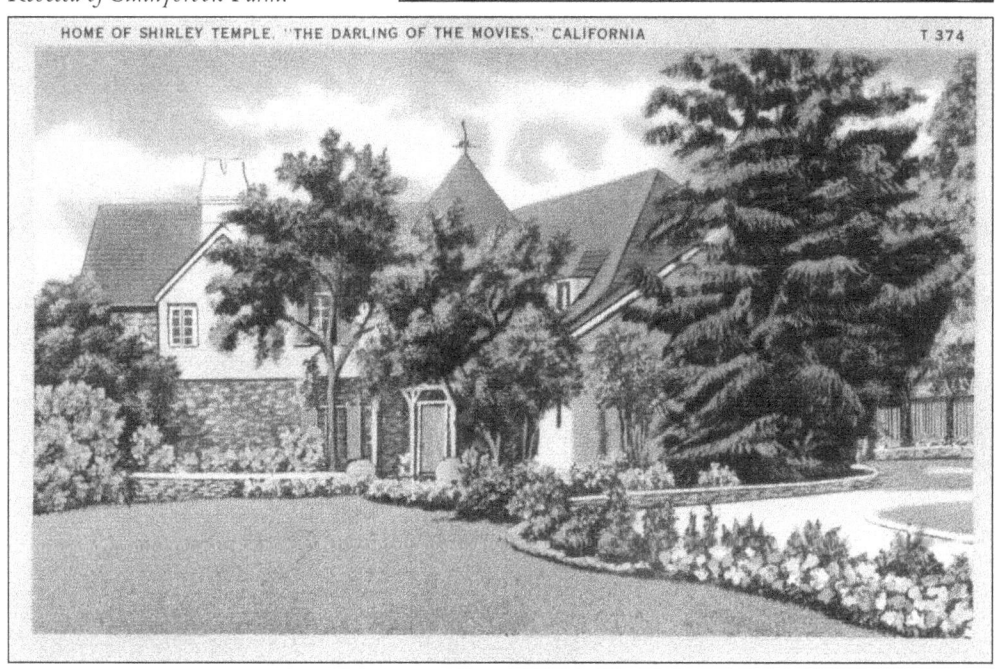

HOME OF SHIRLEY TEMPLE, "THE DARLING OF THE MOVIES," CALIFORNIA   T 374

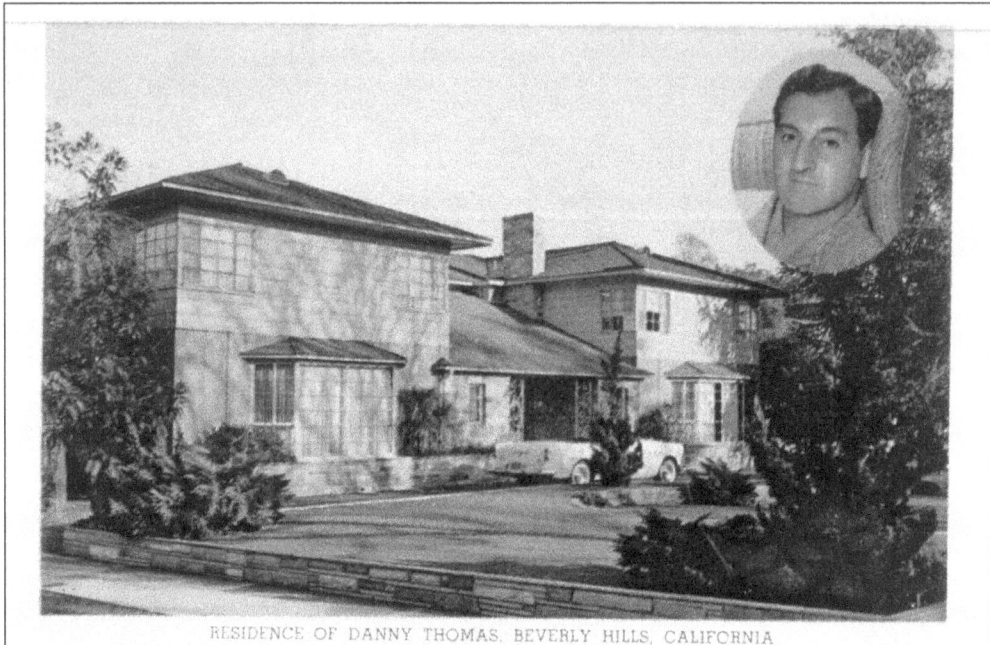

RESIDENCE OF DANNY THOMAS, BEVERLY HILLS, CALIFORNIA

DANNY THOMAS. Although comedian Danny Thomas (1912–1991) made his start in radio and films and did well, it was on television's *Make Room for Daddy* (1953–1964) that cemented his national appeal. Two of his best films are *The Jazz Singer* (1952) and *I'll See You in My Dreams.* Built in 1924, Thomas's Beverly Hills mansion at 630 North Elm Drive had large, spacious, elegant rooms and lovely grounds.

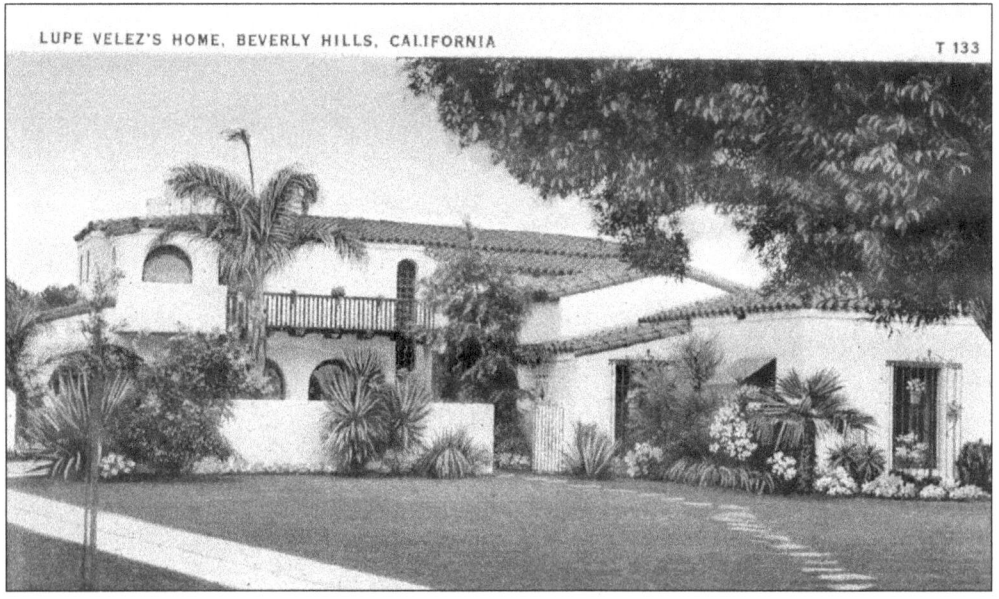

LUPE VELEZ'S HOME, BEVERLY HILLS, CALIFORNIA   T 133

LUPE VÉLEZ. Lupe Vélez (1908–1944), the celebrated actress known as the "Mexican Spitfire," lived at this house at 732 North Rodeo Drive, Beverly Hills. Although she optimistically dubbed it Casa Felicitas, it was later the site of her tragic suicide. Her films include *Lady of the Pavements*, *Wolf Song*, *The Storm*, *Hot Pepper*, *The Half-Naked Truth*, *Laughing Boy*, *Gypsy Melody*, *Stardust*, and eight delightful Mexican Spitfire comedies with Leon Errol.

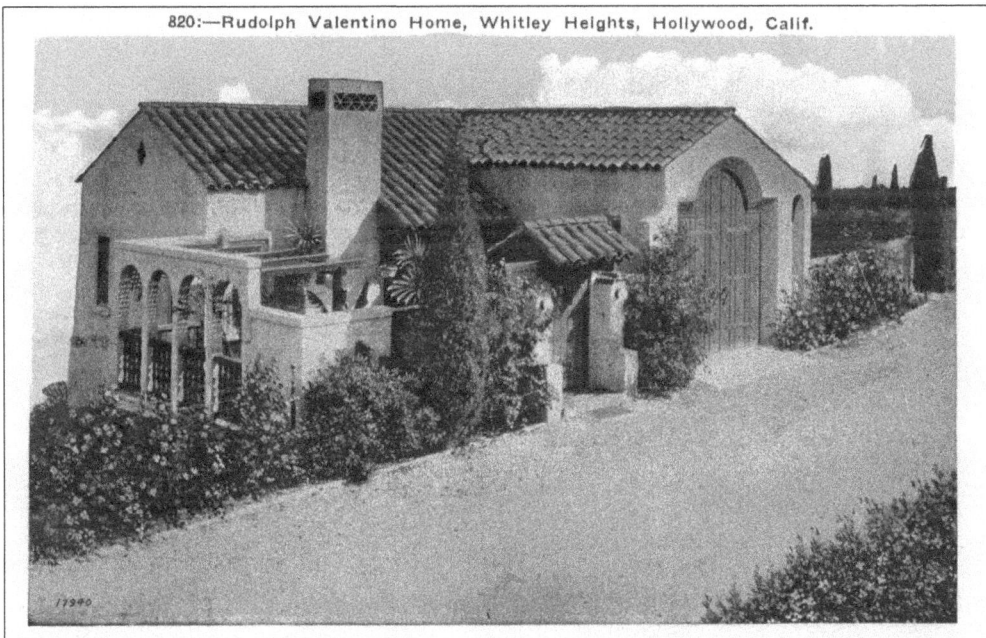

820:—Rudolph Valentino Home, Whitley Heights, Hollywood, Calif.

RUDOLPH VALENTINO. Before buying his famous estate, named Falcon Lair, silent screen heartthrob Rudolph Valentino (1895–1926) lived in this house at 6776 Wedgewood Place, Whitley Heights. The villa was built in 1922 and decorated by his wife, Natacha Rambova. Valentino's most acclaimed films include *The Four Horsemen of the Apocalypse, The Sheik, The Conquering Power, Camille, Beyond the Rocks, Blood and Sand, The Young Rajah,* and *Son of the Sheik.*

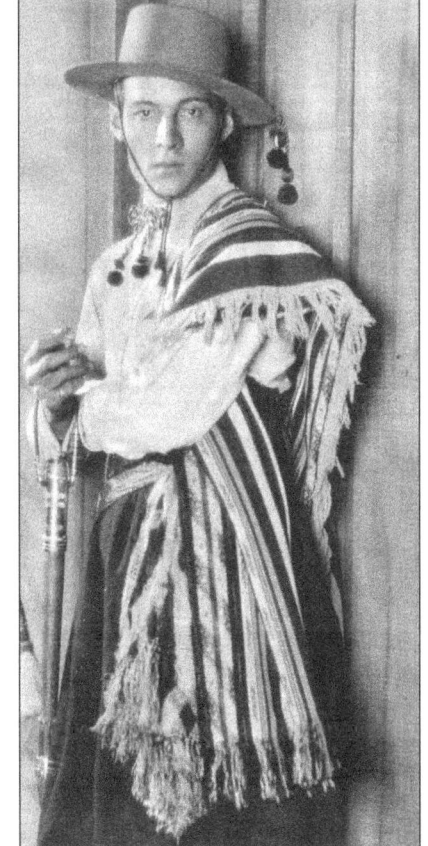

RUDOLPH VALENTINO PORTRAIT. Born in Castellaneta, Apulia, Italy, Valentino was christened Rodolfo Pietro Filiberto Raffaello Guglielmi. His father died when Rodolfo was 11 years old. Coddled by his mother, he did poorly in school. At 17, he sought his fortune in Paris; but at 18, Rodolfo sailed for New York, where he rose from menial jobs to dancing the tango in vaudeville. Eventually, he came to Hollywood and became one of its greatest stars.

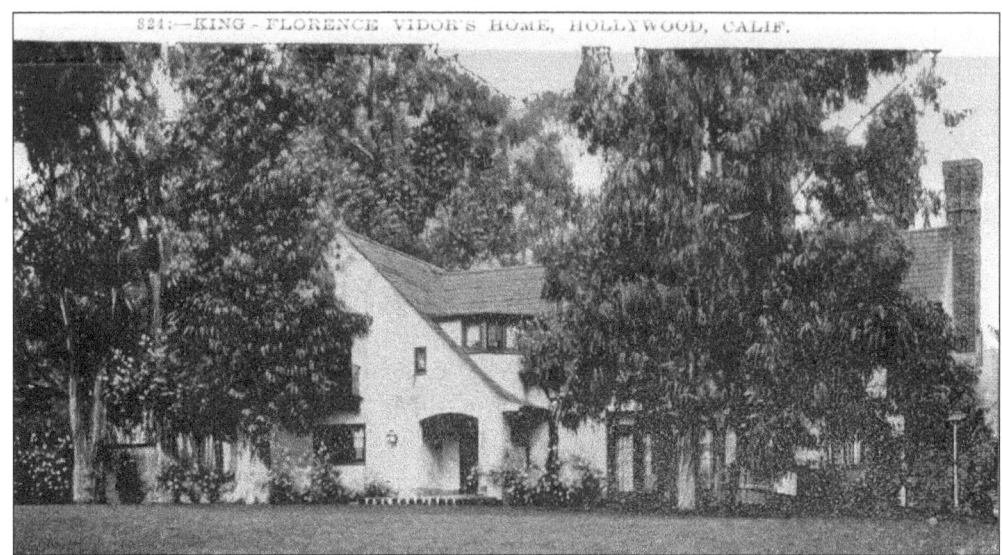

KING AND FLORENCE VIDOR. Director King Vidor and his wife, actress Florence, purchased the Tudor-style mansion at 7919 Selma Avenue, Hollywood, around 1917. The couple's marriage lasted from 1914 to 1925. King Vidor (1894–1982), one of the era's preeminent directors, made the war classic *The Big Parade* (1925). Silent screen actress Florence Vidor (1895–1977) starred in *The Countess Charming*, *Hail the Woman*, *The Virginian*, *Barbara Frietchie*, and *Afraid to Love*.

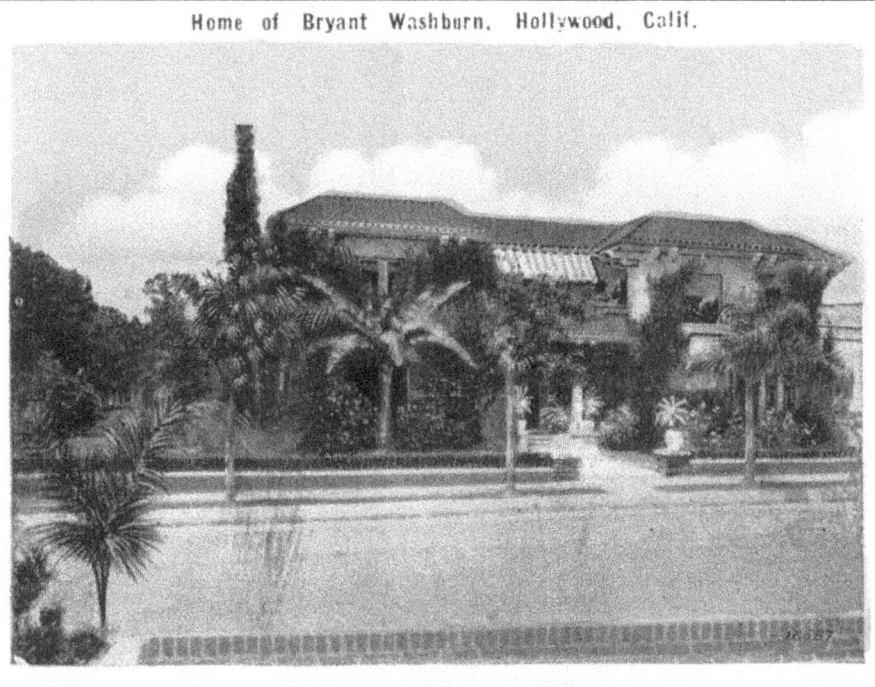

Home of Bryant Washburn, Hollywood, Calif.

BRYANT WASHBURN. Bryant Washburn (1889–1963) was a star of romantic comedies and dramas in the silent era. During the height of his fame, he and his wife, Virginia, lived at 7003 Hawthorn Avenue, Hollywood. His films include *The Whistling Man*, *Hungry Hearts*, *Too Much Johnson*, and *It Pays to Advertise*. Later, he was prominent in such films and serials as *Ellis Island* (1936), *The Spider Returns* (1941), and *Captain Midnight* (1942).

MAE WEST. When Broadway star Mae West (1893–1980) came to Hollywood in 1932, Paramount Pictures moved her into the luxurious Ravenswood Apartments at 570 North Rossmore Avenue. West liked it so much that she stayed there for the rest of her life. Mae West made a huge splash in Hollywood with *She Done Him Wrong, I'm No Angel, Belle of the Nineties, Goin' to Town*, and *Every Day's a Holiday*. Pictured is West in *Myra Breckinridge* (1970).

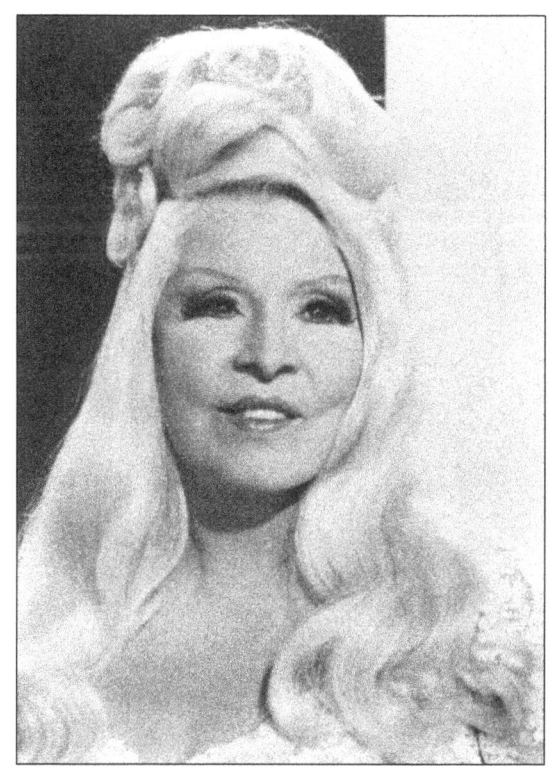

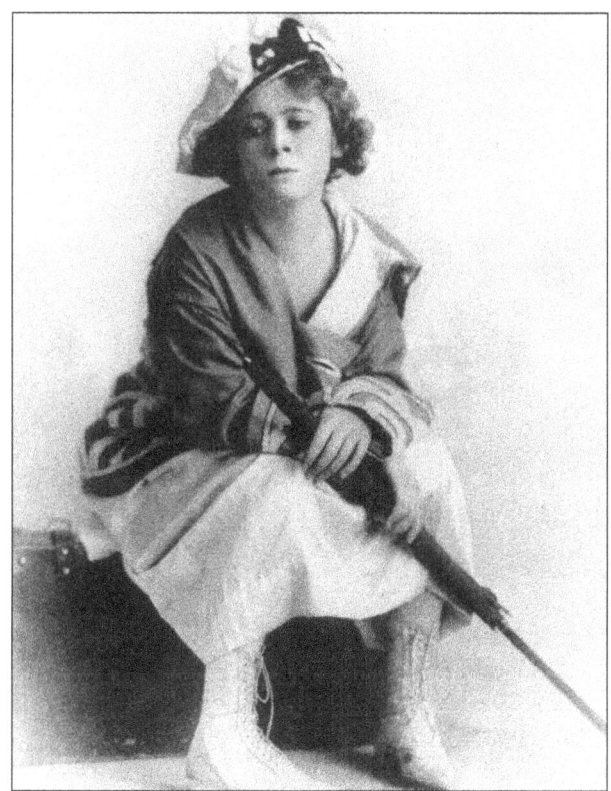

YOUNG MAE WEST. Seen here is Mae West in vaudeville in 1919. In her 1959 autobiography, *Goodness Had Nothing to Do with It*, Mae West wrote that she was born "on a respectable street in Brooklyn." Her parents, John West and Matilda Delker West, had her christened Mary Jane. Her father, a pugilist, retired from the ring and opened a private detective agency; he later worked as a masseur. Before moving to Hollywood, Mae West lived at 200 West Fifty-Seventh Street, Manhattan.

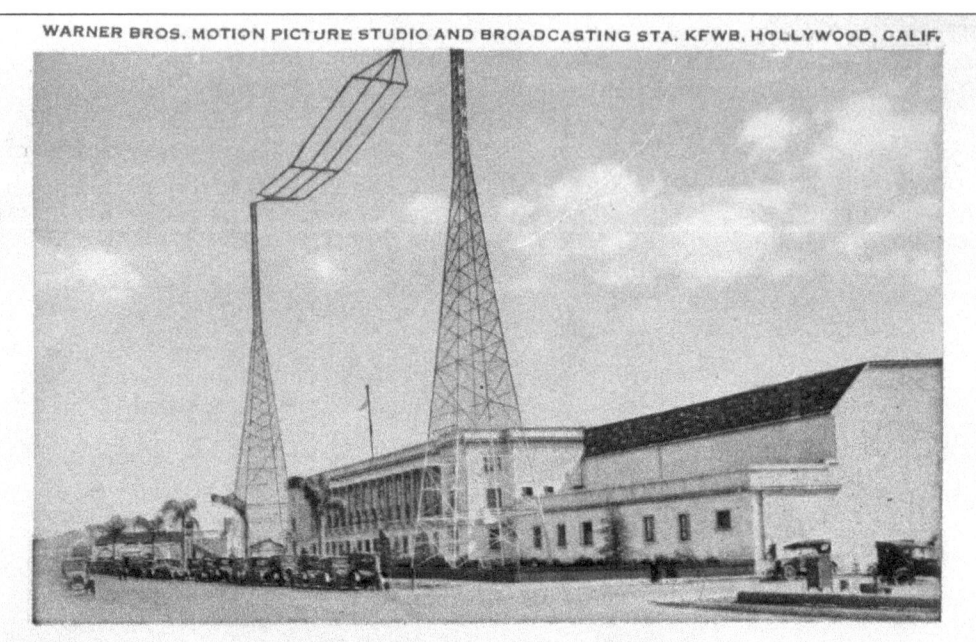

WARNER BROS. PICTURES, INC., 1926. In 1923, Warner Bros. Pictures was formally incorporated. In 1927, it caused a sensation by introducing the first talking feature film, *The Jazz Singer,* ending the silent era. The studio's stars included John Barrymore, Corinne Griffith, Richard Barthelmess, Al Jolson, George Arliss, Warren William, Edward G. Robinson, Paul Muni, James Cagney, Bette Davis, Dick Powell, Joan Blondell, Humphrey Bogart, Olivia De Havilland, Errol Flynn, Ann Sheridan, Ronald Reagan, Jane Wyman, and Doris Day.

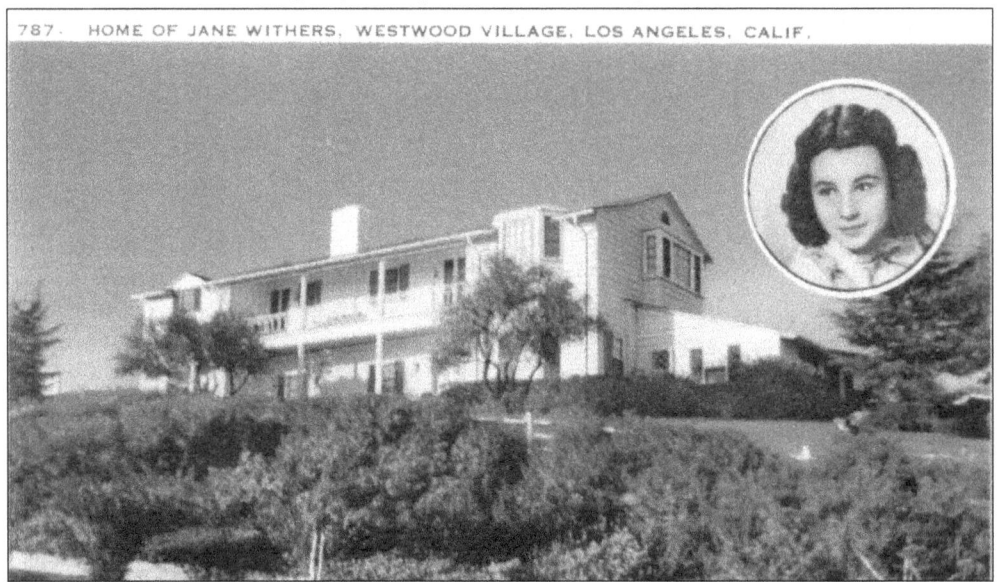

787. HOME OF JANE WITHERS, WESTWOOD VILLAGE, LOS ANGELES, CALIF.

JANE WITHERS. In 1936, child star Jane Withers (born 1926) and her parents, Walter and Ruth Withers, bought this fully modern Old California–style mansion. The "Janns Model Home," christened La Californiana, stood at 10731 Sunset Boulevard, Westwood. It was furnished by Bullock's Department Store. Among Withers's starring films are *This Is the Life, Paddy O'Day, Little Miss Nobody, The Holy Terror, Angel's Holiday, Wild and Woolly,* and *Always in Trouble.*

ANNA MAY WONG. A star of silent and sound films, Anna May Wong (1905–1961) brought not only her talent and beauty to the screen but also her style and panache. Her films include *The Toll of the Sea*, *Song*, *Piccadilly*, *Chu Chin Chow*, *Daughter of the Dragon*, *Limehouse Blues*, and *Dangerous to Know*. On television, she hosted *The Gallery of Madame Liu-Tsong* (1951). She lived at 326 San Vicente Boulevard, Santa Monica.

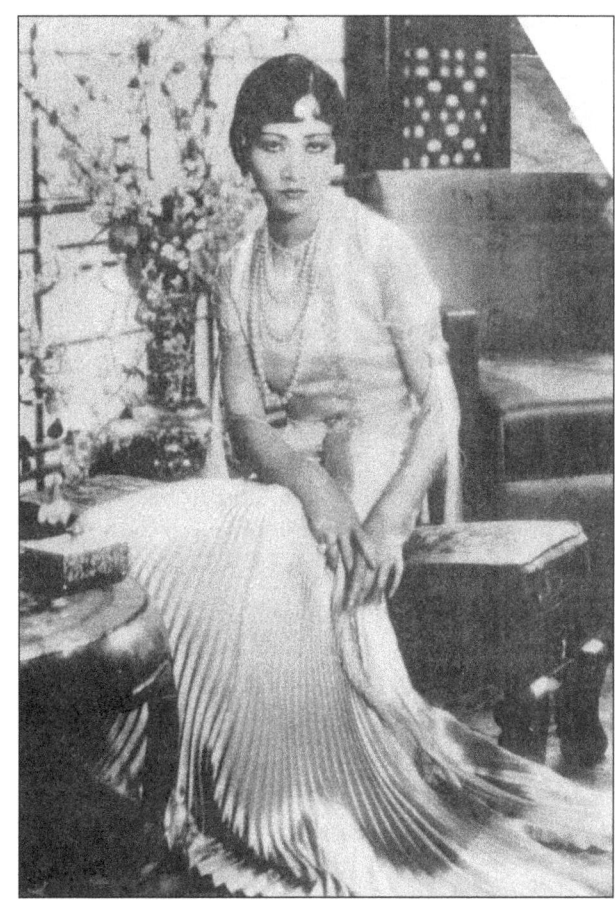

JANE WYMAN. This 1960s postcard shows Jane Wyman's mansion on Rexford Drive, Beverly Hills. Jane Wyman (1917–2007) slowly rose from a Warner Bros. bit player in 1932 to a "B" actress in 1937 and, finally, to an "A" star by 1945. Wyman made four films with her husband, Ronald Reagan, before starring in *The Yearling*, *Johnny Belinda* (Oscar, 1948), *Stage Fright*, *The Glass Menagerie*, *So Big*, *Magnificent Obsession*, and *Miracle in the Rain*.

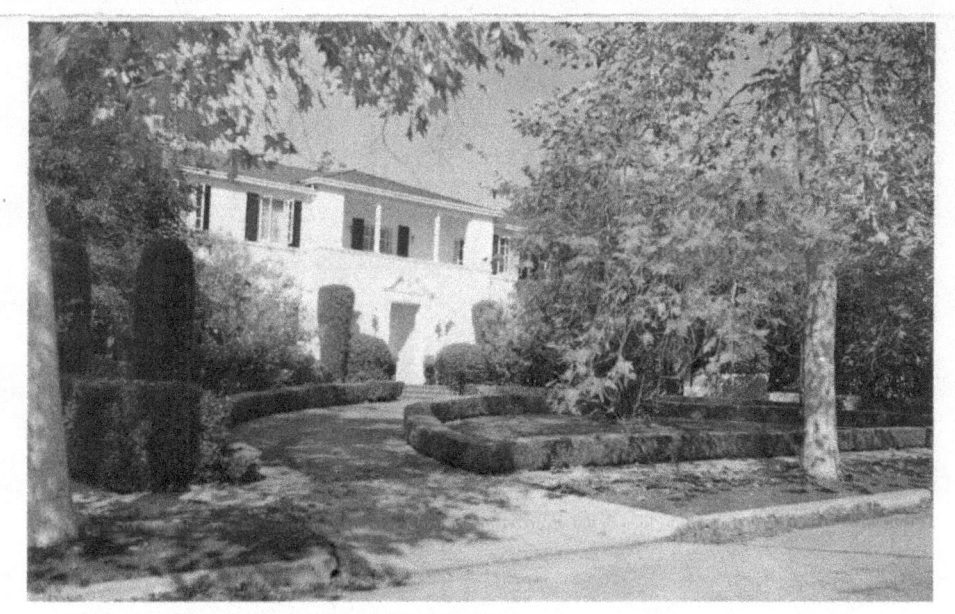

HOME OF JANE WYMAN LOCATED IN BEVERLY HILLS

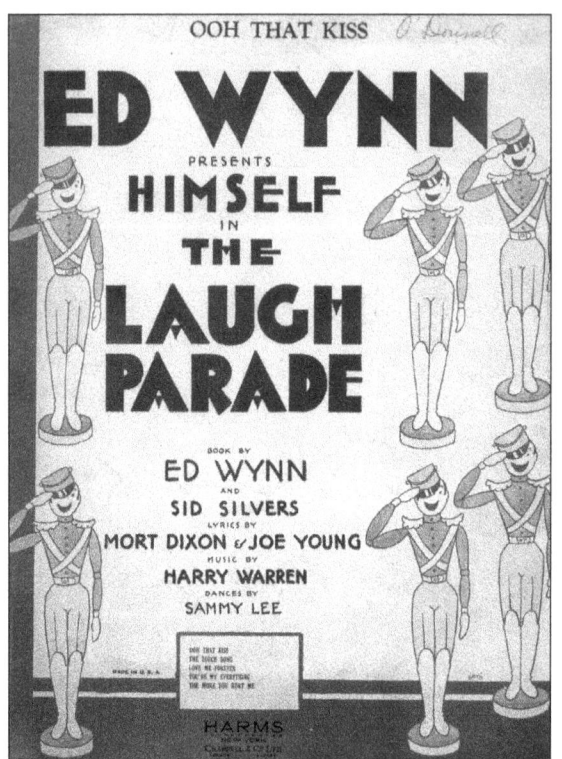

ED WYNN. Comedian Ed Wynn was a vaudeville and Broadway favorite before entering motion pictures and radio. His stage triumphs include *Ziegfeld Follies*, *The Perfect Fool*, and *Simple Simon*. From 1932 to 1935, he scored on radio with *The Fire Chief*. In 1939, MGM offered him the title role in *The Wizard of Oz*, but he turned it down. In his last years, Wynn (1886–1966) lived at 441 North Rockingham Road, Brentwood.

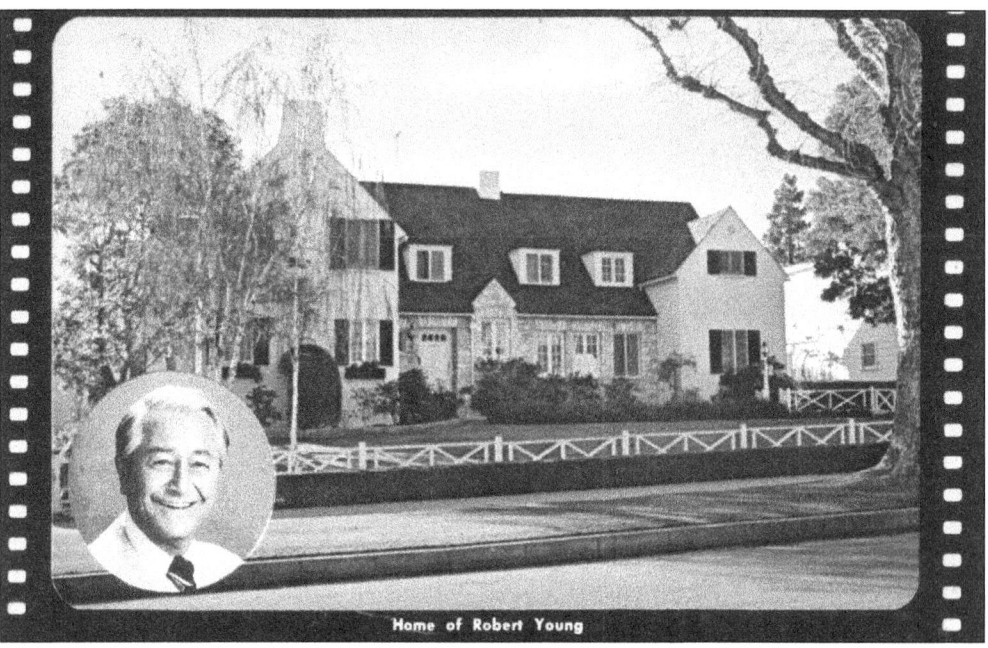

Home of Robert Young

ROBERT YOUNG. Actor Robert Young (1907–1998) lived in this mansion at 607 North Elm Drive, Beverly Hills, which formerly was the home of Billie Burke. Originally a stage actor, his first film was *Black Camel* (1931). Among his later films are *Claudia*, *The Enchanted Cottage*, *They Won't Believe Me*, *The Second Woman*, *Crossfire*, and *H.M. Pulham, Esq.* Television lengthened his career as he was the star of two hit series, *Father Knows Best* and *Marcus Welby, M.D.*

LORETTA YOUNG PORTRAIT.
Before her marriage to Col.
Thomas Lewis in 1940, Loretta
Young lived in a Holmby Hills
mansion with her mother and
teenaged half sister, Georgiana.
Four years after her marriage,
she and her husband, producer
Thomas Lewis, bought
Constance Bennett's elegant
French-style mansion, also in
Holmby Hills. There, they
reared their sons and daughter.

LORETTA YOUNG. In 1933,
screen beauty Loretta Young
(1913–2000) bought this white
brick-and-frame house; it
stood on a knoll. The address
was 10539 Sunset Boulevard,
Holmby Hills. Having been
a child actress in silent films,
she had an easy transition to
talkies and secured stardom in
films, like *Employees' Entrance*,
Midnight Mary, *Eternally Yours*,
And Now Tomorrow, and *The
Farmer's Daughter*, for which she
won an Oscar in 1947.

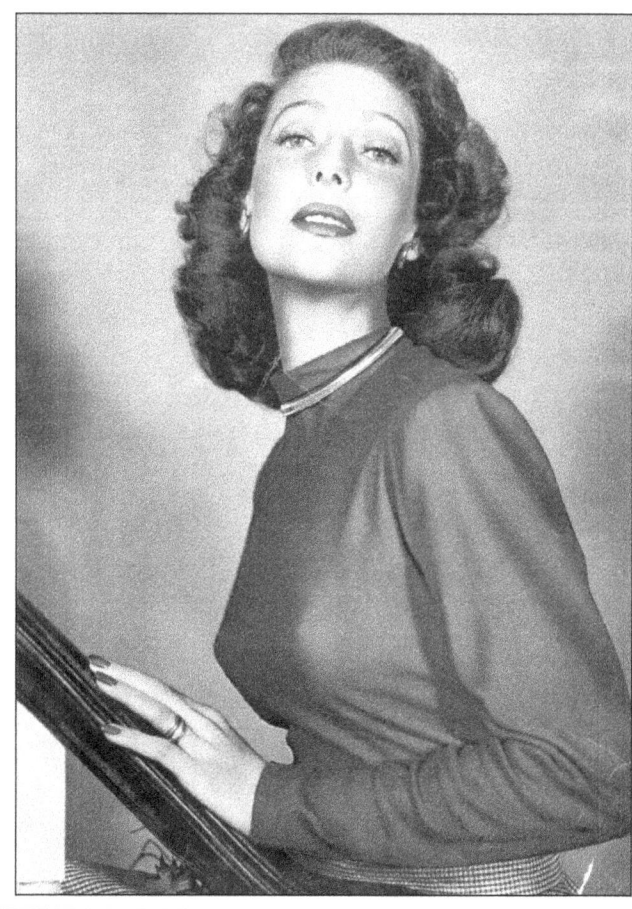

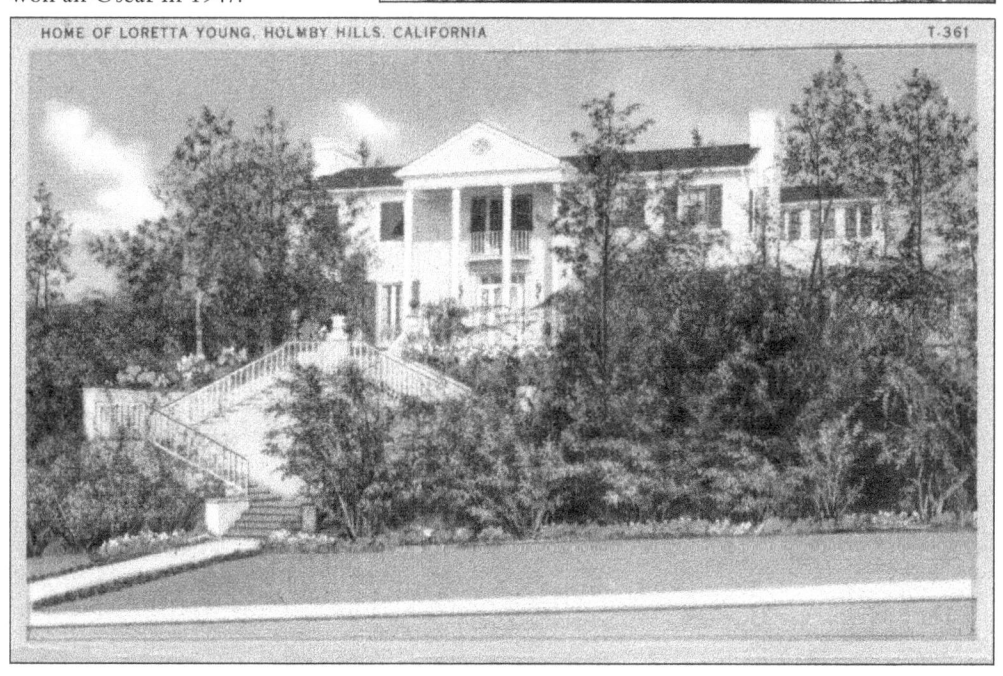

HOME OF LORETTA YOUNG, HOLMBY HILLS, CALIFORNIA   T-361

Visit us at
arcadiapublishing.com

www.ingramcontent.com/pod-product-compliance
Lightning Source LLC
Chambersburg PA
CBHW052144170526
45159CB00018B/3153